Embedding Counselling and Communication Skills

Embedding Counselling and Communication Skills provides step-by-step learning for those looking to gain theoretical and practical understanding of using counselling and communication skills within the helper role and explores how to apply these skills in the context of professional practice.

Rebecca Midwinter and Janie Dickson introduce the reader to a new Relational Skills Model, which demonstrates the phases of relationship development. The authors show what happens within each phase and identify how and when to use skills appropriately. Learning is brought alive through the use of online unscripted video clip sessions of a real helper/client relationship, giving the reader opportunities and encouragement to reflect and evaluate their learning, available at www.routledge.com/9780273774921.

Written in a clear and accessible teaching style, Embedding Counselling and Communication Skills progresses through the 'initial helper' communication skills that are used in everyday life, to the more complex and in-depth counselling skills required in a helper relationship. Knowledge of reflective practice, aspects of the relationship and how to manage change ensures the text considers the full range of general and specific skills and abilities required in a helper role situation, while the supporting online material is an invaluable tool to deepen and embed theoretical understanding, practical application and self-reflection. This book will be an essential resource for students taking an introductory counselling skills course and qualified professionals who wish to enhance their knowledge of embedding counselling skills into their work and practice.

Rebecca Midwinter Rebecca Midwinter has many years of experience working within the helping professions. She is a Senior Lecturer at Bath Spa University and her teaching career includes her role as Senior Teaching Fellow at the University of Bristol. She is a BACP accredited counsellor/psychotherapist and is UKRCP registered. She has completed her EMDR training and has extensive experience of working within the field of trauma counselling. Rebecca is also the Director of Alpheus Training Ltd.

Janie Dickson is a practising psychotherapist, clinical supervisor, trainer and Honorary Teaching Fellow at the University of Bristol. Originally from a social work background, Janie has extensive experience of working within the NHS. She is a BACP accredited counsellor/psychotherapist and is UKRCP registered. She has completed her EMDR training and currently specialises in trauma therapy.

Embedding Counselling and Communication Skills

A Relational Skills Model

Rebecca Midwinter
and Janie Dickson

LONDON AND NEW YORK

First published 2015
by Routledge
27 Church Road, Hove, East Sussex, BN3 2FA

and by Routledge
711 Third Avenue, New York, NY 10017

Routledge is an imprint of the Taylor & Francis Group, an informa business

© 2015 Rebecca Midwinter and Janie Dickson

The right of Rebecca Midwinter and Janie Dickson to be identified as authors of this work has been asserted by them in accordance with sections 77 and 78 of the Copyright, Designs and Patents Act 1988.

All rights reserved. No part of this book may be reprinted or reproduced or utilised in any form or by any electronic, mechanical, or other means, now known or hereafter invented, including photocopying and recording, or in any information storage or retrieval system, without permission in writing from the publishers.

Trademark notice: Product or corporate names may be trademarks or registered trademarks, and are used only for identification and explanation without intent to infringe.

British Library Cataloguing in Publication Data
A catalogue record for this book is available from the British Library

Library of Congress Cataloging in Publication Data
Midwinter, Rebecca.
Embedding counselling and communication skills: a relational skills model/Rebecca Midwinter, Janie Dickson.
pages cm
ISBN 978-1-138-79111-4 (hardback)
1. Counseling. I. Dickson, Janie. II. Title.
BF636.6.M53 2015
158.3 – dc23
2014030578

ISBN: 978-1-138-79111-4 (hbk)
ISBN: 978-0-273-77492-1 (pbk)
ISBN: 978-1-315-73049-3 (ebk)

Typeset in Frutiger and Joanna
by Florence Production Ltd, Stoodleigh, Devon, UK

Contents

Preface   viii
Acknowledgements   xiii

Introduction   1
A window into our classroom   1
Introducing you to our book   1
Introducing you to our Relational Skills Model (RSM)   2
Our teaching structure   4
Introducing you to reflective practice   6
Introducing you to the learning partner relationship   8

1 The skill of communicating   9
The skill of communicating   9
Defining the terminology   10
The differences between counselling and counselling skills   10
Embedding counselling skills   11
The theoretical underpinnings and existing models   12
The Relational Skills Model   20

2 Setting up the relationship   23
Building rapport   23
Setting the climate   24
Attending and listening skills   25
Barriers to active listening   28
Non-verbal communication   30
Contracting   31
Setting up the learning partner relationship   43

3 Developing the relationship — 47

Phrases that help/hinder communication 47
Paraphrasing 48
Summarising 49
Identifying and reflecting feelings, content and meaning 50
Asking questions 56

4 Working with the relationship — 64

The skill of challenging 64
Confronting 66
Use of immediacy 68
Use of self-disclosure 71
Use of silence 78
Clarifying 84
Reassessing 87
Probing 87
Giving feedback and sharing information 88

5 The established relationship — 97

Working empathically 97
Focusing 100
Use of metaphor and hunches 101
Drawing together themes 108
Clarifying and developing goals 111
Action planning 123

6 Maintaining the relationship — 129

The nature of change 129
Theory of change and change models 131
Resistance to change and systems awareness 147
Maintaining change and ending the relationship 149

7 Deepening your understanding — 156

The powerful tool of counselling skills 156
Working within your competencies 158
Working across difference and diversity 161
Introduction to transactional analysis and the ego-state model 163
Dealing with difficult clients 170
Getting it wrong and accountability 174

8 Becoming a reflexive practitioner   **184**

How do we learn?   184

What do we mean by reflective/reflexive?   187

How can we understand ourselves better?   189

The levels of reflection   191

Applying a model of reflection to our case work   195

Conclusion   201

Future learning   201

Further reading   204

Appendix 1: The Relational Skills Model   205

Appendix 2: The qualities of a helper   206

Appendix 3: Skills sheet   207

Appendix 4a: Working with the relationship (Video Clip 4d) (blank transcript)   208

Appendix 4b: Working with the relationship (Video Clip 4d) (completed transcript)   213

Appendix 5: Blank milestone table   218

Appendix 6: Prejudices and judgements   220

Appendix 7: Session to critique – Janie and Becky (Video Clip 7a)   221

Appendix 8: Boniface levels of reflection   227

Appendix 9: Gibbs framework for reflection   228

Core reading	230
References	231
Index	235

Preface

This book was born out of a discussion between us (the authors) about how we have taught counselling skills over the past few years on various levels of counselling courses. We have received consistent, enthusiastic feedback on the practical demonstrations that we have given in front of the class as we took on the roles of counsellor and client to *show* what we do. Throughout this book, students access online video clip demonstrations of unscripted counselling skills in action, modelling the same format as many of the counselling skills courses that we have either attended or taught on.

The book aims to provide:

- comprehensive training for those who embed counselling and communication skills within professional roles;
- continued professional development (CPD) for professionals working with (or intending to work with) the welfare of others, who wish to enhance and improve their counselling and communication skills; and
- an introductory training for students who will be progressing to a formal counselling training or other therapeutic training.

Over the years that we have worked as counselling skills trainers, we have increasingly come to understand the importance of skilled communication within professional helping roles and how 'counselling' skills are an essential component of training. We envisage that this book will be beneficial for those working within the NHS and social services such as medical professionals, audiologists, nurses, health-care professionals, occupational therapists, social workers, occupational heath advisors and alternative therapists, as well as professionals within public-sector roles such as welfare officers, teachers, police officers, personnel and legal representatives.

While this book does not aim to teach counsellors to become qualified, it provides an introductory training for those who wish to pursue a formal counselling qualification and can provide essential learning for those where an introduction to counselling skills training is an entry requirement to other therapeutic programmes.

As this book is a joint authorship, when we share a personal story or reflection, we point out which of the authors is talking. Hopefully, this gives you the experience of being in the classroom and a sense of building a relationship with us, as well as with the helper and client, as you journey through the book.

HOW THE BOOK IS STRUCTURED

Introduction

We introduce the helper to:

- A window into our classroom
- Introducing you to our book
- Introducing you to our Relational Skills Model
- Our teaching structure
- Introducing you to reflective practice
- Introducing you to the learning partner relationship

Chapter 1: The skill of communicating

In this chapter, we set out an overview of the framework and context of counselling skills and the relevant theoretical models, and highlight the differences between counselling and counselling skills. We will be introducing the helper to:

- The skill of communicating
- Defining the terminology
- The differences between counselling and counselling skills
- Embedding counselling skills
- The theoretical underpinnings and existing models
- The Relational Skills Model

Chapter 2: Setting up the relationship

We describe the first phase of the Relational Skills Model. Each chapter will look at the individual phases in detail.

The first phase is about contacting and meeting the client, getting to know the client, communicating with the client and contracting with the client. Initial core skills within this phase are attending skills, active listening skills and contracting skills. In this chapter, we will be discussing the essential elements of setting up a helper relationship. These include:

- Building rapport
- Setting the climate
- Attending and listening skills
- Barriers to active listening
- Non-verbal communication
- Contracting
- Setting up the learning partner relationship

Chapter 3: Developing the relationship

This phase enables the helper to create an environment where the client feels safe enough to bring his or her story and issues. The focus within this chapter is on developing the relationship, problem identification and assessment. Additional core skills to develop communication and build upon the earlier skills are: the presence and communication of the core conditions; paraphrasing; summarising; identifying and reflecting feelings, content and meaning; and asking questions. The additional core skills we will cover in this chapter are:

- Phrases that help/hinder communication
- Paraphrasing
- Summarising
- Identifying and reflecting feelings, content and meaning
- Asking questions

Chapter 4: Working with the relationship

Now that the relationship is established, the emphasis is on exploring the issues in more depth and creating an empathic understanding of the client's situation. The focus within this chapter is through challenging and creating new meaning, different possibilities and perspectives. Enhanced skills to progress the communication are the skills of challenging. Different ways of challenging are:

- The skill of challenging
- Confronting
- Use of immediacy
- Use of self-disclosure
- Use of silence
- Clarifying
- Reassessing
- Probing
- Giving feedback and sharing information

Chapter 5: The established relationship

At this phase, the helper and client are able to clarify and focus on likely changes and work collaboratively to make plans, set goals and consider and evaluate possible strategies and directions. The focus within this chapter is on goal setting and evaluation. Intuitive and learned skills within this phase are:

- Working empathically
- Focusing
- Use of metaphor and hunches
- Drawing together themes

- Clarifying and developing goals
- Action planning

Chapter 6: Maintaining the relationship

The helper and client are now ready to consider how the client's goals could be implemented. It is useful here for the helper to hold an awareness and understanding of the theory of change and transitions. The focus is on supporting and encouraging the client to implement and maintain change and support self-management strategies. We will also discuss the ongoing relationship where we might continue to review, monitor and evaluate the client's progress with them, to facilitate an ending, or signpost him or her on to other agencies. This chapter covers:

- The nature of change
- Theory of change and change models
- Resistance to change and systems awareness
- Maintaining change and ending the relationship

Chapter 7: Deepening your understanding

This chapter will help to deepen the helper's understanding of the value of the use of these skills and will cover some of the common issues or situations that may arise as he or she works more formally with them.

This chapter will examine:

- The powerful tool of counselling skills
- Working within your competencies
- Working across difference and diversity
- Introduction to transactional analysis and the ego-state model
- Dealing with difficult clients
- Getting it wrong and accountability

Chapter 8: Becoming a reflective practitioner

We anticipate by this stage that the helper will begin to integrate all aspects of the skills into his or her work. He or she will be building on this knowledge through growing self-awareness and reflection.

This chapter will examine:

- How do we learn?
- What do we mean by reflective/reflexive?
- How can we understand ourselves better?
- The levels of reflection
- Applying a model of reflection to our case work

Conclusion

In this chapter, the authors reflect on their own learning journey and the development of the Relational Skills Model, and consider its impact and application for future training. This chapter includes:

- Future learning
- Further reading
- Appendices

Acknowledgements

We are extremely thankful to our helpers Jacqui Erskin-Crum and Glyn Williams for their courage, generosity and unquestioning belief in our project from the outset. Your skill and congruence in the video clips led us to conceptualise the Relational Skills Model.

Caz Thomas-White and Rob Omielan: thank you for your bravery and openness as 'clients'; without you, this project could not have happened.

To Dave, Laura and Jack: you all understood my desire and determination to fulfil my ambition to write this book and never waivered in your support and encouragement. Thank you for that.

To Fiona: thanks for being alongside every step of the way.

To all our past students: this is our legacy to you.

Introduction

We begin our book with:

- A window into our classroom
- Introducing you to our book
- Introducing you to our Relational Skills Model (RSM)
- Our teaching structure
- Introducing you to reflective practice
- Introducing you to the learning partner relationship

A WINDOW INTO OUR CLASSROOM

When we teach counselling skills in the classroom, we follow a specific teaching structure. Helpfully, this structure translates into the acronym TERMS.

Teaching: A session introducing the helper to the theory and the skills, and their relevance and importance to the helper role.

Example: A demonstration of a helper and client session.

Reflect, practise and evaluate: Reflections and observations on a counselling skills example to help the helper make links between practice and theory. Practise is through setting up and maintaining a relationship with a learning partner to practise the skills and to give and receive feedback. A transcript of the session enables the helper to critically evaluate the session.

Model box: An overview of the model(s) and how they relate to the skills taught.

Summary: A summary of learning and reading list to embed knowledge and deepen understanding and interest.

We have followed the same structure in this book, creating a programme of study that allows you to have a similar study experience to a 'live' taught course.

INTRODUCING YOU TO OUR BOOK

This book is pitched at an appropriate academic and practical level to enable you to evolve from 'initial helper' communication skills that you use in everyday life, to the more complex and in-depth skills required in a professional helper role. There are many different professional 'helper' roles within our society. We use the term 'those working with the welfare of others' in the preface to acknowledge that a 'helper' is anyone whose professional interest is in the well-being, happiness, health and prosperity of another.

Chapter by chapter, you will learn the theory attached to each skill; you will be able to see a demonstration of that skill being used within a helper relationship and will be given opportunities and encouragement to reflect upon your learning and to give and receive feedback. You will undertake exercises to practise the skill with a learning partner and will see how those skills fit within the model you are using. You will be encouraged to participate in further reading that will enhance and embed your knowledge.

We will also introduce you to some of the leading experts in the counselling field and explore how their ideas and models have influenced our teaching over a number of years and influenced the development of our new and innovative counselling skills model – the Relational Skills Model (RSM).

INTRODUCING YOU TO OUR RELATIONAL SKILLS MODEL (RSM)

Years of experience in various professional roles as counsellors, helpers and trainers have led to our understanding of the process involved in working with the welfare of others. We have tried and tested a range of well-established theoretical skills models and integrated these into our own ways of working. Many of these models incorporate 'stages' that a helper is encouraged to follow, encompassing within each stage a set of relevant skills and strategies. Most theories acknowledge that helping is not a linear process and that the skills and strategies are interchangeable within each stage, but these skills are often taught stage by stage.

What is missing for us is: (i) the connection between the different phases of the relationship development between the helper and the client; and (ii) how and when the various skills can be appropriately embedded within those phases. In order to understand the development of the skills, we need to understand the development of the relationship. Through the process of creating video clips and reflecting on how the skills are applied within a helper/client relationship, we came up with a model that we believe emphasises the importance of *embedding skills within the relationship*, instead of looking at the skills as a distinct set of 'tools' to be implemented. Our model looks at the process of relationship development and then embeds the use of appropriate skills within each of the various phases. This has the effect of moving away from the helper thinking that they 'ought to do a paraphrase' or 'should be challenging' at this stage to a more relational process of 'it seems OK to challenge this client at this point' and 'it feels appropriate to start action planning now'.

The term 'relationship' is often used to infer an established connection or affiliation between two people, but in the helper/client role we are using it to describe two people *in relation to each other* and the phases that they move through. In this context, we feel that a 'relationship' can be made both within a 10-minute meeting or a longer-term contact.

We have used the term 'phase' within our model, rather than the more commonly used 'stage', as it suggests to us a flexibility of the process of embedding the skills into the relationship. As the relationship develops, we are able to embed more skills. A 'phase' also indicates to us a fluid use of skills, at times building upon each other and at other times being interchangeable. As the phases of the relationship develop, so do the skills within them. Each phase can be as short or as long as the time boundaries allow, and therefore the model is suitable for either short- or longer-term working. Each relationship is different and has a number of internal and external factors influencing it. Once you become familiar with the different phases of relationship development, your skills and judgement will enable you to become responsive to and decide upon which skills to introduce and when – for example, when you meet a client for the first time, it may not be appropriate to go straight

FIGURE I.1 The Relational Skills Model

Phases of relationship development	Process	Skills
Setting up the relationship	Contacting/meeting the client Getting to know the client Communicating with and contracting with the client	**Initial core skills:** Attending skills Active listening skills and contracting skills
Developing the relationship	Developing the relationship Problem identification and assessment	**Additional core skills:** Presence and communication of the core conditions Paraphrasing Summarising Identifying and reflecting feelings, content and meaning Asking questions
Working with the relationship	Challenging and creating new meaning, different possibilities and perspectives	**Enhanced skills:** The skill of challenging: Confronting Use of self-disclosure, immediacy and silence Clarifying Reassessing Probing Giving feedback and sharing information
The established relationship	Clarifying and focusing on likely changes Working collaboratively to make plans, set goals, and consider and evaluate possible strategies and directions	**Intuitive and learned skills:** Deeper empathy Focusing Use of metaphor and hunches Drawing together themes Clarifying and developing goals Action planning
Maintaining and ending the relationship	Implementing and maintaining change Supporting self-management strategies	**Embedded skills:** Encouragement, support and affirmations Review, monitor, evaluate and facilitate ending Signposting/referring on

© Copyright 2012 Midwinter and Dickson. All Rights Reserved.

into goal setting. You would first need to take some time to develop and establish the relationship. This way of working might feel daunting initially, but the more you practise, the easier it becomes. Our model is fully explained in Chapter 1, together with the models that have influenced and informed our thinking.

OUR TEACHING STRUCTURE

From Chapter 2 onwards, we follow the specific teaching structure 'TERMS'.

Teaching

There is a *teaching* session where you are introduced to specific skills embedded within the RSM. We, as the 'tutors in the room', introduce the skills within the chapter and inform you, the 'students in the room', of any further models and underpinning theory, giving examples from experience of how it applies in practice and its relevance to the role of 'helper'. While we might refer to you as students, we understand and appreciate that some of you reading this book will be professionals looking to improve and enhance your skills as helpers. It is essential, therefore, from the outset that we clarify what we see as the difference between formal psychological counselling and *embedding* counselling skills within a role, and we will explain what we mean by the terms 'helper' and 'client' and their relevance to students and to professionals who work with the welfare of others (this is discussed in detail in Chapter 1).

Examples

Examples will be through the viewing of video clips of counselling and communication skills in action. You will be directed to watch clips at a certain point in your reading, to fit with the learning structure and at an appropriate point to embed and enhance the learning from the taught session.

Many of us have discovered in our learning journey that we understand more when we have seen something done and have an opportunity to do it ourselves, and we hope that the inclusion of the examples at relevant points will enable you to participate in and be part of the learning process. We wonder whether the anxiety of 'showcasing' skills by qualified counsellors could be the reason why counselling skills books are restricted to the written word with client examples being laid out as 'thought-through' transcripts. There are videos of counselling sessions but it is our experience that these are not integrated into a skills textbook. We feel that the 'unscripted sessions' in our examples provide an arena for constructive criticism and developmental learning. These sessions are not hour-long counselling sessions, as the purpose of our book is not to train professional counsellors undertaking 50–60-minute counselling sessions, but they are short sessions, typically 10-minute extracts, of the type that we consider helpers might encounter within their professional roles.

We feel strongly that in order for the helper relationship and the skills to *feel* real, they have to *be* real. However, we needed to keep in mind ethical issues about asking a real client to be involved in recording his or her session for a book, so we have decided to use qualified counsellors in both the helper and the client role, but nevertheless with the client bringing a real issue to the session. These are never perfect sessions. Indeed one might argue that there is no such thing. These examples model the exercises that we set for our students on taught programmes. The helpers have not been briefed on the subject matter and have not discussed the client material prior to the recording. We have used clients who are known to the helper and others who had not met the helper prior to the recorded session. This enables us to demonstrate the differences between using counselling skills with someone you know in a dual-role relationship and working with someone you have not met before. Some of the clips will show the sessions in their entirety, and others will be an extract to draw your attention to something in particular and/or give you a flavour of the session or skill we are demonstrating. When we ask students on our courses to be clients, we ask them to bring 'mild anxieties' to the practice sessions. The reasons for this are twofold – to keep the client safe as they are working with a student within a practice environment, and to enable the student in the role of counsellor to practise and demonstrate the skills. To model this, we have asked the clients in these video clips to do the same – to bring a mild anxiety to explore with the counsellor, to enable the counsellor to demonstrate the skills in the clips. These issues may not be of the nature that some readers of this book are used to their clients bringing. For others, who are new to using counselling skills in this way, the issue that the client brings can be less important and it will be learning about the skills of building the relationship that is paramount. However, in our view, there is no such thing as a 'bad client' or a less important issue. If it matters to the client and they choose to explore that issue with you as a helper, then it matters. Often, 'mild anxieties' can be the presenting issue that leads to a much earlier, deeper and value-based issue, and we have been very mindful of working ethically with our volunteer clients to ensure that the level of self-disclosure is relevant to the publishing of this book.

Reflect, practise and evaluate

We believe that, as students, you are not 'passively taught' so it is important that you are active in your learning. Throughout the book, you are given reflective prompts, exercises and questions to stimulate your thoughts and feelings, encourage participation in the learning and encourage you to *reflect, practise and evaluate* your learning. Most courses teaching counselling skills work in triads when they do practice work – having helper, client and observer roles. We model this by providing the opportunity for you to take part in both helper and client roles. This is by undertaking the exercises in this book and within a relationship that you will set up with a learning partner. You will take the observer role through watching, learning and constructively critiquing the examples in the video clip. This will encourage you to reflect upon how the theory and the practice work together. You will be given various exercises to undertake with your learning partner in order to practise and embed the learning and skills. This relationship will become very important as you work through the book, and it is essential that you set up the learning partner relationship from the outset. Details of how to do this are set out in Chapter 2. You will also be directed to a transcript of the session as a way for you to check out your observations in order to critically evaluate, identify and recognise skills and, through reflection, to decide whether it aligns or differs with our observations and reflections. You will be encouraged to keep a *reflective learning journal* to record, analyse and reflect upon your learning experiences.

Model box

Each chapter will have a *model box* giving a brief overview of the counselling models to form a framework and context for the use of counselling skills. This model box will be a useful guide to reference and pinpoint the theoretical underpinning of the models used within each chapter.

Summary and reference list

Having seen the examples of the skills in use, you can then progress through the learning structure by completing exercises and tasks that will help to link the theory to the practice. At the end of each chapter, there will be a *summary* to deepen theoretical understanding and awareness of the skills shown. There is a full reference list at the end of the book and a further reading list to help put the learning into context. The reading list at the end of the book is an important part of learning where we will indicate the core reading book(s) and recommend further reading to develop your counselling skills practice.

INTRODUCING YOU TO REFLECTIVE PRACTICE

> When we go about the spontaneous, intuitive performance of the actions of everyday life, we show ourselves to be knowledgeable in a special way. Often we cannot say what it is that we know. When we try to describe it we find ourselves at a loss, or we produce descriptions that are obviously inappropriate. Our knowing is ordinarily tacit, implicit in our patterns of action and in our feel for the stuff with which we are dealing. It seems right to say that our knowing is in our action.
>
> (Schön 1995: 49)

We, as curious human beings, gather up our knowledge in a number of different ways. We may 'know' something through first-hand experience of doing it, or through reading it, being taught it or being shown it. It is often the case that these different ways of knowing are held in isolation – we may have read about Chinese culture in a book but we have no personal experience of having visited China and experienced that culture first-hand. Or we may have the personal experience of having migraine headaches, without ever having read about the causes or symptoms of them. You may have read about the use of counselling skills, but have no practical experience of using them professionally. It is, of course, the aim of this book to enable you to have both the academic knowledge and the practical experience of using counselling skills within your professional roles.

Reflection is widely accepted as an important part of a helper's way of working. Practitioners are encouraged to 'reflect on action' (Schön 1983) to turn 'experience into knowledge'. In other words, to think back to the experience and ask yourself questions about how you did it, why you did it, what you would have changed about it and so on. Reflection on action gives you a greater understanding of the experience, your judgements and meanings, and enables you to challenge and modify your way of working. The reflective prompts, transcripts and actions set out within this book encourage you to reflect on action as you undertake the tasks and exercises.

There are many different levels of reflection that lead you to become more reflexive workers and to reflect on action, and we will talk more about this towards the end of the book.

One example of learning to reflect on action is through writing a *reflective learning journal*.

> A journal is a record of happenings, thoughts and feelings about a particular aspect of life, or with a particular structure. A journal can record anything relative to the issue to which it pertains. So a reflective practice journal is like a diary of practice but in addition includes: 'deliberative thought and analysis related to practice'.
>
> (Holly 1988: 78)

A reflective journal is unlike a log or a diary. The journal can be used for a variety of purposes, whether personal or professional. They are solely for your own use, do not need to be shared and can be 'written' in any way you like. We encourage the use of a reflective learning journal alongside this workbook, and throughout the book you will find reflective learning journal exercises, to encourage you to reflect upon your process of learning and discovering as you proceed through the chapters, video links and activities.

Where you see this logo in the reflective learning journal box, we are inviting you to video the skills session with your learning partner and reflect upon it.

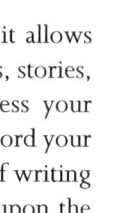

A learning journal should be reflective and creative. Written spontaneously, it allows feelings and thoughts to evolve. It can include photographs, drawings, mind maps, stories, poems and illustrations. Be as experimental as you want to be! It can express your celebrations and your frustrations, the thoughts on your decisions and choices, record your insecurities and anxieties, and reflect on the things that have gone well. The joy of writing the journal is that there are no rules; you decide what you put in, you decide upon the things you wish to explore, question, monitor and feel. It can become a confidant, critical friend, internal supervisor and helpful tool for analysis.

Johns (1996: 91) lists the aims and purposes of a learning journal as including:

- reflecting on experience, thoughts, feelings and behaviours;
- exploring ideas, reactions changes in self and others;
- clarifying personal beliefs, attitudes, values;
- evaluating movement in understanding, skills, knowledge;
- setting objectives for the next stage of learning and growth; and
- monitoring assumptions, achievement and blocks.

Furthermore, the journal can reflect *who you are* at any stage of development. Often, students who have read back through their journals make comments such as 'I can't believe that was me who wrote that back then'. The journal captures a moment in time in your learning journey, and as you grow and develop, the journal reflects this.

To begin this process, we invite you to undertake the following exercise:

> **REFLECTIVE LEARNING JOURNAL EXERCISE**
>
> Using photography, painting, poems or stories or any other metaphor to represent a portrait of you at the beginning of your journey, begin your reflective learning journal by asking yourself the following questions:
>
> - Who am I?
> - Where am I at this moment in time?
> - Where have I come from?
> - What do I want to achieve?

We will return to these questions in the final chapter of the book.

INTRODUCING YOU TO THE LEARNING PARTNER RELATIONSHIP

The aim of this book is to help you to embed and enhance counselling and communication skills through mirroring the counselling skills training experience in the classroom. To assist this process, we ask that you set up a relationship with a *learning partner*. A learning partner should be someone who is also studying this book or someone who is familiar with the use of counselling skills. This can be either a peer on a training programme (if the book is being used as part of a formalised training programme) or a peer or mentor at work if you are using it as part of your continued professional development. Your learning partner also needs to be someone that you have regular access to. Throughout the book, you will be invited to evoke feedback from your learning partner and to reflect on your learning journey together. As new skills are put into practice, it is hoped that learning partners will be able to share experiences, discuss challenges and learning edges, and celebrate successes. We will discuss this partnership in more detail in Chapter 2.

Chapter 1
The skill of communicating

In this chapter, we will be introducing you to:
- The skill of communicating
- Defining the terminology
- The differences between counselling and counselling skills
- Embedding counselling skills
- The theoretical underpinnings and models
- The Relational Skills Model

TEACHING

THE SKILL OF COMMUNICATING

Jake had gone to Mr Smith for advice on his problem.

> 'Did Mr Smith tell you what you should do?' asked Jake's wife when he got home.
>
> 'Do you know', replied Jake, 'the funny thing is, that looking back on our conversation he never told me what to do. We talked around it quite a lot, he gave me some other ways of looking at it, and I am not sure how it happened but I think I know what I want to do now and how I want to be. Did he "tell me" what to do? Now I think about it. No he didn't do that at all!'

This book is aimed at those people working with (or wanting to work with) the welfare of others, who want to embed counselling and communication skills into that role. These skills are founded on the ethos of empowering others rather than advice giving and often this role has been referred to as the 'helper' role (Egan 2002: 3). It does not mean providing others with a solution; rather, it is an attempt to help people find their own solution or ways of coping with their problem situation. In order to embed and enhance these skills, we need to practice them and incorporate them into our supporting roles. These skills are fundamental to counselling and psychotherapy, but they are not exclusive to these professions, and our aim in this book is to share these skills with you, demonstrate them and aid you in embedding them into your work with others.

DEFINING THE TERMINOLOGY

In the preface, we set out who this book is intended for and why we have decided to write it. Equally important for us is to outline the limitations of this book. We recognise that most of us have natural communication skills that we use in our everyday lives. Our book aims to teach the reader how to enhance and improve those natural skills and to embed them into his or her practice when working alongside others.

So why have we included the word 'counselling' in our title?

The British Association for Counselling & Psychotherapy (BACP) is the largest professional body representing counselling and psychotherapy in the UK (www.bacp.co.uk). To train as a counsellor on a current BACP accredited training course, you must undertake 400 hours of direct teaching or instruction time, undertake 100 face-to-face counselling placement hours and attend fortnightly clinical supervision. Counselling training is in-depth and leads to a professional qualification (BACP 2012). There is no book (that we are aware of) that can replace that level of training. However, underpinning all counselling training, regardless of the orientation or theoretical positioning of the training, is knowledge and application of the *core counselling skills* that we discuss in this book. The teaching of these core counselling skills can be included within a counselling training course, but often knowledge of the core counselling skills are a prerequisite to joining any training course focussed on a 'helping' role.

The confusion may arise because, while the term 'counselling' applies to the role carried out by the professional, qualified *counsellor* and relates to '*psychological counselling*', it is also the generic term for those who use *counselling skills* within their work with other people, as part of another role.

Knowledge of counselling skills alone will not enable you to practise as a qualified counsellor. However, knowledge of core counselling skills will enable you to become a better *communicator* by enhancing your knowledge and understanding of the theoretical underpinnings of counselling skills models, by learning how to apply counselling skills competently and appropriately, by raising your self-awareness and by enabling you to work ethically with the welfare of others. So it is important that the term 'counselling' is included and defined, as this book is all about those core counselling skills and how they can be communicated and used effectively and competently.

THE DIFFERENCES BETWEEN COUNSELLING AND COUNSELLING SKILLS

Within the following chapters, we will make frequent references to these distinctions and how they will affect the working relationship between the helper and the client.

This book aims to provide helpers with the skills they need to embed these core counselling skills into their working roles.

We thought long and hard about what to call the *roles* of those who use and receive core counselling skills. Often, in counselling skills training courses and books, they are referred

FIGURE 1.1 The differences between counselling and counselling skills

	Counselling	Supportive help using counselling skills
Role	Explicitly identified as a counsellor to clients; strives to avoid or minimise any role conflict and ambiguity	Combines offering support with other roles; may involve some role conflict and role ambiguity
Authority	Has neither managerial nor other formal authority over client	May have managerial or other formal authority over client
Contract	Explicit agreement to offer counselling to client, including clarity about confidentiality and boundaries	Uses discretion about whether to have a contract or to use counselling skills spontaneously; confidentiality often implicit and boundaries may not be explicitly defined
Time	Planned and protected from interruptions	May not be planned; can be a spontaneous response to someone needing help
Professional support	Works to ethical guidelines that require regular supervision to enhance quality of service	May not have either a professional ethical framework or receive supervision
Process	Assist clients to make their *own* decisions and take action for themselves	May advise, coach, distribute physical resources or act on behalf of clients
Focus	The 'person in context': the client is at the centre; the context provides a perspective for both self and practitioner assessment; the goals and aims of others are considered to the extent that they relate to the client	The 'person and context(s)': the helper may have a dual focus and be required to take account of the context in which the help is offered; for example, to balance organisational needs and requirements with those of the individual seeking help

Source: Culley and Bond (2004: 6)

to as 'listeners' (those who actively use the counselling skills) and 'talkers' (the recipients). However, because this book is aimed at a wide range of readers, some of whom will be practitioners, professionals and/or students on professional courses and so on, we have decided to use the terms from the dictionary definitions of '*helper*' (person that helps) and '*client*' (person using the services of a professional person), as these are generic terms that apply across a range of professions and activities. Throughout this book, we have used alternate genders sometimes referring to the client as her and sometimes as him.

EMBEDDING COUNSELLING SKILLS

It is important for us to acknowledge the idea of 'embedding' counselling skills into practice and how this terminology first came to the forefront of our minds when we were thinking about writing this book. After many years of training students to become qualified counsellors, one of the authors (Becky) was asked to teach two Counselling Skills modules to students undertaking a BSc in Audiology. These students were taught an Introduction to Counselling Skills module in year 2 of their degree, and a Developing Counselling Skills module in year 4, after undertaking a year in a clinical setting with supervised patient contact. From the outset, it became clear that Becky needed to formulate a clear distinction between teaching '*counselling skills*' and teaching '*counselling*', as she had taught previously. Audiologists may often have less than 15 minutes with a patient and have many conflicting demands and tasks that they need to respond to within that time. Becky's role, as their tutor, was to help them identify and become familiar with core counselling skills that they could use in their everyday encounters with patients and within their workplace roles.

While she was teaching on the BSc in Audiology, Becky's attention was drawn to McLeod's (2007) book *Counselling Skill*, in which he sets out a framework 'for making sense of episodes of counselling that are *embedded* in other activities and roles' (McLeod 2007: 1, original emphasis).

> [A] useful counselling conversation can take place within about eight to ten minutes. This length of time represents the typical window of opportunity that a teacher, doctor or manager has to allow someone to talk through something that is troubling them.
> (McLeod 2007: 2)

McLeod's concepts of '*embedded counselling*' (McLeod 2007: 17) fitted well with the aims and objectives of audiologists, who were dealing, in a very tight timescale, not only with the clinical practicalities of those with hearing loss, but also with the complex area of problem management and the changing beliefs and behaviour associated with hearing loss. McLeod and McLeod (2011: 23) describe these as '*empathic opportunities*' that the helper can learn to recognise as potential openings for using their counselling skills within a consultation setting.

Teaching on the degree programme gave Becky first-hand experience of seeing the benefits of embedding the core counselling skills into all roles that involve working with the welfare of others and how knowledge of the core skills becomes mutually beneficial to the practitioner and the patient. The audiology students improved their counselling skills in their practical exercises with each other, thereby leading to better interventions with their patients, and, following their year in placement, they reported that they were able to analyse the skills they had learned and identify when and where they were embedding these skills themselves and where they were being used, or not, by practitioners within their placements.

THE THEORETICAL UNDERPINNINGS AND EXISTING MODELS

In the preface, we introduced you to our Relational Skills Model. In formulating the Relational Skills Model, we have drawn from a range of well-established theoretical models. In particular:

- Rogers (1961)
- Egan (2002)
- Culley and Bond (2004)
- McLeod and McLeod (2011)

We will make links to theories within the *model boxes* contained in each chapter, but in this chapter we will give a general overview of the theories and models that have underpinned the development of our model.

Rogers: person-centred model

The core conditions

Carl Rogers played a major part in originating and developing the person-centred approach to therapy. He believed that:

> Individuals have within themselves vast resources for self-understanding and for altering their self-concepts, basic attitudes and self-directed behaviour; these resources can be tapped if a definable climate of facilitative psychological attitudes can be provided.
>
> (Rogers 1980: 115)

In his paper 'The Necessary and Sufficient Conditions of Therapeutic Personality Change', Rogers (1957: 96) identified several conditions that seemed to him to be necessary and sufficient for 'constructive personality change' to take place:

1. Two persons are in psychological contact.
2. The first, whom we shall term the client, is in a state of incongruence, being vulnerable or anxious.
3. The second person, whom we shall term the therapist, is congruent or integrated in the relationship.
4. The therapist experiences unconditional positive regard for the client.
5. The therapist experiences an empathic understanding of the client's internal frame of reference and endeavours to communicate this experience to the client.
6. The communication to the client of the therapist's empathic understanding and unconditional positive regard is to a minimal degree achieved.

While all six conditions are considered '*necessary and sufficient*' in a counselling relationship, there are three of the 'core conditions' that we consider need to be present in the helper relationship:

Congruence (genuineness)
The ability, as a helper, to be open, genuine, non-defensive and real. To be congruent, you need to be self-aware and make decisions about what you would like to share with the other person. This not only relates to what you say, but also to what you show to the other through your non-verbal communications.

Unconditional positive regard (acceptance)
To be able to respond with respect and in a non-judgemental manner; to accept the other person; to value the other person.

> **Empathy**
> The ability to see and feel from the other point of view; to tune into another's feelings; to stand in the other's shoes.
>
> Source: Adapted from Rogers (1980)

Communication of the 'core conditions' is crucial (condition no. 6) – the helper may hold all of the above qualities but if these are not communicated to the client, will not be able to appreciate their value or feel the helper's encouragement and support.

Over the following chapters, we will teach you the skills of developing a helping relationship based on the principles of 'person-centredness' and holding and communicating these core conditions.

Egan: three-stage skills model

Gerard Egan is a Professor Emeritus at Loyola University of Chicago. His book *The Skilled Helper: A Problem-Management and Opportunity-Development Approach to Helping* is widely used as a core text in counselling skills training.

Egan gives an overview of the helping process by breaking it down into three stages and describing these stages in detail with guidance to the skills required by the helper and potential issues that might arise, giving scenarios and examples throughout the text. His work is aimed at helping professionals who are not necessarily 'formal' helpers, but rather those that 'often deal with people in times of crisis and stress' (Egan 2002: 3).

Initially, the three stages may appear to be linear, but in reality, like life itself, the helping process can go back and forth between the stages and they are not intended to be sequential, but rather can be seen as an interactive model within which the skill sets are situated. The model consists of three stages, each of which has three steps, and Egan suggests that the helping model is used flexibly (Egan 2002: 33), with clients' needs taking precedence. Clients may start at a different point in the model and also might engage with the stages and steps differently. Although focus and direction is required from both helper and client, individual needs and diversity need to be considered, and he recommends using this model as an underlying framework to the helping process.

An overview of Egan's model's stages and skills

Egan stresses the flexibility of using the helping model, and consequently the skills used during each stage are not neatly prescriptive. Egan warns against the 'purity' of the model becoming more important than the client, and at all times we need to hold what Egan refers to as the values of respect, empathy and genuiness of the helping model (see also Rogers' core conditions).

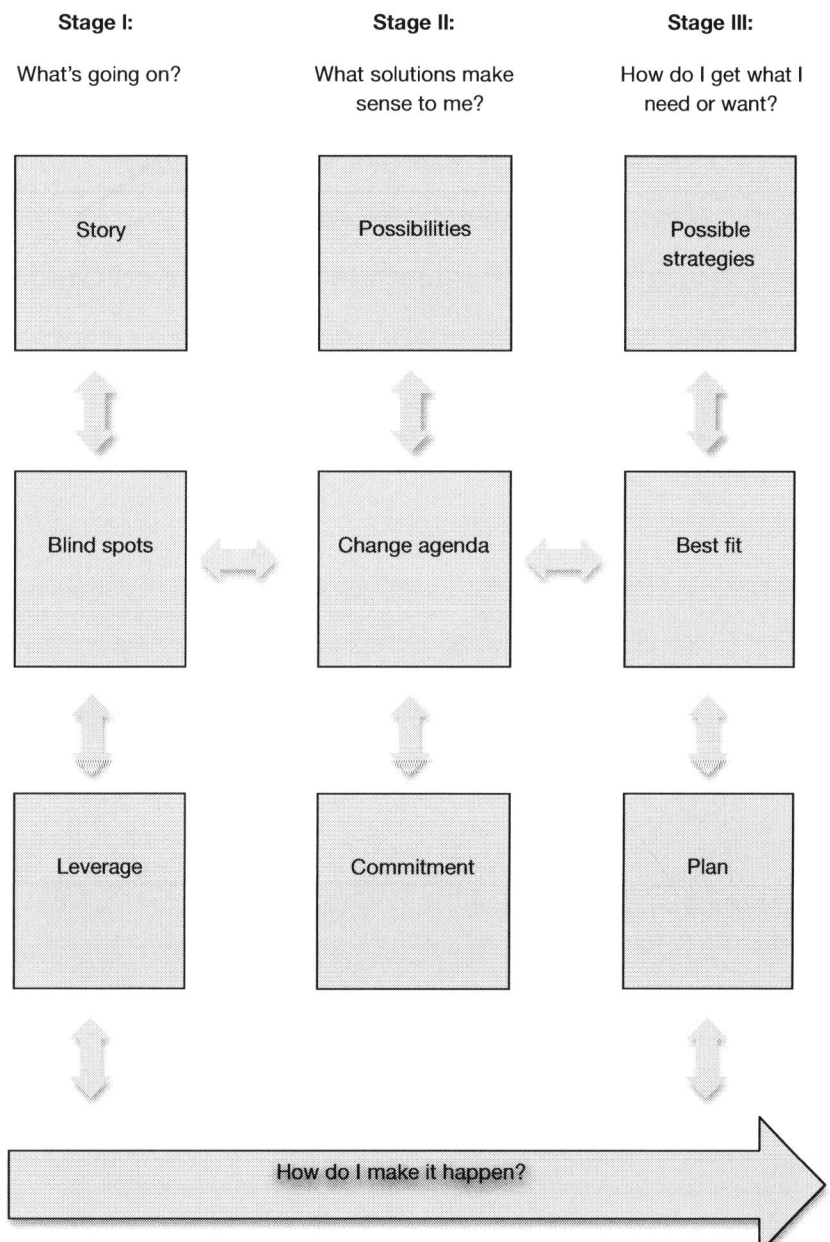

FIGURE 1.2 The skilled heper model
Source: Egan (2010)

Stage I: what's going on?

In Stage I, you, the helper, are exploring the client's story with him or her, or 'what is going on'. This might be at the beginning of your contact or could be through further clarification later on in the time you have together. The diagram of the skilled helper model illustrates how you may be listening and/or checking that you have heard their story correctly (Step I-A), or you might have had a hunch about potential blind spots that your client is experiencing (Step I-B).

In Step I-C, leverage questions help the client to prioritise, clarify and decide what they would like to *focus* on, which may lead on to Stage II and further exploration of potential solutions to the problems. Egan sees Step I-C as acting as a stimulus for client action.

Stage II: what solutions make sense for me?

The helper's role for Stage II is in supporting and enabling the client to explore options and possibilities; it also deals with self-worth and motivation to change. The important aspect about these agendas for change are that the helper respects the client's autonomy and ability to make informed choices. This might involve helping the client to explore existing competencies or past experiences that they might draw on.

Step II-B involves helping the client to move from possibilities to choices and formulate a change agenda. Egan's model for shaping goals is similar to the common SMART goals (Doran 1981) that are often used in workplace training, which are that goals are **S**pecific, **M**easurable, **A**ttainable, **R**elevant and **T**ime-bound. In addition, Egan (2002: 276) suggests they should be both relevant and prudent, flexible and congruent to the client's values. Step II-C is about client commitment. Egan stresses the need for client self-efficacy, and this is an important stage for the helper to more deeply explore with the client the commitment and motivation for the proposed change. This differentiates the helper from an advice giver.

Stage III: how do I get what I want or need?

In Stage III, the helper and client work together to find best-fit strategies and plans that are realistic and they look at the tools and information that might be necessary to carry out the plan of action.

In Stage III-B, the client explores the 'best-fit' strategy, suggesting a simple balance sheet of pros and cons.

Egan (2002: 357) refers to Stage III-C as 'action-focused self-contracts'. This stage is drawing together all the ideas and conclusions with the client and creating a map with which to move forward.

The helper uses these tools with the aim of *following* the client's process and not *leading*, at the same time *challenging* any inconsistencies that he or she observes and using active listening skills as a way of helping the client 'hear him or herself' so he or she can make informed choices.

Culley and Bond: integrative skills model

The framework Culley and Bond have used in their model is one of 'stages'. They have named these stages beginning, middle and end. Each stage has its own aims, strategies and named skills, which are 'the basic tools by which you put the strategies into operation and fulfill the aims of each stage' (Culley and Bond 2004: 15).

Beginning stage

AIMS

- to establish a working relationship;
- to clarify and define problems;
- to make an assessment; and
- to negotiate a contract.

STRATEGIES

- exploration;
- prioritising and focusing;
- communicative core values; and
- being concrete or specific.

SKILLS

TABLE 1.1 Foundation attending and listening skills

Foundation skills	Attending and listening	
	Reflective skills	Probing skills
Attending and listening	Reflecting a word/phrase (restating)	Questioning
Observing clients	Paraphrasing	Making statements
Being concrete	Summarising	

Middle stage

AIMS

- to reassess problems and concerns;
- to maintain the working relationship; and
- to work to the contract.

STRATEGIES

To challenge by:

- confrontation;
- giving feedback;
- giving information;

- giving directives;
- self-disclosure or self-sharing;
- immediacy; and
- communicating core values.

SKILLS

The foundation skills from the beginning stage provide the basis for the above strategies.

Ending stage

AIMS

- to decide on appropriate change;
- to implement change;
- to transfer learning; and
- to end the working relationship.

STRATEGIES

- goal setting;
- action planning;
- evaluating action and sustaining change; and
- ending.

SKILLS

The listening skills from the foundation skills and the challenging skills from the middle stage.

(Taken and adapted from Culley and Bond 2004)

McLeod and McLeod: the counselling menu

> the kind of micro-counselling that takes place when counselling is embedded in other work roles is necessarily more flexible, time-limited and improvisational, often more like a snack than a full meal.
>
> (McLeod and McLeod 2011: 69)

The counselling menu model is a clear response to the challenges presented to those who embed counselling skills into their professional helping role. It is especially applicable to those professionals who may not be able to form longer-term relationships with their clients or patients but who are nevertheless offering micro-counselling in response to their client's need to explore an issue or situation. The authors stress the importance of client-led decision-making, and the metaphor of the model is the drop-down menu of an Internet website as a brief concise menu that might be used in the micro-counselling situation within a professional helping role, typically the 8–10-minute slot available, for example, in many medical consultations.

The key aspects of this model are:

- clarifying the client's goals;
- counselling tasks; and
- methods.

Clarifying the client's goals

The authors examine what goals are achievable within a professional helping role and suggest that *specific* goals are appropriate in a micro-counselling relationship.

The helper may not have the luxury of time or appropriate setting to go into the bigger goals, but nevertheless the helper needs to be aware of the existence of the 'bigger questions' and take them into account when setting goals with the client. The helper needs to hold awareness that the specific goals may be related to the *life* goals within a micro-counselling situation. For example, a specific goal may be to set out prompts to remember to take medication but this may be part of a life goal of coming to terms with a difficult prognosis or, as another example, a specific goal of a care plan for hearing aid use when the larger life goal is accepting increased hearing loss.

Counselling tasks

The helper works with the client, acknowledging that there are two parts to this process – *planning* and *consequent action* of working towards a goal. Within the counselling relationship, appropriate tasks are identified and planned for in order to work towards the goals that the client has identified with the help of the helper. It is important to remember the client's self-advocacy. After exploring possibilities and plans within this stage, the expectation is that the client will go forward to put these plans into action, thereby moving closer to the agreed goal.

Methods

This model suggests a toolkit of *methods* available to the helper, while at the same time valuing difference:

- conversation;
- specific interventions developed by counsellors and psychotherapists;
- arts-based creative activities;
- cultural resources; and
- the personal resources of the counsellor.

(McLeod and McLeod 2011: 79)

The main strength of this model is the flexibility of the counselling relationship and the importance of client autonomy in a shared decision-making process, and the model is particularly sensitive to the organisational constraints of an embedded helper role.

THE RELATIONAL SKILLS MODEL

The phases of our model are (see also Appendix 1):

1. Setting up the relationship
2. Developing the relationship
3. Working with the relationship
4. The established relationship
5. Maintaining and ending the relationship

Setting up the relationship

This phase is about contacting and meeting the client, getting to know the client, communicating with the client and contracting with the client. Initial core skills within this phase are attending skills, active listening skills and contracting skills.

Developing the relationship

This phase enables the helper to create an environment where the client feels safe enough to bring his or her story and issues. The focus within this phase is on developing the relationship, problem identification and assessment. Additional core skills to develop communication and build upon the earlier skills are the presence and communication of the core conditions: paraphrasing, summarising, identifying and reflecting feelings, content and meaning, and asking questions.

Working with the relationship

Now that the relationship is becoming more established, the emphasis is on exploring the issues in more depth and creating an empathic understanding of the client's situation. The focus within this phase is through challenging and creating new meaning, different possibilities and perspectives. Enhanced skills to progress the communication are the skills of challenging. Types of challenging are confronting, the use of immediacy, self-disclosure and silence, clarifying, re-assessing, probing, giving feedback, and sharing information.

The established relationship

At this phase, the helper and client are able to clarify and focus on likely changes and work collaboratively to make plans, set goals, and consider and evaluate possible strategies and directions. The focus within this phase is on goal setting and evaluation. Intuitive and learned skills within this phase are deeper empathy, focusing, use of metaphor and hunches, drawing together themes, clarifying and developing goals, and action planning.

Maintaining and ending the relationship

We have found that some of the models end with the goal-setting and planning stages, whereas our experience shows that there is often a further phase where clients need ongoing support in order to manage and integrate the changes into their everyday life. If the relationship develops into this phase, further skills can be introduced to support and encourage the internalisation of the work that has been undertaken. The focus within this phase is on implementing and maintaining change and supporting self-management strategies. The development and communication of the core and enhanced skills will enable the helper to deepen awareness of the core conditions, help a client to unlock his or her potential through encouragement, support and affirmations, and review, monitor, evaluate and facilitate an ending with the client.

FIGURE 1.3 The Relational Skills Model

Phases of relationship development	Process	Skills
Setting up the relationship	Contacting/meeting the client Getting to know the client Communicating with and contracting with the client	**Initial core skills:** Attending skills Active listening skills and contracting skills
Developing the relationship	Developing the relationship Problem identification and assessment	**Additional core skills:** Presence and communication of the core conditions Paraphrasing Summarising Identifying and reflecting feelings, content and meaning Asking questions
Working with the relationship	Challenging and creating new meaning, different possibilities and perspectives	**Enhanced skills:** The skill of challenging: Confronting Use of self-disclosure, immediacy and silence Clarifying Reassessing Probing Giving feedback and sharing information
The established relationship	Clarifying and focusing on likely changes Working collaboratively to make plans, set goals, and consider and evaluate possible strategies and directions	**Intuitive and learned skills:** Deeper empathy Focusing Use of metaphor and hunches Drawing together themes Clarifying and developing goals Action planning
Maintaining and ending the relationship	Implementing and maintaining change Supporting self-management strategies	**Embedded skills:** Encouragement, support and affirmations Review, monitor, evaluate and facilitate ending Signposting/referring on

© Copyright 2012 Midwinter and Dickson. All Rights Reserved.

MODEL BOX

In this chapter, we have referred to:

- The differences between counselling and counselling skills (Culley and Bond 2004: 6)
- The core conditions from the person-centred model (Rogers 1957: 96)
- The three-stage model (Egan 2002)
- Foundation skills and beginning, middle and end stages (Culley and Bond 2004: 15)
- Counselling menu: goals, tasks and methods (McLeod and McLeod 2011)
- An overview of the Relational Skills Model (Midwinter and Dickson 2015)

SUMMARY

This chapter has outlined a number of traditional models that have led to the creation of the more contemporary Relational Skills Model. It is useful for you to understand the framework that underpins the model, and throughout the following chapters we will take you through the Relational Skills Model phase by phase in order for you to integrate this into your practice.

Chapter 2
Setting up the relationship

This phase is about contacting and meeting the client, getting to know the client, communicating with the client and contracting with the client. Initial core skills within this phase are attending skills, active listening skills and contracting skills. In this chapter, we will be discussing the essential elements of setting up a helper relationship. These include:

- Building rapport
- Setting the climate
- Attending and listening skills
- Barriers to active listening
- Non-verbal communication
- Contracting
- Setting up the learning partner relationship

You will also be introduced to the first of the video clips. The video clips in this chapter are very short and focus solely on building rapport and setting up the working alliance. Over the following chapters, you will see various clips, going through each phase of the relationship development. It is important that these clips are viewed in sequence to build upon your learning.

TEACHING

BUILDING RAPPORT

People talk to my (Becky) gran. Wherever we go, people talk to her. Not just polite, small talk, but sharing information, often very personal, about themselves. I've often wondered why. Is it because she has a cheerful smile? Or maybe she is a good listener? Or is it because her own life experiences combined with her warmth, genuineness and instinctive empathy somehow encourages this kind of person-to-person relationship to develop. People interconnect with others every day of their lives. We take these relationships for granted; we share our thoughts and feelings with some, we help or are helped by others, or sometimes we just '*be*' with another person. Relationships affect our lives. They are crucial to our overall well-being. As helpers, we need to be able to quickly build a rapport with others and be aware of the qualities that need to be present in order to enable people to talk and interact with us. How often have you heard people describe someone who has helped him or her as being 'really nice'? What makes a person seem 'really nice'? It seems to me that such a person would immediately put me at ease; they would smile, they would make appropriate eye contact, they may pass a pleasantry, perhaps commenting on the weather or my journey, and they would seem genuinely interested in what I was about to say.

From the beginning of the interaction, those everyday rapport-building skills are really important as they let the other person know that you are 'attending' to him or her. They are the building blocks to setting the climate for a successful helping relationship to develop.

So what distinguishes a successful helping relationship from an everyday interaction?

SETTING THE CLIMATE

The key to a successful helping relationship is often based on creating the right climate for the interaction to take place.

A crucial aspect of setting the climate is building the relationship between the helper and the client. This is achieved through the building of rapport, setting up the contract, good communication and listening skills, asking open and curious questions, accepting and reflecting feelings, and allowing a space for the client to tell you his or her story and explore his or her difficulties.

However, as helper, it can be easy to 'get lost' in clients' stories, to identify with aspects of the story that they are telling you, to allow your own judgements and prejudices to filter into the space and to feel inadequate or unable to 'fix the issue'. We might also discover a strong pull to lead the client to solutions that might work for us. It is important, therefore, as a helper, to develop our self-awareness and to be aware of our own strengths and limitations. We need to understand the dynamics of the helper relationship and be able to recognise and hold professional boundaries. It is important that we communicate to the client our ability to hold a helper relationship to reassure that within this role, we are boundaried, safe and can work professionally.

> ### REFLECTIVE LEARNING JOURNAL EXERCISE
>
> Think of a time when you have shared a problem with someone and he or she has really helped you. What qualities did that person have that encouraged you to go to him or her for support and what was it about that interaction that was helpful?
>
> List these qualities in your learning journal and in Appendix 2.
>
> How do you imagine a person meeting you for the first time would describe you? What qualities do you think he or she would list? Do you consider he or she would list any aspects of yourself that were less helpful, and what do you think these might be?
>
> Later, when you watch the video clip, look out for these qualities and add in any more that you observe in the helper or that you consider you hold.

Underpinning all counselling skills training is the emphasis on the human relationship and how this is set up, developed, established and maintained. While the helper is undertaking a role and using particular skills, fundamentally a helper is one human being talking to another human being, and the success of that relationship depends on how real, genuine and respectful that helper can be. Whether these interactions are referred to as holding values (Egan 2002) or core conditions (Rogers 1961), the meaning is the same. Communicating these values or core conditions effectively is an essential element in establishing the helping relationship. So, how do we communicate these?

ATTENDING AND LISTENING SKILLS

What does it mean to listen well? Listening can be the ability to be absorbed in a concert or focusing intently on a lecture. This ability to concentrate is an essential listening skill, but counselling skills require more than this; perhaps we could describe this as the '*doing*' of listening.

Active listening means we are demonstrating to someone else that we are really hearing him or her; that we understand and we are empathic to his or her situation. Even though others might have told us that we are a really good listener, we can improve our active listening through self-awareness and practice. Active listening involves both verbal language and non-verbal body language, and through it we are trying to convey to our clients that we hear them, understand them and empathise with them.

Active listening means that we are not only listening, but fully engaged with what our client is telling us, that we are responsive and attentive and that our facial expressions and body language convey this.

We can convey this by *attending* to the other person through our posture, eye contact, facial expressions and the way that we are seated (Culley and Bond 2004). Egan (2010: 77) talks of 'visibly tuning in to clients' and he summarises these skills using the acronym SOLER:

S	Face the client *squarely*
O	Adopt an *open* posture
L	Remember that it is possible at times to *lean* toward the other
E	Maintain good *eye* contact
R	Try to be relatively *relaxed* or natural in these behaviours

SOLER is a useful framework for checking how we are *attending* to our client but we also need to be culturally aware that these responses are *appropriate*. For example, in some cultures, direct eye contact may feel intimidating and overly familiar. When working with cultural differences, we should try to develop an awareness of the cultural norms and be sensitive to these differences – for example, when working with opposite genders or different age groups. We discuss more on cultural differences in Chapter 7.

At the end of this chapter, we will be introducing you to a short video clip of a helper setting up a session. When reflecting on the session, notice how the environment has been set up to enable both the helper and the client to feel relaxed and comfortable. The two chairs are set at an angle – being opposite each other can often feel intimidating and result in knees banging together! There is water on the small table, a box of tissues and a clock – all essential items to maintain comfort and ensure time boundaries are met. Notice how the room is set up when you view the video clip.

We appreciate that often these interactions take place in a working environment and it is not always possible to have a bespoke setting, purely for counselling use. If this is the case, always ensure you have access to two chairs and that these can be placed away from any desks or computer stations, creating the more intimate setting seen on the video clip. Water and tissues can be placed on the floor and the clock placed at a distance in front of you so that you can easily glance up to monitor timing, without the need to keep looking at your watch. Once again, if this is not practical, just mention at the beginning of the session that you will be monitoring the time and therefore you hope it will not be too distracting if you glance at your watch. Bringing these issues out into the open at the beginning of the session saves you the embarrassment of trying to sneak a glance without the client noticing and hopefully stops the client thinking they are taking up too much of your time. If you are working within a medical setting, you may have a different workplace where two chairs are not available and your client is on a consulting couch or other clinical situation. In this case, you might want to consider any adaptations you might make to support your client to feel more relaxed. We will explore this further when we look at the use of touch and dual roles in the helping relationship.

Being fully engaged

We have looked at the importance of the environment and setting the climate, and we appreciate that this may be challenging within a busy work environment. In order to be fully engaged with our client, we need to make sure there are minimum distractions to both our client and ourselves. If we have other pressing work issues, or things that may distract us, we might be better to reschedule, turn on our voicemail, or try to ensure we will not be disturbed in any way. Don't forget, we can also ask our client to turn his or her mobile to silent. Taking into consideration our own ability to be a helper at this time is also important. If we are hungry, preoccupied or really tired, we are in danger of being distracted and cannot give our full attention. If our minds are elsewhere, it is harder to be fully engaged with our client. We want to convey that we are really interested in our client and, for the time that we have allocated, we are fully present for him or her. As an extreme example, I (Janie) can remember a previous work supervisor who was so exhausted that she nearly fell asleep! While I felt sorry for her, I also felt unimportant, boring and definitely *unheard* by her.

> **REFLECTIVE LEARNING JOURNAL EXERCISE**
>
> Can you think of a time when you have been in conversation with someone and he or she appeared distracted and not really listening?
>
> What did that feel like to you?
>
> Consider how you are going to prepare for your helping role so that you are fully engaged with your client.
>
> What preparations will you need to make?

Being responsive

When we *respond* to our clients, we learn to 'track' them rather than 'lead' them. We respond to what they are saying and we stay alongside them rather than impose our own agenda. This can be a challenge and, like all skills, needs practice to embed into our ways of working with others.

In the following chapters, we will examine in more detail the ways we can verbally and non-verbally respond to our clients through counselling skills – for example, summarising, paraphrasing or reflecting. Throughout this book, we will learn the ways to embed these skills in a way that is a relevant response to our client.

Being attentive

When we are attentive, we can begin to notice clues as to how the other person might be feeling. These might be strong words that are said with intense feeling and phrases that seem to 'carry weight', or it might be prompts from a client's stiff body posture or quavering voice. As we acquire our counselling skills, we also learn if and when to respond to these clues. We learn to have an inner dialogue where we question if a response would be helpful. This might sound daunting at this stage but practice will help to embed these skills and observations. If you drive a car, you may remember what it was like when you first began to learn and how you never thought you would remember to check the mirror, release the handbrake and put the car into gear. Embedding counselling skills is a little like that. You do not entirely lose your awareness because you still choose how to use your skills, and practising will help you to more easily embed skills into your work as it gradually becomes a more instinctive process.

Eye contact, facial expression and body posture

A large percentage of our communication is silent – through our faces, eye contact and physical posture and mannerisms, we convey subtle messages through our interaction with others (see non-verbal communication, p. 30). Psychologists have discovered that there are 100 facial expressions that convey we are angry (Ekman 2008: 128). We need to develop an awareness of how we are appearing to other people and what messages we are projecting that are out of our awareness. In common with many mammals, we communicate a great deal through eye contact; intense staring can be uncomfortable, but equally if we are not looking at the other person, we can appear disinterested or bored. When my eyesight started to deteriorate (Janie), people would say that I frowned a lot when in fact I was trying to concentrate on seeing them clearly. Even after having contact lenses, this continued to be an unconscious habit and I have to check myself occasionally to ensure that I don't inadvertently appear stern! We can learn to be aware of how we appear to others by asking for feedback and watching videos of ourselves.

Listening

And finally we need to fully *listen* to the other person. This requires a lot of concentration if we are to do it well, and as we begin to embed these counselling skills it can be a surprisingly tiring activity as it involves vast amount of effort on our part. We are focused on the person in front of us and, if we are listening well, we should be able to repeat what he or she has just said. Although it is highly unlikely that we will have perfect recall, we should be able to summarise and stay on track with him or her. Not only do we need to listen to what is being said, but we must also listen out for the 'gaps' and the things that are not being said. This could be conveyed through gestures, facial expressions, intonations, body posture and a mismatch between what is being said and what is being shown. An example might be someone telling you something really sad but giggling and smiling while he or she relates it. A good listener will be able to reflect this back to the client, sharing his or her observations. We will examine this in more detail in the next chapter.

BARRIERS TO ACTIVE LISTENING

There are some blocks to listening that are easy to slip into and while we do it in everyday conversations, they are not conducive to the helping role. However, we should not worry if we recognise our own patterns of interacting in the following examples, as most people will have one or more of these. This is an opportunity to develop an awareness of your own blocks and learn to recognise them when practising your counselling skills.

'Me too' moments or identifying

When our experiences are similar, it can be easy to get lost in comparing the client's experience with our own. There may well be times when we identify with what our client is saying, but when we get lost in the 'me too' moments we can stop listening. All at once, we find ourselves daydreaming and back in our own past experiences. It is easy to find that we have not heard our client's story for the last few minutes of the interaction because we have become lost in our own memories.

Second-guessing

We may have a real sense of where our client's dialogue is going next and it is tempting to jump in with your next intervention through this 'second-guessing'. We need to beware of mind reading and remember that we are *tracking* our client and not *leading* him or her.

Planning what we are going to say next

When we first start to use counselling skills, it is easy to find ourselves rehearsing how we might use them, which can have the effect of missing what our client is saying because our minds are planning what we are going to say next.

Filtering

Our aim is to try to hear *all* that our client is telling us. When we filter, we listen to some things and not others.

Value judgements

Our aim is to provide an open environment where our client feels respected and safe. We attempt to reserve judgement until we have heard what our client wants to say. When we are quick to judge, we can stop listening fully because we have an inner critical dialogue going on in our heads. A basic rule of listening is that judgements should be held until we have heard and evaluated the content. This will enable us to 'respond' to what we are hearing, rather than 'reacting' from an impulsive position.

Losing concentration or dreaming

If we are not *fully engaged* because we are tired or distracted, it can be easy to lose concentration or get lost in our own thoughts. We might be reminded of an experience in our own lives and find our minds wandering off to that memory. Later, we will examine the way we can use skills to check with our client that we have heard and understood them.

Advising and having the right answers

'If I were you', or 'In your position, I would' might be a response we would want from a friend, but as a helper we are trying to support our client to explore and to find his or her own answers. We need to remind ourselves that we are all different and our answers may not be suitable answers for our clients. In this situation, our role is to help our client solve his or her own problem and not to provide solutions. If our head is busy planning the solution, we may stop listening fully.

Changing the subject

This could be going back to a subject that has aroused our curiosity but is not relevant to the client. When we do this, we are leading, not tracking. We also need to be mindful that we use humour sensitively and appropriately as this can also have the effect of derailing the train of conversation away from the subject and can blind us to our client's current feelings.

Going along with everything

'Absolutely . . . oh yes, I know . . . right, right'. We want to be pleasant and likeable, but if we agree with everything a client says, we may slip into half-listening. We get the drift of the conversation but we are not really involved.
(Adapted from McKay *et al.* 1995)

NON-VERBAL COMMUNICATION

Verbal language is a small percentage of the way in which we communicate and interact with others. We pick up hundreds of small visual clues about the other person and process these consciously and unconsciously. When a stranger walks into a room, we have made all sorts of assumptions and judgements based on the way he or she walks, the way he or she looks, dresses, holds his or her posture, makes eye contact and any mannerisms he or she may have. This *body* communication is an integral part of active listening.

Imagine you are talking to a helper about a problem you have. He is sitting opposite you slouched right down in his chair with his legs stretched out in front of him and his arms behind his head. Sometimes he yawns and looks out the window or looks down at his feet. His clothes are a little scruffy and he has not shaved for a few days. Do you think he is listening to you? What do you imagine about him? Why do you think that?

A helper is sitting bolt upright in her chair. She is staring at you intently and her hands are fidgeting consequently. She frowns as she speaks and does not respond to your smile. You can see that she keeps checking the time in an agitated way. How easy do you imagine it might be to talk to this woman? If it does not feel easy, what is it about her way of being that does not feel comfortable?

Through non-verbal messages, we can communicate many different emotions – boredom, agitation, disinterest, tension, anger, dislike, judgement, anxiety and so on. We can also show warmth, empathy, respect and acceptance. The latter may, in some ways, come naturally but also we might want to adapt some of our ways of being in order to convey this. We are all different, and self-observation and awareness of how we present to others can develop these important skills.

Often, when we watch a video of our skills practice, we notice that the client and the counsellor are sitting in a similar way, with their legs crossed and their heads occasionally tilted in the same direction.

This is termed *mirroring* and it is a form of 'body listening'. When it is pointed out by an observer, both the client and the counsellor have often been unaware of doing it, but

FIGURE 2.1 Mirroring

it is a good example of how unconscious body gestures are part of the listening process because mirroring can be a demonstration of empathy.

CONTRACTING

Before embarking on any kind of helper relationship, it is really important to set up a contractual agreement (first coined by Greenson 1965); Clarkson (2003) calls this 'the Working Alliance'. This contract sets up the relationship and is a way of ensuring both parties know and understand any of the important aspects that affect their working together. Often in life, people get together and talk about the common problems of their daily experiences. They share their thoughts and feelings, let off steam, laugh together and cry on each other's shoulders. Creating a helper relationship, however, is very different. Both adults are making a decision that in some way they will be working together, with one person taking the role of helper and the other the role of the client. In making that decision, they will no longer be two equal human beings simply sharing their experiences, but they will be embarking on a relationship where they 'contract' to work on a problem or a set of problems. In setting up the working alliance, the helper will be assessing whether he or she has the capacities to help the other person with the problem(s) he or she brings, and the client will be assessing whether he or she feels safe, respected and understood and whether he or she would like to invest further in the relationship.

The contractual agreement is about developing the quality of the working relationship – deciding on the *boundaries* of the relationship and thinking about and discussing *confidentiality* and how that might affect the relationship. It is also crucial to talk about *realistic expectations* and what the client might hope to achieve (and, of course, whether those expectations are realistic and achievable). In a workplace setting, there might be *dual relationships* involved, and it is important to negotiate these various roles and examine any possible tensions, which might influence the helper relationship. There will be *ethical issues* that need to be explored and *guidelines* to follow. In our view, the success of the relationship is depicted by how well the working alliance has been set up, how it is negotiated throughout the relationship and how well it is managed. There may be occasions when aspects of the working alliance need to be reviewed and amended.

Let us consider the various elements that could make up the working alliance.

Boundaries

Time boundaries

Often, in our enthusiasm and willingness to help, we overestimate how much time we can realistically give to the relationship. For the purposes of this book, we are not setting up contracted counselling sessions that occur on a regular weekly basis for a period of 50–60 minutes, as might happen in a professional counselling contract. As a helper, you might be only offering a one-off session that lasts for 30 minutes, or you may be able to offer a number of sessions that each lasts for 10–50 minutes. You need to be clear about what you are able to offer and transparent with the client about this. If you realise your time frame is going to be unrealistic, then this needs to be discussed with the client and a new time frame negotiated.

Space

Are you always able to see the client in the same environment? If so, will there be a room that you can regularly book and how might this work? Will you or your client do this? Have you ever had one of those moments where you have stood outside of a restaurant or meeting room with someone and you both look blankly at each other when you realise that you both thought the other person was making the reservation? So it is important from the outset that these issues are discussed and a process confirmed. Is the space quiet with minimal risk of being overheard? If it is not your own room, or you often have to change environments, it is useful to take in a pre-written sign that you can put on the outside of the door that lets others know that the room is engaged to ensure some privacy. Also always take tissues with you and a bottle of water and two disposable cups, just in case there is no access to water. These simple things often make the difference in setting up a caring and empathic working alliance.

Self-disclosure

We will talk more about self-disclosure in Chapter 3, but it is important to acknowledge that in the helper role, the boundaries of sharing information are very different to other relationships. In a friendship, for instance, it is usual for two people to take turns in sharing information – one person tells his or her story and then the other person takes his or her turn. In a helper/client relationship, the client will maximise the time and space to engage in self-disclosure, whereas the helper will minimise the amount of self-disclosure to information that is helpful to the session.

Touch

Touching is a way of communicating and can be a way of relating. There are many types of touch – physical, nurturing, sexual, disciplinary, practical and protective. However, there are a number of sensitive and problematic issues when considering using touch in a helper role. The use of touch must be appropriate to the role and setting of the helper relationship. While physical touch may be routinely used in a nursing or physiotherapy role, this level of touch would be inappropriate in other settings. People have different experiences, in life and cultures, and what is OK to one person might be totally inappropriate to someone else. We need to be aware of, and sensitive to, the use of touch and be respectful of personal space. If we are unsure, it is always better to avoid touch altogether. Sometimes, it may be more appropriate, less threatening but caring, to pass across a box of tissues when someone is in tears rather than to lean across and give a hug.

> Questions that are important when thinking about the use of touch are:
> - Does the client invite and want touch, and, if so, are you, as helper, comfortable with this?
> - Are you and the client clear that the touch is appropriate in the setting of the session?
> - Is the touch intended for the client's benefit?
> - Is the client fully able to give consent?
> - Could the client misinterpret the touch?

Some people are less comfortable with touch than others, and this applies as equally to the helper as it does to the client. Physical touch is only one way of communicating empathy and care, and there are many different ways that a helper can convey support without the use of touch.

Confidentiality

Clear, accurate information about confidentiality is crucial to a good working alliance. However short the session is, it is vital that the client knows where and with whom the information he or she discloses will be shared and/or stored. This can be a difficult area, especially where there is more than one relationship involved. As a helper, you need to be clear of the confidentiality framework within which you will be working.

> Questions that need to be explored when considering confidentiality will be:
> - Will the information shared be confidential to only you and the client or will it be shared with anyone else? If it is to be shared, agreement must be reached with the client before the information is divulged to anyone else.

> - Will you be taking notes, and, if so, how are you going to store these? Has the client given you consent to take personal data and have you informed the client what you will be doing with these data and their purpose? Are you aware of your responsibilities and obligations with regards to the Data Protection Act? If you hold personal information, you must use it fairly, keep it secure, make sure the information is accurate and keep it up to date. Will you be storing the notes on a computer, and, if so, do you need to notify the Information Commissioner's Office (www.ico.gov.uk)?
> - What happens if the client meets you in another setting? How will you both hold the confidentiality boundaries outside of the session?
> - Is the client fully informed of the limits of confidentiality and able to give informed consent that he or she wishes to continue with the sessions?

Confidentiality is never clear-cut, and the above questions will need to be considered alongside more specific workplace guidelines relating to the confidentiality framework within which you are employed. Unexpected situations may arise resulting in a need to revisit the confidentiality contract you have made with your client, so it is important from the outset that both you and your client know what to expect in terms of sharing and storing the information. This will enable the client to feel safe and reassured in sharing personal information, and you will be confident that you are aware of your responsibilities to enable you to work in an ethical and respectful way.

Realistic expectations and dual relationships

In Chapter 1, we discussed the differences between counselling and using counselling skills. An important aspect of the working alliance is to ensure that both the helper and client understand the boundaries and limitations of this relationship and we attempt to clarify this with our client from the beginning. It is important that the client is given an opportunity to discuss his or her wants and expectations from the relationship, and it is equally important that the helper is clear as to whether those expectations are achievable within the boundaries of the relationship.

In the helping role, it is essential that both you and the client understand the context of the relationship. An example might be:

> A personnel officer using counselling skills when discussing employment issues and his client discloses a recent diagnosis of breast cancer. While it would be appropriate for the helper to be empathic and use good listening skills, this helper would also be considering how to signpost the client to more appropriate professional counselling support. It would be important for this helper to understand and acknowledge the limitations of his knowledge and expertise and to understand when to refer the client on to more appropriate support.

If we are embedding counselling skills into our professional role within the workplace, there is likely to be unavoidable dual roles that need to be clarified. If, for instance, we practise counselling skills in our role as a manager in a health setting, responsibilities might arise if our client discloses issues that could impact on his or her ability to carry out his or her work effectively. Conflicts of responsibility to service users could affect confidentiality, and our working alliance needs to clearly set down these limitations from the outset.

Dual roles can be less obvious through other relationships – for example, mutual friends or social circles, or historical relationships in a previous role. Any existing relationships, outside of the helper role, will have an impact on the interaction between helper and client. These different relationships need to be acknowledged and a way of working within them needs to be established when setting up the working alliance. It is important for you and the client to agree on the boundaries and information that can be shared within the different roles. An example of this might be a client who shares a personal story with you during a helper session, who later meets you in the office kitchen but does not want to continue the conversation that they shared with you earlier. In this case, you might already have discussed with the client, when you set up the working alliance, how you will manage such boundaries when you meet outside of the session.

Ambiguity around dual role clarification can lead to distress and insecurity, so it is essential that roles are continually reviewed and clarified to match the climate of the relationship.

In the second of the video clips, later in this chapter, you will see the helper raise the issue of dual relationship as she sets up the contract and the working alliance with the client.

Cultural expectations and diversity

It is also essential to be aware of cultural expectations and diversity. Diversity is about more than race and culture; it is also about gender, age, sexual orientation, beliefs and disability. Diversity is about the human qualities that are different to our own and may be outside of our own experiences or cultural norms, but are present in other individuals or groups. Recognising and having acceptance of these differences is crucial within the helping relationship. We need to educate ourselves about diversity and equality and have knowledge about different client cultures to provide a culturally appropriate service. It is important to be self-reflexive and aware of our own culture and values and to consider the impact of these on the helping relationship. It is important that we do not fall into the trap of 'stereotyping' clients or making assumptions that clients share the same values and cultural norms as us. There is a huge diversity of experience of people who might come from the 'same social or cultural group', and we should not assume that they share similar personal qualities, skills, experiences or cultural values.

Ethical issues and guidelines

Relational ethic in counselling and psychotherapy has been described as 'a medium through which decisions, actions and interactions associated with a relationship are mindfully approached' (Gabriel and Casemore 2009: 11), and this can equally be applied to the use of counselling skills. We need to remain ethically 'mindful' that we are *not causing harm* and are *respectful, fair* and *honest* in our interactions, and that our aim is to *benefit* the client and *his or her interests*. As we develop our counselling skills practice, we will begin to realise how powerful and evocative these simple skills can be, and potentially open to manipulation and exploitation of others. We have a responsibility to be mindful of this as you may be surprised how much personal information and life history can be disclosed by our simply using open questions and reflecting back during our interactions. Therefore, we have a responsibility to use these skills appropriately.

The BACP outline in their Ethical Framework (BACP 2013) principles that inform counselling practice and these principles apply equally when embedding counselling skills into the helper role. For the purposes of embedding counselling skills, we see these principles as:

> *Being trustworthy*: the helpers are honest and act in good faith.
>
> *Autonomy*: the client's right to have and make choices of his or her own free will.
>
> *Beneficence*: to work in the best interest of the client and others.
>
> *Non-maleficence*: to do no harm to the client.
>
> *Justice*: to offer services fairly and equally to all.
>
> *Self-respect*: to acknowledge your strengths and have an appreciation of your limitations.

We need to continually review our ethical stance to ensure we are working within the ethical principles, because these can change throughout our work with our clients. For this reason, the contract is often returned to. While we set up the working alliance at the beginning of the relationship, there will be times when it needs to be reviewed and amended in order to ensure the principles are being adhered to. At the time of going to press (winter 2014), the BACP ethical guidelines (www.bacp.co.uk) are under review again, and it is useful for us to keep up to date with any changes in these policies.

EXAMPLE

VIDEO CLIP 2a
SETTING UP THE RELATIONSHIP:
Jacqui and Caz

It is now time to watch the following clips, paying particular attention to the way in which the helper sets up the climate and the working alliance with the clients and think about how the various skills are utilised.

This first clip is with Jacqui setting up the relationship with Caz, a client who is not known to Jacqui.

Video Clip 2b is with Jacqui and Becky, and you will see from the clip that they have had a previous relationship and are setting up the working alliance for this session.

Video Clip 2c is with Glyn and Rob. Glyn knows this client but they have not been involved in a helper/client relationship before.

VIDEO CLIP 2b

SETTING UP THE RELATIONSHIP – DUAL RELATIONSHIP: Jacqui and Becky

VIDEO CLIP 2c

SETTING UP THE RELATIONSHIP: Glyn and Rob

REFLECTIVE LEARNING JOURNAL EXERCISE

Having watched the three short clips, reflect on the following:

- What qualities did you notice the helper had in building rapport with the client?
- How did the helper set the climate for working with the client and what skills did he or she use?
- What information did the helper discuss in setting up the working alliance?
- How did the helper deal with issues of confidentiality? What were they?
- In Video Clip 2b, you will notice that the helper spent time going through with the client the possible impact of this dual relationship upon the session. What aspects of your working environment or working relationships do you think will be helpful/hindering to client sessions?

Now you have had an opportunity to view the clips and answer the questions, take a look at the observations and skills that we have reflected upon in the transcripts. You might find it helpful to compare your answers with our listed skills and observations. In the following chapters we will use these transcripts for each session and as you become more familiar with labelling the *process* (what is going on between the counsellor and client) and *skills* (identifying which skills they are using), you will be able to reflect, practise and critically evaluate your own learning in a similar way.

> ***Process*** is what we notice is going on between the two people and also what is going on for us internally as we watch the video clips.

TABLE 2.1 Transcript of Video Clip 2a: Setting up the relationship – Jacqui and Caz

Content	Process	Skills
J: Caz, hi. Really nice to see you after all the organising that has been going on and the emails that have been passed between us and the others, and now you are here and I can see your face and it's really great	The relationship is clarified, as although they have not met, the helper acknowledges the email contact. The helper maintains good eye contact, smiles at the client and mirrors her body language The helper is relaxed, has an open posture facing the client, they are sitting in a similar way. She is fully engaged and attentive	Building rapport Setting the climate SOLER (Egan)
C: Yes, it's nice, it's really good		
J: So, one of the purposes of today is to do a 10–15-minute counselling skills demonstration, OK, so just to sort of tell you about the time boundary more than anything else. So what's the best thing? I'll probably wrap it up in about 10 minutes so then that gives us a few minutes extra just to bring the conversation to a close. Is that OK?	The helper sets up the working alliance with time boundaries. While these are part of the 'contract', this is done in a tentative voice and the helper checks that client is OK and understands these parameters	Contracting (setting up the relationship RSM) Setting up working alliance (Clarkson and Egan) Time boundaries
C: That's absolutely fine	The client confirms her agreement, which helps the helper know she is on the right lines	
J: Also to think about confidentiality. Now the confidentiality that we are going to have in here is going to be very different to be normal counselling session, because this session has the potential to be read by many, many people and we have got a cameraman and an observer. So just for you to think you know what issues you bring and for you to be comfortable with you what you say. Have you thought about this at all, Caz? I just wondered	Second, the helper sets up confidentiality, is congruent that this situation is different from the norm and checks that the client has considered this and so the client feels she has options (Although on this occasion the agreement is about a cameraman being present, which is obviously not a usual occurrence, the helper demonstrates here the importance of establishing the boundaries of confidentiality, whatever they may be)	Setting up working alliances (Clarkson and Egan) Setting up the contract (setting up the relationship RSM) Confidentiality boundaries

table 2.1 continued

Content	Process	Skills
C: Yes, I have beforehand; it's to think through. There are things I obviously will not want to . . . I think if we touch on an issue where I don't want to . . . I will signal that is something maybe that is not appropriate within that context. So if that's OK with you		
J: Yes	The helper is attentive and also gives a non-verbal indication of listening in her posture and eye contact. She is continuing to negotiate with her client	Non-verbal communication Attentive listening
C: Cos you never know		
J: Well, we all know the dangers that sometimes you get talking about, around an issue, and things can go further than you imagined. So will you just say? How would you like to do it? Say 'Look I'm not comfortable with this' or do you want to wave at me! (shared laughter) What would you like?	The helper has listened to the client and is responding to her by negotiating how she might signal if she feels they have reached an inappropriate subject for this public arena	Attending and responding Ethical guidelines (BACP) Being concrete (Culley and Bond)
C: I'm happy to say if there is anything that I find is a little bit near the knuckle or a little too raw. I am more than happy and confident enough to say, 'Sorry Jacqui not going there'.		
J: Great, no, I think that is a really important issue that, and for you to take the lead in that	Confirmation again with this summary	Summarising
C: Absolutely, thank you		
J: Is there an issue you would like to think about now, to start the ball rolling, that you have had in your head, or where would you like to go from here?		Allowing the client to tell her story (Egan stage I: what's going on?)

table 2.1 continued

Content	Process	Skills
C: I think there is something that is very prominent for me personally at the minute. I've just come back from holiday with my children and my husband and when you have a little time to reflect and a bit of space, things come up don't they when you are lying by the pool. And one of the things actually was where am I going next with my life really. I was looking at my children, who are 10 and 12 but rapidly growing up, and they have been the centre of my practical day-to-day work. I've always worked part time. Things are changing there and my relationship with my husband is changing as well, and I'm just at the time of my life where I'm just very aware of periods of transition and fears around that. But I think it's all caught up . . . I'm in my mid-40s, things are changing. I've recently undertaken quite a lot of study, which I've loved doing. And I'm moving into a time where I'm changing where I work, my placement, all sorts of things, so it feels like a little scary place, a very good place but my children within it are very much uppermost in my mind, and especially how I'll manage that especially when they've been arguing. There's quite a lot of things in there I realise		
J: Yes, several strands growing out of that transition		Reflective skills (Culley and Bond)

TABLE 2.2 Transcript of Video Clip 2b: Setting up the relationship – dual relationship – Jacqui and Becky

Content	Process	Skills
J: Another thing we need to just think about is the fact that we know each other, we've worked together, in fact you've been my boss, we've become friends, and again what impact that might have on what you want to bring to this session. Have you thought about that at all?	The helper openly acknowledges dual roles and checks the client's feelings around this	Building rapport Boundaries Congruence
B: Yes, I have, and I've always felt really comfortable with you and I think our relationship has always been as equal as it can be in our various roles, so I don't feel intimidated by that or strange about our relationship, certainly for the purposes of this demonstration, and I feel comfortable in bringing the issue that I have thought about to bring in this environment, so yes I feel fine about that	The client demonstrates being fully aware of the possible issues and fully consents	Communicating and contracting
J: OK, that's great, that's lovely (*fade out*)		

TABLE 2.3 Transcript of Video Clip 2c: Setting up the relationship – Glyn and Rob

Content	Process	Skills
G: Rob, great to see you, thanks for coming down		
R: It's OK, it's OK		
G: How are you feeling about it all?		Attending skills and getting to know the client
R: I'm a little bit nervous		
G: I get a little bit nervous with these types of things as well So you are not alone. I've got a couple of things to run through before we start		Communicating with the client through use of immediacy
R: OK, all right		
G: We now have an opportunity to meet for a couple of sessions, to talk about what's going on, and during those sessions I will maintain a confidentiality in relation to things you tell me as we have already agreed previously	The helper is using a visual prompt to remind him of the areas he has to cover in the contract	Contracting (RSM)
R: Yeah, OK		
G: During our time together I will respect your right not to answer any questions you do not wish to answer and do not undertake anything that you do not wish to do	Although using a visual prompt, the helper still maintains eye contact	Contracting
R: OK		
G: Have you got any questions for me?	Checks understanding and smiles	Contracting
R: No I don't, not at the moment anyway		
G: OK		

SETTING UP THE LEARNING PARTNER RELATIONSHIP

Now is the time to set up the relationship with your learning partner. You may recall that at the beginning of this book, we suggested that your learning partner should be someone who is either studying this same book or someone who is familiar with the use of counselling skills in order for you to have the experience of being in the role of both helper and client. This can be either a peer on a training programme (if the book is being used as part of a formalised training programme) or a peer or mentor at work if you are using it as part of your continued professional development. He or she needs to be someone that you have regular access to. Your learning partner is someone that you can practise your skills with and someone with whom you will be able to give and receive feedback about your individual and joint progress. How you work together is entirely up to you but, as discussed above, setting up your contractual agreement is a very important part of the relationship.

It is really helpful to video our skills practice, and in these days of small video cameras we do not need a studio and expensive cameras to try this out. During this book, we will be encouraging you to observe yourself. Many of our students find this part of the course the most daunting and often say, 'I hate to see myself on camera'. However, at the end of the course, they usually come to see this as one of their most useful learning processes. Try to go beyond your initial embarrassment and ask your learning partner for feedback. These video clips will be useful to keep for revision and future learning.

Through evaluating your sessions, you can discover the things about your body language that you had not noticed before. For example:

> Do you look relaxed or tense?
>
> How are you sitting?
>
> Are you too close to the other person or is there sufficient personal space between you? (Note: this may not be applicable if you need to sit close to fit in the camera viewfinder.)

Giving feedback to each other

When giving feedback to each other, remember that feedback needs to be about the behaviour or situation rather than the person – for example, 'I feel frustrated' as opposed to 'you are frustrating'. It is often said that feedback should *always* be 'sandwiched' – for example, negative feedback sandwiched between positive feedback – but this can lead to someone feeling that positive feedback will always be followed by something negative and they will not hear the positive while they are waiting for the 'but' to follow – 'you are doing really well but . . .'. Rather, always ensure that feedback is balanced between positive and negative and that negative feedback is constructive and clear, and trust your own process about which feedback to give and when.

The method of feedback most widely cited in academia and business is CORBS:

> **Clear** Say your feedback clearly, honestly and precisely.
>
> **Owned** Your feedback is just one opinion and not the 'truth'. Ensure the other person knows and understands that he or she can reject your feedback if he or she wishes to. Ask the person if he or she has received similar feedback before so he or she has something to measure your feedback against.
>
> **Regular** Give feedback regularly and do not store it all up for one occasion. Sometimes, it is wise to think about the feedback and give yourself time to consider the implications of giving the feedback rather than just 'blurting' it out but try to give it as near to the event as possible.
>
> **Balanced** Try to balance positive and negative feedback and check out with the person that he or she has heard both (we are inclined to only remember negative feedback). Be mindful of not overwhelming the person with feedback but only give as much as he or she is able to process at that time.
>
> **Specific** It is hard to learn from generalised feedback. Feedback about specific situations or behaviour is much easier to process and learn from. Check out with the person that he or she understands what you have said and what the feedback relates to.
>
> (adapted from Hawkins and Shohet 2012: 160)

Some examples of feedback using CORBS:

'I felt you were really listening to me when you summarised what I had said at the end.' (*Specific and owned*)

'I wonder whether you could have used an open question to encourage your client to explore the problem themselves?' (*Clear, owned and specific*)

'I think you listen really well but this client is extremely talkative and I wonder if you could have used your skills more?' (*Balanced and regular*)

> ### REFLECTIVE LEARNING JOURNAL EXERCISE
>
> What do you think the other person sees when he or she is sitting opposite you?
>
> Ask your partner for feedback on this.
>
> Reflect in your journal what you feel about his or her feedback.
>
> Does it fit with how you see yourself?

In later sessions, you can begin to notice:

> what skills you are applying;
>
> the content of the session;
>
> the climate of the relationship and the rapport;
>
> the process – what is going on between you in the session;
>
> how you are improving;
>
> your strengths and weaknesses with regards to using the skills.

Being a client

You may have been on other courses where you have been asked to role-play being a client. In our opinion, being asked to role-play can be a highly anxiety-provoking situation for both the client and the counsellor, and can feel set-up and unrealistic. In all the training we provide, we always encourage students to bring their own issues to work with. Initially, this may be something that makes you 'mildly anxious': situation-based issues such as a minor conflict with a colleague, friend or partner; feeling anxious about attending a meeting or an event; managing an anticipated transition or a difficult situation at home or work. As you build up trust with your learning partner, you may wish to explore some deeper value-based issues such as 'I'm not assertive enough', 'I get angry too easily' or 'I find it hard to show my emotions'. You may want to explore a personally important issue such as 'I'd like to work out why I can't lose weight' or 'I always seem to argue with my partner'. When counselling skills are used well, they can be extremely powerful and can take you into areas you were not thinking about or feeling. It is important, therefore, to remain boundaried and safe during these exercises, and only bring material that you are happy to explore with your learning partner, remembering that the objective is to undertake an exercise and practising his or her skills. Having said that, students can find these mini practice sessions extremely rewarding and they often report gaining a lot of insight through engaging in these exercises.

REFLECT, PRACTISE AND EVALUATE

Identify your learning partner and arrange a meeting to set up your relationship. Pay particular attention to setting up a good working alliance, having regards to the skills of contracting set out in this chapter. Think about how the helpers in the video clips set up their contractual agreements with their clients. Setting up the contractual agreement with your learning partner is a really good way of practising setting up a contract with your clients.

This is also a good opportunity to think about what issues you might like to bring to these practice sessions as a client.

Video all the sessions with your learning partner so you can watch them back, reflect on them and evaluate them. Each session is usually about 10 minutes in each role.

MODEL BOX

In this chapter, we have referred to:

- The Relational Skills Model – setting up the relationship
- The skill of visibly tuning in to clients – SOLER (Egan 2010)
- 'What's going on?' (Egan 2002)
- Ethical framework for good practice (BACP 2013)
- Five relationship model – the working alliance (Clarkson 2003)
- The relationship as working alliance (Egan 2002)
- The foundation skills – attending skills and listening skills (Culley and Bond 2004)
- CORBS model (Hawkins and Shohet 2012)

SUMMARY

- The essential framework of a helping relationship is setting up the contract and working alliance, building rapport, and providing a safe and conducive climate.
- Consideration of the initial core skills of what constitutes good listening can develop our awareness of the barriers to active listening.
- Underpinning all counselling skills training is the emphasis on the human relationship and how this is set up, developed, established and maintained.
- Observation of video clips of the helper/client relationship is a key aspect of learning.
- Setting up a relationship and working with a learning partner is essential to learn, to give and receive appropriate feedback, and critically evaluate progress.

Chapter 3
Developing the relationship

This phase enables the helper to create an environment where the client feels safe enough to bring their story and issues. The focus within this phase is on developing the relationship, problem identification and assessment. Additional core skills, which can be used to develop communication and build upon the earlier skills, are the presence and communication of the core conditions, paraphrasing, summarising, identifying and reflecting feelings content and meaning, and asking questions. The additional core skills we will cover in this chapter are:

- Phrases that help/hinder communication
- Paraphrasing
- Summarising
- Identifying and reflecting feelings, content and meaning
- Asking questions

TEACHING

PHRASES THAT HELP/HINDER COMMUNICATION

There are some very useful 'tips' to aid effective communication and help you communicate to the client the core conditions of empathy, unconditional positive regard and congruence. Phrases such as:

- 'It seems as though . . .'/'It seems as if . . .'
- 'What would happen if . . .'
- 'Can you tell me more about . . .'
- 'How do you feel?'/'How do you feel about . . .'
- 'Can I just check out that I've got this right . . .'
- 'You seem/look/appear [a bit/very] upset/angry/sad/pleased'
- 'Could you explain a little more about . . .'
- 'Let me know if I got this right . . .'
- 'I'm wondering . . .'

These all encourage tentative exploration of the issue and encourage a client to think about his or her feelings and the meaning of the issue and the impact and reason for bringing it to the session. It is useful to use some of these phrases to check out and explore with the client that you understand his or her story and its importance and relevance.

There are also some phrases that are less effective such as:

- 'You should/ought to/must do this . . .'
- 'You obviously are/feel . . .'
- 'Oh don't worry, it's not important/everything will be OK'
- 'Don't cry, it's not that bad'
- 'I know exactly how you feel'
- 'Don't be silly'/'That's really silly'
- 'You don't really mean that'/'Don't be angry/upset'
- 'It could be worse . . .'
- 'If I were you, I'd . . .'
- 'Moving on . . .'

These phrases often shut people down, thereby stopping them from exploring the feeling and/or meaning of the issue for them. While, on the one hand, it might be reassuring for a helper to tell the client 'I'm sure everything will be OK', in reality it might be useful for the client to explore how it feels for him or her when things are not OK and to express his or her apprehension and fear within a safe place in the session.

As helpers, it is useful to keep the helpful phrases 'up your sleeve', and while it could sound contrived or even patronising to start every sentence the same way, it is good to get familiar with using the effective phrases (and not using the less effective ones) as part of your counselling skills language.

PARAPHRASING

The skill of paraphrasing is listening to the meaning of what your client has just said and *rephrasing* it, showing your understanding of what he or she has just said back to him or her, *using your own words*. So you are picking up the essence of what has been said without interpreting it.

The client can find this helpful in various ways. He or she can feel 'heard' by you, the helper, and can see that you have been listening and understood him or her, and it also helps him or her to reflect on his or her own thinking processes. This is a really important skill to learn and it requires practise to embed paraphrasing into your way of working. In the beginning, paraphrasing might feel strange and perhaps a bit contrived, but as you develop into a skilled helper you will be able to integrate paraphrases in a way that sounds natural and empathic. Paraphrasing can develop trust and understanding between a client and a helper, and the helper can check that he or she has understood and is 'tracking' his or her client and not 'leading' him or her.

Good paraphrases are brief, focused on the client's experience and could contain both facts and feelings. They are tentative, non-directive and non-judgemental. The helper tries to follow the tone and feeling behind what the client is saying and attempts to match this in the paraphrase. Here are some examples to consider:

Client: I have been referred to a specialist by my doctor because I can't hear properly in my left ear. Both my parents went really deaf when they were older I am really worried what will happen next. How can I be a music teacher if I can't hear properly! It's a disaster!

Helper: You sound really anxious that the consultant will discover something seriously wrong with your hearing that is perhaps hereditary and I can hear you're worried how it might affect your work.

Client: Yes, that's it, because since my husband was made redundant we have totally relied on my earnings to support the whole family.

Helper: You're the main 'bread winner'.

Client: Absolutely! My earnings as a teacher are essential, particularly as we are hoping the kids will go to university and you know how much that costs these days.

Helper: This sounds like a lot of worries for you. I wonder if we were to make a list of these worries, which one would be at the top of that list?

You will notice that in the first two interventions, the helper is relating back to the client what she is saying but with his own words.

> ### REFLECTIVE LEARNING JOURNAL EXERCISE
>
> How do you think this conversation in the example sounds?
>
> Does it flow well?
>
> Does the helper sound empathic? Does he seem as though he is following what his client is saying and understanding her?

A paraphrase enables the client to hear what he or she has said and to focus on the meaning; the client can recount his or her story and a paraphrase can show him or her that he or she has been listened to, respected and encouraged. The final intervention ('I wonder if we were to make a list of these worries') is intended to focus the client on one aspect of her concerns, having shown that he has listened to a number of her presenting problems.

SUMMARISING

Summarising is gathering together the content, themes and feelings of what the client has presented to you. It provides some order to the information and process, and again demonstrates that you have listened and made sense of what the client is bringing. Summaries are helpful when a client brings multiple issues and the helper needs to check he or she has heard accurately. It gives the client an opportunity to define and agree on what has been said. Some useful opening words to a summary can be:

- 'What I have heard you say is . . .'
- 'I understand from what you are saying that . . .'

A summary can be a good skill at the end of a meeting but equally can be used within the session to help the conversation move forward:

> Client: It has been quite a challenge for us since my husband, Ben, has returned from Afghanistan. The kids and I got so used to doing things with the three of us.
>
> Helper: A big change for everyone.
>
> Client: Certainly. Don't get me wrong it is just wonderful to have him home and safe but it's really hard to adapt to it. For instance, I've become really good at some DIY and now Ben sees that as his job. I had a settled routine with the kids' schoolwork and bedtimes.
>
> Helper: You were doing the things around the house that Ben would have done and had a settled routine that worked for you all.
>
> Client: Yes it ran really smoothly. I did my Open University work after they went to bed and I've even got myself a part-time job. Now he has asked me to be a stay-at-home mum and give up my work. How am I going to continue with my studies and how does he think we managed without him for those two years?
>
> Helper: That sounds like a shift for everyone and you are wondering if Ben understands that. I think you are saying that you are really happy to have him home and safe but he is asking you to give up some important things that you enjoyed when he was away and a routine that worked for you.
>
> Client: Now you put it like that, I can see that I am feeling like he is asking me to give up a lot but I do want to have time free to be with him.

The client has heard a summary of her own words from the helper and it has led to her to create her own conclusion from this.

IDENTIFYING AND REFLECTING FEELINGS, CONTENT AND MEANING

In our usual everyday conversations, we often choose which direction we want a conversation to go in. We might focus on one particular theme that catches our attention or try to change the subject when we realise the conversation is going to bore us. We might want to ask lots of questions about a certain area as we are curious and we want to find out more about the content of the subject matter. We often interpret the meaning of the story that fits for us and filter out meaning or content that does not fit. This is all perfectly acceptable in our normal, daily interactions.

However, for a helper/client conversation to be useful, the helper needs to be able to 'track' the client (Culley and Bond 2004) and help the client to explore different elements of the conversation. Where we choose to direct and lead the conversation is important and can help or hinder the communication.

As we listen, we become aware of key disclosures that the client is choosing to share. These could be expressions of feelings, they could be the 'content' of the story – the people, places, actions – or they could be about the meanings that the client is making. As helpers, we need to listen out for these various elements of the story and reflect back to the client what we have heard. Focusing only on one area – for example, the content of the story – can dramatically change the direction of the conversation, resulting in the client satisfying the helper's curiosity but not exploring the area that the client wishes to focus upon. It is more useful to 'capture' both the content and the feelings that are being expressed, reflect these back to the client and then explore with the client what this means for him or her.

Below is a fictitious example to illustrate.

Identifying content

Helper: Hi Sheila, are you OK? You don't look your usual cheery self.

Client: Actually, I'm really angry. I've just found out that one of my colleagues at work has applied for the same job that I am going for and hasn't said a word to me about it.

Helper: Which job is that?

Client: It's the administrator's post.

Helper: Are you both being interviewed for the post?

Client: Yes, her interview is before mine on the same day.

Helper: Do you know if anyone else is going for the post?

Client: No, I don't but now I know she is going for it I'm feeling really deskilled.

Helper: Would it be helpful in this session to go through what skills you do have and what made you feel you were suitable for the post when you applied for it? Maybe that will help raise your confidence?

Client: Yes that would be very helpful . . . but I'm so angry at my friend at work I'm not sure how I'm going to work with her now.

Identifying feeling

Helper: Looking at you now, I can see that you do look really angry.

Client: I can't believe that someone who I thought had been my friend would do this without telling me.

Helper: You seem let down by your colleague.

Client: Yes I do feel let down. To be honest, I feel very hurt. I told her about the job and how excited I was about applying for it as I thought I stood a really good chance of getting it. It feels like she has gone behind my back and used the information I gave her to apply for the job herself. And now I'm scared that she is going to be better than me and she will get the job. I think that's why I feel so angry.

Helper: It sounds as if you have several things going on at once. First of all you feel hurt and let down because you thought of your colleague as a friend. You are angry because in sharing that information, she is now a competitor and you feel scared that you have jeopardised your own chances of getting the job, as your colleague might be a better applicant.

Identifying meaning

Client: Yes, I'm angry with her for using me and I'm angry with myself for giving away too much information about the job and trusting her not to apply for it herself. Thinking about it, all our jobs are really precarious at the moment and we are all concerned about losing our jobs, so I'm not surprised she is applying for it. It's just the fact that I thought she was my friend and if she had said something like 'Would you mind if I applied too?' then I wouldn't feel so hurt or angry, as it's a free world and anyone can apply for the post.

Helper: Let me know if I've got this right. It sounds like it's not so much that you are angry that she has applied for the job, but more about the fact that she has done it secretly?

Client: Yes that's exactly it. I can't believe she has applied without telling me. I'm not sure how I can trust her now.

Helper: I'm wondering how our session might help in thinking about your ongoing relationship with your colleague but also about how you might regain your confidence in time for your interview? What might be the most useful aspect for you to explore?

You will see from the example that the helper's interventions determined the direction and focus of the conversation. Using listening skills, the *helper* is able to reflect all aspects of the conversation, identifying and reflecting the content, the feelings and the meaning. The *client* is then able to choose which area she would like to focus on within the session, having had an opportunity to acknowledge all three aspects of the issue.

EXAMPLE

Now you have watched the clip, answer the following question:

VIDEO CLIP 3a

DEVELOPING THE RELATIONSHIP – IDENTIFYING FEELINGS, CONTENT AND MEANING: Jacqui and Caz

> ### REFLECTIVE LEARNING JOURNAL EXERCISE
>
> What skills did the helper use to help the client decide upon the area to focus on in her session?
>
> Note down the skills you can identify and compare your examples with the following transcript . . .

TABLE 3.1 Transcript of Video Clip 3a: Developing the relationship – identifying feelings, content and meaning – Jacqui and Caz

Content	Process	Skills
J: Hello, Caz. Welcome back. So this is our second 15-minute session following the one where we set up the boundaries and talked about confidentiality, didn't we, in this setting and you then started talking, sort of gave us a little bit of a vignette really of your, some of the things you wanted to talk about and what I remember mostly is sort of transition for you and maybe the way you feel some of your roles are going to change? Is that where you were going with that?	The helper summarises to check boundaries and contract. This summary is tentative to clarify. She re-establishes the focus and she is checking and clarifying. You will see a mirroring of hand positions The helper communicates the core conditions through this summary and her body language	Good summary
C: Definitely, yeah. I think it's a period of looking back. And I feel like I am in a situation where looking back at things I've achieved and having a space to enjoy motherhood, the roles I've done so far. But also a little trepidation of looking to the future as well. So I feel that there's … it's quite a strange sort of mixture of celebration of my life as it is but also just that worry of … well what do I do next because it is changing enormously	'Definitely' concurs that the helper is on the right track. Note the client mirrors the hand gestures that the helper has just been using	
J: And where it's going to take you perhaps?	Clarifying that she has heard the client with a tentative closed question	Paraphrase
C: Yes, where am I going to go. And I think I've always been up until recently quite a … I've been a very planned person, if you like, I like planning, having a route to follow		
J: So would it be useful then, thinking about, perhaps feeling safer within a plan that we use this time to explore where your next plan might go? Or do you have a plan in mind or maybe there's no plans at all? I don't know	Focusing and continuing the contracting	Identifying content and meaning (developing the relationship RSM)

table 3.1 continued

Content	Process	Skills
C: I think that's it, there's no plans at all. I think for the first time I have sort of been through a process where through my study, through experiences that have happened in my family and in my extended family. I've been very lucky to take some time over the last few months and just reflect and *be* within my family and the roles that I have and that's been a really positive thing to do. To take the sort of burden off myself of 'you must do this, you must . . .' Very much career with me, "You must attain this. You must move into a new career. You must achieve'. Achieve is a big word in my life and I think I have just gone through a period where I have reflected on what I have achieved in my life and given credence to that but now . . . I don't know where I'm going so I am at a period, yes, where maybe exploration would be a . . .	This client is identifying the content and meaning of what she wishes to explore	
J: Sounds like a nice place to be, though. Is it? What does it feel like being there?	The helper is congruent about how she has seen this but clarifies with an open question	Identifying feelings
C: Yes, it is really nice. I feel really proud of myself and happy that I have come to that place because I think I was very much a, definitely a hamster on a wheel before. With just moving things forward, getting on day to day, but striving. Striving is the word a lot of my friends and colleagues would say about me. Striving, driven person and it's interesting talking with people now and they say, 'Oh we don't hear you talking so much about what you're going to do this week and next week', and I actually really like that. I like that I've had the time and the ability to stand back and go – actually this is really good that I can just stop for a little while and think and before I move, especially with work, where I'm going to go with that. But with my family as well		

ASKING QUESTIONS

If you stop to notice what happens when you chat with a friend, you will probably find that you are asking quite a lot of questions in everyday conversation. 'How are you?' 'What have you been up to?' 'How's your mum?' As a helper, we will also be asking our clients some questions but in this case we need to become mindful of how and why we are doing this because some questions help but others can hinder.

Mindful guidelines to asking questions

Am I asking too many questions?

Questions require an answer. Too many questions can feel overwhelming for the client. Questions are only part of our skill set and should be used among and with other skills. Combining a question with a paraphrase or summary can be really helpful – for example, 'It sounds as though it has been a really difficult time for many reasons. What would you say was the biggest worry?'

Have I heard the answer to the question?

If we listen carefully to the answer to our question, we can often follow it with a reflection, paraphrase or summary. Questions alone can feel interrogatory. 'What would you say was your biggest worry?' 'What did you do next?' 'Who did you tell?' 'What did they say?'

Who is this question for? Who benefits from me asking it?

Am I asking this out of my own curiosity because it relates to me ('me too' moments) or because I need the information to help and track my client? 'What happened next?' questions could be helpful to clarify your understanding of the story or they might be purely for your own curiosity.

Am I asking this question to fill a gap?

Some people find silences uncomfortable but they can be useful breathing spaces to allow clients to reflect and process. New helpers can be tempted to fill those silences with questions because these gaps feel awkward.

Is this question relevant to what is being said?

It can be easy to be sidetracked into asking questions from something that was said earlier but effectively we are changing the subject. We ask questions that are relevant and that move the client on. We are tracking the client and not leading.

Closed and open questions

How we ask questions is really important and our aim is to help someone examine his or her issues in more detail and perhaps to look at them from different perspectives.

Open questions lead to further exploration by opening up and shedding further light on what is being discussed. They might encourage further description and clarification or could prompt further investigation. Open questions can demonstrate varying viewpoints of the issue or subject.

Open questions can focus down on one aspect at a time. They could be questions that neither of you have an answer to beforehand. They can prompt an exploration of feeling and experience or could clarify understanding and information that is relevant to the context.

Questions that are *open* will show the client that you are listening and attending rather than imposing your point of view.

Closed questions prompt a yes/no answer so they can lead to a shutting down of the dialogue – 'Are you unhappy?' 'Did they do that?' – or can have the effect of *leading* to the questioner's assumptions or hunches – 'Don't you think it would have been easier to . . .'.

It is better to avoid closed questions, particularly if working with a client who is finding it hard to communicate, as it will interrupt or shut down the flow of the conversation and can be controlling. However, there are times when it is appropriate for the helper to use closed questions – for example, when establishing the working alliance, contracting or checking specific details, information gathering and clarifying – 'Will you be able to come every Tuesday at this time?'

Questions starting with 'who', 'what', 'where', 'when' and 'how' help to clarify information, description and context. They indicate that the helper is interested, engaged and attempting to follow, and they can lead the client to further exploration:

> 'Who else do you know that might have experienced that?'
>
> 'What was in your thoughts just then?'
>
> 'Where might you find support for that?'
>
> 'When did you first know that about yourself?'
>
> 'How would you describe that to a colleague/friend?'

However, 'why' questions can invite blame or justification. The client might feel they have to defend or explain themselves. 'Why did you do that?' 'Why did you feel that?' Putting the words 'I'm wondering' before a 'why' question can have the effect of 'softening' the question – for example, 'I'm wondering why you did that?'

Socratic questions

> [Socratic questioning] draws the client's attention to relevant information that may be outside the client's focus, asking questions to increase the range of attention and memory.
>
> (Sanders and Wills 2005: 109)

Asking open and Socratic questions gives the client the opportunity to think about his or her beliefs and to revalue and re-evaluate them. Asking Socratic questions can help a client to become used to asking him or herself the 'right' questions – questions that enable him or her to generate new ideas and more positive beliefs about him or herself and his or her current situation.

> There are three types of Socratic questions:
>
> 1. Questions of clarification:
>   - What do you mean by . . .?
>   - What do you think is the main issue here?
> 2. Questions that probe assumptions:
>   - What are you assuming, and is that always the case?
> 3. Questions that probe reasons and evidence:
>   - How do you know that?
>   - What difference does that make?
>
> *(Centre for Coaching 2011)*

Questions that can be unhelpful

When we are interested and involved in the client's stories, we must beware of asking questions that are purely to satisfy our own curiosity:

> 'What happened next?'
> 'What did he say then?'

It may be the information or clarification is important, but we should be mindful that it is relevant to the client and not just for our own interest and ourselves.

Leading questions could take the form of advice or opinion giving:

> 'Have you thought of leaving the job instead?'
>
> 'Don't you think you should talk to your mother then?'

Useful check

We now understand that questions can be powerful or empowering and they need to be used carefully and economically. Before we use this skill, it might be helpful to ask ourselves the 'why' or 'who' questions:

> 'Why am I asking this question?'
> 'Who am I asking it for (them or me)?'

> ### REFLECTIVE LEARNING JOURNAL EXERCISE
>
> With your learning partner:
>
> Practise a conversation for five minutes each without asking any questions (even disguised ones!).
>
> How easy was that?
>
> Discuss what it felt like for:
>
> - the person asking the questions; and
> - the person responding.

EXAMPLE

Having identified and discussed some of the skills, you now have the opportunity to watch them being demonstrated in the next session between the helper and the client.

This is an example of skills being used in a helper relationship between Glyn and Rob, who are developing the relationship in this first session together.

> **REFLECTIVE LEARNING JOURNAL EXERCISE**
>
> While you watch the video clip, fill in the skills sheet. There is a spare copy at the back of the book (Appendix 3) and online. See if you can identify any of the skills we have outlined above.

eResources: Video your skills session

Figure 3.1 Skills sheet

Skill used	Examples
Identifying and reflecting content	
Identifying and reflecting feelings	
Identifying and reflecting meaning	
Phrases that helped communication	
Phrases that hindered communication	
Paraphrasing	
Summarising	
Open questions	
Closed questions	
Challenging questions	
Probing questions	

eResources

VIDEO CLIP 3b

DEVELOPING THE RELATIONSHIP: Glyn and Rob

> **REFLECTIVE LEARNING JOURNAL EXERCISE**
>
> Giving examples from your skills sheet:
>
> - How easy was it for you to identify the skills?
> - What do you think worked particularly well?
> - Were there any parts that you thought didn't work so well?
> - Can you give examples of how the relationship was developing and what additional core skills were being introduced?

TABLE 3.2 Transcript of Video Clip 3b: Developing the relationship – Glyn and Rob

Content	Process	Skills
G: OK Rob, can you tell me what's going on for you?	Problem identification. The helper has open body language and good eye contact	
R: Um, yeah, yeah, it's about my mum and my brother moving house last week, and it's the place I've known since I was pretty small really and I think I just wanted to come and have a chat about that really. You know?		
G: Absolutely, sounds quite important to you		Empathy and immediacy
R: Well, er, I don't know. In one sense it is but at the same time I'm trying to kind of . . . I have a few conflicting feelings and thoughts about it and you know I, er . . . I'm not sure		
G: Where is the conflict do you think?		Open question Identifying meaning The helper picks up the word 'conflict' and reflects it back
R: It's somewhere I've known for a lot of my life so I guess I'm just wondering whether I miss the place and even before that it feels quite unusual to think that it's somewhere that I can't go back to any more, um, you know? And at the same time excited about the new place, not that I live there, but it's somewhere that they call home now and what I leave behind and what's coming and . . .		Active non-verbal listening skills
G: And how far is the new place from where it was?	The helper moved away from the material. He could have just used active listening skills and stayed with the client rather than asking a curious question	Identifying content
R: It's about a hundred miles or so, maybe a bit further. So it's not a huge amount but it's fair enough		
G: And what sort of memories do you have of the old place?	The helper returns to the client's material	Identifying content Open question

table 3.2 continued

Content	Process	Skills
R: Well that's it, they're a bit mixed. I have lots of pretty bad memories, lots of memories like when I was little like my parents shouting at each other when they were still married and I have lots of memories of being little and growing up with my brothers and my sisters, so us playing, and I have memories of the new guy coming in and that being quite difficult and being quite, um … fun at the same time so I think that's to do with why I can't quite make sense of it. It's lots of different things. I feel good about it and I feel not so good about it. I feel ….	The client responds very positively to the open question ('that's it, that's it')	
G: And what sort of emotions are coming up with it all?		Identifying feeling Open question
R: I feel pretty sad actually and I can kind of feel it behind my eyes, you know? Yeah, I feel sad, but at the same time … I can't put my finger on it yet, I don't know what it is but it's … it's an OK kind of feeling, you know … yeah, I can't describe it more than that at the moment		
G: And it sounds like, because it's so mixed, that you're having trouble locating it within yourself and …	Empathic response	Paraphrase
R: I can feel it in me but I can't put a name to it, I can't sort of settle it down and because it's not one particular feeling or even a couple that I can make sense of. You know, I thought that I would be really upset, and for a while I was, but it passed a lot quicker than I expected it to. And that's unusual, I think that's got something to do with why it won't settle		
G: Um		
R: Before then, we'd moved around a lot. I mean I lived in about four or five different places in the space of … well, eight years. But this place was the place I'd been the longest, so yeah, I suppose it was a reference. It was stable. You know, like I said, some of the stuff that went on there I don't particularly want to remember, it's not a good memory but, um, I knew it was there and I knew it was home in a way	The client returns to the story now there is mutual understanding ('yeah, I suppose it was a reference')	

table 3.2 continued

Content	Process	Skills
G: And is there some sort of movement within those mixed feelings that you're talking about, that's causing this?	The helper is tentative at this point	Identifying feeling and meaning
R: There is, there is a little, but I don't want to say there is when there isn't, I don't want to look for something that's not there, I guess I feel a bit more, I feel a bit . . . happy is the wrong word, but relaxed about the fact that I did spend some time there. That actually whatever went on was a part of the other things that were going on at the time and wasn't all my fault. Wow, I don't know where that came from! But yeah, um, and yeah, I don't know where that came from	This enables the client to explore in more detail and consider	
G: So it sounds like there is part of you that wants to move but there's still something there that you've got a connection with from the good and bad times	There is evidence of the relationship developing as the counsellor gently communicates acceptance. However, we notice the helper does not pick up on the client's surprise at connecting with feelings of 'all my fault'	Using a paraphrase as a summary Use of empathy
R: There is definitely a part of me that wants to move on from it, but I definitely do have a connection to it and that's it, that's it. You know? It feels less complicated now. You know that we've been talking about it, somehow, um		
R: And part of what it is, is that it surprises me that I want to move, that I'm OK, that I'm OK with, well, my mum and my brother moving but me not going back there. And I've never really dealt with moves very well before. I've always felt unsettled so I guess part of the being, you know, not sure of what I'm feeling is actually maybe that I've grown up a bit this time that, um, you know, like that I do feel that it's a good thing and it's not as painful as all of my other moves	The client responds to the presence of the core conditions ('it feels less complicated now . . . that we've been talking about it'). The client is beginning to connect with the emotional connections of this to the past	

Now you have had an opportunity to view the video clip, and see where you can identify the skills, you can now compare your worksheet with the skills that we have identified in the transcripts. We have also drawn to your attention our thoughts on how effective (or otherwise) the interventions were and given our observations of the relationship between the helper and the client and how this fits with the Relational Skills Model.

REFLECT, PRACTISE AND EVALUATE

With your learning partner:

- Continue with the conversation you had earlier but this time take 10 minutes each to see if you can include paraphrases, some helpful questions, identify and reflect content, feelings and meaning, and summarise.
- Video the session and watch back to reflect and evaluate.

MODEL BOX

> In this chapter, we have referred to:
>
> - The Relational Skills Model – the developing relationship (Midwinter and Dickson 2015)
> - Stage 1: 'What's going on?' Helping clients clarify the key issues calling for change (Egan 2002: 21):
> - Stage 1-A: Help clients tell their *stories*
> - Stage 1-B: Help clients break through *blind spots* that prevent them from seeing themselves, their problem situations and their unexplored opportunities as they really are
> - Help clients choose the *right* problems and/or opportunities to work on
> - The foundation skills – reflective skills – paraphrasing, summarising, probing skills (Culley and Bond 2004: 25)

SUMMARY

- The use of additional core skills will enhance and encourage good communication.
- It is important to identify content, feelings and meaning of interactions.
- In developing the relationship, the presence and communication of the core conditions are essential.
- It is important to be mindful of the skills we use and how we might use our everyday communication differently in the helper role.

Chapter 4
Working with the relationship

Now that the relationship is established, the emphasis is on exploring the issues in more depth and creating an empathic understanding of the client's situation. The focus within this phase is through challenging and creating new meaning, different possibilities and perspectives. Enhanced skills to progress the communication are the skills of challenging. Different ways of challenging are:

- Confronting
- Use of immediacy
- Use of self-disclosure
- Use of silence
- Clarifying
- Reassessing
- Probing
- Giving feedback and sharing information

TEACHING

THE SKILL OF CHALLENGING

Challenging is an umbrella term for a number of skills that are used. We might decide to use challenging skills when we have moved to this phase of 'working with the relationship'. People that we experience as 'challenging' are often seen as hard to work with or relate to, and so it might feel difficult to incorporate challenge within our empathic way of working where we have begun to set up and develop the relationship.

In deciding whether a challenge is appropriate, we need to carefully consider why, when and how we might do it. We acknowledge challenge as part of the helping relationship and a supportive way of working and that, for our client, being challenged can promote change and develop self-awareness.

> **REFLECTIVE LEARNING JOURNAL EXERCISE**
>
> Can you think of someone that you have worked with, or been taught by, that has helped you develop further with your life or work?
>
> Think about whether you felt challenged by him or her. What was that experience like?
>
> What was it about that relationship that helped you move forward? It might not have been particularly comfortable to feel challenged but in retrospect we can often see this has been an important part of our personal growth.

Challenging within this stage of the relationship can be empathic as well as tough, gentle as well as strong. We have observed that all counselling skills theorists acknowledge the importance of challenging and all of them acknowledge that this is not a skill to be used in the very beginning of a relationship when we are setting up the contract, but rather when a certain amount of trust has developed and we, the helper, have earned the right to challenge by providing a safe environment in which our client can consider our response and not feel unduly threatened.

What are we challenging and why? Challenging negative thinking has been embraced as a therapeutic skill in cognitive behavioural therapy (CBT), termed by Beck et al. (1979: 244) as 'dysfunctional assumptions or maladaptive rules'. Egan (2002: 177) refers to them as 'blind spots' and the act of challenging as 'reality testing' (Egan 2002: 176). We can learn to recognise these blind spots by looking out for discrepancies in things people are saying, inconsistencies, and the things that do not quite fit. Sometimes, these indicators are very subtle. People smiling or laughing when they are telling you something really sad or using words such as 'ought', 'should' and 'must'. These internalised rules for living may be self-limiting within the client's views of his or her own life and in his or her expectations or views of others. As helpers, we are looking for incongruences in the story or descriptions and we then decide whether it would be helpful to our client to point these out. We are embracing one of the core conditions of congruence but alongside this must be the other main conditions of unconditional positive regard and empathy for challenge to be effective and helpful. Our aim is to support the client to challenge him or herself and to broaden perspectives or try out new ones. Within this chapter and the transcript, you will be able to recognise examples of challenging skills.

Challenging can be subtle or tentative as we offer the challenge to our client and invite him or her to challenge him or herself. We may bring immediacy into the challenge, perhaps in the form of self-disclosure, or we can use more direct confronting, but we remain aware that our ideas may not fit with his or her ideas and our answers or choices may work for us but not be appropriate for him or her. We remember our role of supporting our client in his or her decision-making rather than imposing our preferred agenda.

CONFRONTING

It might feel that confrontation is quite a strange word to use in connection with the use of counselling skills. When we think of the word, we may imagine aggression, attack or argument. However, it is difficult to think of a different word in relation to the general strategy of challenging. Confrontation, used as a form of challenging, is more about bringing something to the forefront of the conversation – coming face to face with the problem, if you like. As a helper, you might be noticing inconsistencies – between the different stories the client tells you, between what he or she says and what he or she does, or between his or her verbal and non-verbal communication. Picking up on these inconsistencies can be really valuable and can help a client 'confront' the issues, hopefully leading to different perspectives and choices.

Before any confrontation is carried out by the helper, the helper has to be very sure that the relationship has developed to a stage whereby the confrontation will not be seen by the client as a criticism, a judgement or a 'parental' intervention such as being told what to do. Challenge is an important part of the developing relationship – used well, it can enhance and build on the working alliance, allowing the client to bring inconsistencies and areas of concern that are not 'worked out' yet and face and interpret any blind spots (Egan 2002: 139). There is no set time or stage when confrontation would be appropriate; it is entirely based on the development of the relationship. It might be that a helper never gets to the phase where he or she believes it would be appropriate to confront an inconsistency in the client's story – the risk of damaging the helping relationship could be too high. Tentative, gentle challenging can work much more effectively, rather than a direct confrontation. Reflections, one-word paraphrases, picking up on important or repetitive words used by the client or asking questions that you are curious about can all be effective ways of tentatively challenging inconsistencies or discrepancies – for example:

Client: The baby was up all night and I didn't sleep a wink.

Helper: You didn't get any sleep at all?

Client: Well, I might have had a few hours in between the baby waking and crying but it wasn't enough.

Helper: So you did manage to get some sleep but you don't feel it is enough. Would it be useful to look at alternative ways you might be able to catch up on the missed sleep?

Yet at other times, when the inconsistency or blind spot seems really noticeable in the room and/or the client keeps returning to it, the best strategy might be to bring it out into the open and face it. An example of this is as follows:

> The client, at an audiology appointment, is reluctant to attend a wedding wearing her new hearing aid as 'everyone will be looking at me'. The audiologist asks if the client would like to attend the wedding and the client confirms it is really important, as it's the daughter of her best friend who is getting married. The client says again that she cannot possibly go with everyone looking at her with her hearing aid in.

Helper: So you would like to go to the wedding but you feel you can't go, as you will need to wear your hearing aid?

Client: Yes, I will need to wear it as otherwise I won't hear what anyone is saying, as my hearing is at its worst when there are lots of people talking at once and there is lots of background noise.

Helper: So you realise how important it is to wear your hearing aid to the wedding but you would rather not go because you think that everyone will be looking at you?

Client: Yes, I'm really embarrassed to be seen wearing it.

Helper: I'm going to challenge you a little on the point that 'everyone' will be looking at you. At the wedding, how likely is it that everyone will be looking at you, and not at the bride?

Client: (*smiles*) Well it's very unlikely that will happen. But that's how it feels.

Helper: So it feels like everyone will be looking at you, but in reality you don't see that happening. Looking at it from that perspective, do you still think it is worth missing the wedding of your best friend's daughter?

Client: No, I don't as I really want to go but every time I think about going I start to feel embarrassed about my hearing aid and it puts me off going.

Helper: If you had a friend in a similar situation, what would you say to them?

Client: Well, I'd say don't be so daft, no one will care if you wear a hearing aid – they might be pleased to see you wearing it as you will be able to hear them and communicate better with it in. I'd try to reassure them that it will be OK and everyone will want to see her there. And if all else fails I'd tell them to wear a hat to the wedding so no one will notice! (*shared laughter*)

Sometimes, clients tell you stories about themselves and the picture they paint of themselves is not what you see in your relationship with them. These can be the more negative aspects of themselves, which they perceive as the only aspect of themselves – that is, 'I'm always getting it wrong', 'I'm useless at everything', 'I'll never find a boyfriend'. Confronting the client with the 'evidence' you have gleaned from stories shared before can be helpful and affirming – 'You say you are useless at everything, but didn't you say that you've been in your post for the last 10 years and have successfully been promoted twice?' It is helpful to challenge directly the belief the client has about him or herself and then look for the evidence to support or refute that belief with the client.

On occasions, it may be important to confront any differences between what the client is saying and what he or she is exhibiting in his or her non-verbal communication – 'I notice that when you say "Ah well, it doesn't matter", you look sad and tearful and it looks to me like it does matter to you'.

This gives the client the opportunity to decide upon which is the truer version of events, the one that he or she is are saying or the one that he or she is 'showing'.

As a rule of thumb, always be frugal with confrontation. Only confront when tentative challenging has not moved the session forward or when the relationship feels developed enough to withstand the impact of the confrontation. A more 'gentle' way to challenge is through the use of *immediacy*. Immediacy can be used at any phase in the relationship and can help build rapport and encourage greater understanding of the client's issues that he or she brings and about the helper/client relationship.

USE OF IMMEDIACY

> Immediacy bridges the gap between empathy, which is responsive to the helpee's experience, and confrontation, which is initiated out of the helper's experience of the helpee.
>
> (Carkhuff 1969: 192)

Immediacy, as a form of challenge, can be a spontaneous and highly effective intervention. Immediacy is based on empathic understanding, mutuality, and the sharing of hunches, thoughts and ideas. They are 'in the moment' reflections that focus on what is happening in the here and now. It is a way of holding up a 'mirror' to the client to show him or her what you are seeing, hearing, feeling and thinking, and can be a way of modelling a way of communicating that may be different to his or her own/interpersonal relationships.

> [I]mmediacy of expression serves two purposes. First, the immediacy response assists the helpee in personalizing the helper-helpee relationship. Thus the helpee's understanding is made more real because it embraces an understanding of what is happening then and there with the helper. A second purpose is that the helpee learns something about effective communication by being presented with a model of one person, the helper, who is able to communicate fully and accurately.
>
> (Carkhuff 1979: 114)

Immediacy potentially increases the self-awareness of the client by the helper bringing into the open what he or she is experiencing within the relationship and sharing those thoughts and feelings to deepen understanding.

> Egan (2002: 210) talks of three kinds of immediacy:
> - overall relationship immediacy;
> - event-focused immediacy; and
> - self-involving statements.

In other words, this means what is going on between us generally; what is going on at this moment in time in relation to what we are discussing; and what is going on for me as the helper while I am interacting with you, the client.

What is going on between us generally?

How a client behaves with us, as helpers, can give us an indication of what might be happening for him or her in the 'outside world'. A client who finds it difficult to communicate his or her feelings might be struggling to manage an intimate relationship with a partner. Holding up that 'mirror' to the client by reflecting back to him or her what you notice within *your* relationship with him or her might be helpful for the client's understanding of how he or she is in relationship with others:

> *Helper*: I'm glad you've brought up that you think I might have misunderstood you last week. Over the last few sessions I've noticed that you are beginning to be more open with me about your feelings and letting me know when I've misunderstood you or got something wrong. Why do you think that is?
>
> *Client*: Well, I think it is because you don't seem bothered by my saying it and that you are really trying to understand how it is for me. It's not so easy to do that with my partner as I'm scared I'm going to hurt his feelings or he won't understand what I'm trying to say. He always thinks it's about him but mostly I'm trying to tell him about me and how I feel.
>
> *Helper*: So it's easier for you to say difficult things to me as you trust that I won't take them personally and I will try and understand what's going on for you?

Hopefully, reflecting on this understanding of the difference between the relationship processes can help the client to focus on what might be helpful in improving communication with her partner.

> Very often the expressions of the helpee, whether direct or indirect, reflect his feelings and attitudes toward the helper in the present moment. Depending upon how sensitive the helper is to these expressions, whether or not he chooses to respond to them is critical to the helpee's feeling of really having his experience translated to action or interaction in the immediate context of helping. That is, the helper acts upon what he sees going on between himself and the helpee.
> (Carkhuff 1969: 192)

What is going on at this moment in time in relation to what we are discussing?

Reflecting on what is happening 'right now' in the helper/client relationship can be a way of allowing space for thoughts and feelings to emerge. Focusing on the here and now of the interaction can be useful:

- When the relationship seems stuck or you feel you are going round and round in circles:
    - You might find yourself going over the same things, experience feelings of boredom, long unproductive silences, or feeling like the session is going nowhere.

- When there has been a rupture in the working alliance:
  - These might include trust, boundaries, timekeeping and 'getting the wrong end of the stick'.
- When there are relationship issues or tension in the room:
  - You notice you are feeling judgemental, anger, frustration, unspoken emotions or lack of clarity of emotions.
- When there are diversity issues that need some focus:
  - Such as language misunderstandings, difference of meanings, non-verbal communication and checking out assumptions.
- When there is role ambiguity:
  - These might include attraction, friendship and role conflict.

Asking the client to pause and think about what is going on for him or her, or being congruent about what is going on for you, can strengthen the relationship and rebuild the working alliance and trust, if this has become an issue. Statements such as:

'What's going on for you right now?'

'I'm wondering what's going on for you at this moment as I'm beginning to feel like we are not understanding each other?'

'Is the fact that I am also a colleague of your manager concerning you, as just now you seemed embarrassed about describing your feelings about her to me?'

'I'm noticing that I'm feeling very resentful when you talk about how you didn't get any support from your colleagues and I'm wondering if that is how you are feeling towards me too?'

'Can we just stop a moment while I check out that I have got this right as I am feeling that I might have misunderstood your meaning just then as you look puzzled?'

'You've said a couple of times now how you wish we could be friends and you could see me more often. Shall we take some time to think about our relationship and what that means to us?'

'I notice your face lights up when you talk about the prospect of changing your job.'

What is going on for me as the helper while I am interacting with you, the client?

It is not always appropriate to share with the client everything that is going through your mind. Being congruent is about noticing what is going on for you and making a decision about what is appropriate to share with the client, either in the moment or storing it for a later, more appropriate time. Using immediacy through self-involving statements is often about deciding what is in the interests of the relationship, at that particular moment, to share. It is often a spontaneous intervention – *'When you said that, I felt . . .'* – and it can often be a way of giving the client some feedback, either positive or negative. Statements such as:

'This could be a personal response but I'm aware that I'm feeling . . .'

'I'm glad that you are able to . . .'

'When you talk about . . ., I . . .'

'I can really resonate with what you are describing.'

> Culley and Bond (2004: 133) set out the following guidelines for using immediacy:
>
> 1. Be assertive. Say directly what you think, feel and observe.
> 2. Be open yourself. Immediacy is not pointing out the unproductive aspects of their behaviour to clients. If a pattern is developing between you and clients – for example, a pattern of avoidance or collusion or cosiness – then you have some part in that.
> 3. Describe what you think is happening clearly and specifically. Say what you think is happening, what you observe the client doing and what you are doing.
> 4. Ask the client to comment on what you have said.

Using immediacy often leads to the helper disclosing to the client aspects about him or herself that he or she believes will be helpful to the client. Like immediacy, using self disclosure can be a powerful and helpful intervention, yet it needs to be used with caution.

USE OF SELF-DISCLOSURE

Sometimes, when we are feeling isolated, unheard or misunderstood, there is nothing nicer than hearing a 'me too' moment. The old saying 'a problem shared is a problem halved' comes to mind – sharing a problem with a friend and him saying he understands, or disclosing that he often feels that way too, can be very powerful, affirming and reassuring, and can make us feel a lot better about ourselves and our issues. This type of self-sharing can also be beneficial within a helping relationship but the focus is on the client broadening and deepening his or her understanding of the situation and there is a lot less sharing of the 'me too' moments in a helping relationship.

Yet there are many times when self-disclosure or self-sharing is incredibly helpful. Often clients find it difficult to share how they feel and it can be useful for the helper to 'model' this through appropriate self-sharing such as 'There have been times when I too have felt strong feelings in a situation similar to the one you are describing' and 'I remember feeling really sad at my father's funeral'. Sharing feelings, in a non-defensive manner, can help to build trust in the relationship and 'normalise' a client's feelings and reactions.

The helper can also bring a wealth of experience, insights and knowledge to the relationship. While the focus should always be on the client coming to his or her own understandings and judgements, it can be helpful to share knowledge if it seems like it is in the best interests of the client to share it. When sharing your 'expert' with a client, always remember to do it tentatively and own it as your experience, giving the client the choice to take or leave your 'advice' rather than introducing it with 'In my opinion/ experience . . .'. Introducing your experience can be prefaced with phrases such as:

'I don't know if this is helpful but . . .'

'I wonder if it would be useful for me to share a little of my own experience?'

This can then be followed by disclosures such as:

'I've come across an excellent website/book that might give you some greater clarity on the issue you bring.'

'I'm aware of an agency that has a really good carer's support group that you might consider joining.'

'One thing I've learned through my experience of being a nurse is . . .'

These can all be very useful to the client.

A tricky situation helpers often find themselves in is when a client asks a question to you directly, resulting in you having to choose whether it is appropriate to answer his or her question honestly and thereby self-disclosing information about yourself that you might not wish to share. A trainer once reminded me that confidentiality only stretches one way in a helper/client relationship. The client could choose to tell anyone information that you have shared within your relationship. So while you might consider it to be in the best interests of the client to tell him or her that you also had an eating disorder in your teens, if this is something that you would like to keep confidential to the wider world, then you need to consider the impact of answering a client's question directly. Often, a client will ask you 'What would you do in this situation?' and there is a fine line between being genuine and honestly answering the question and giving the client an idea that if *you* did it that way, then *he or she* should also follow the same route, or a client feeling negative because if you could do it, why is he or she not able to? A genuine response could be something such as 'It's difficult to know really what I would do as there are many different choices. Perhaps it would be useful to look at those different choices and see where that leads us'. Something that we as counsellors often do is reply with the question 'Why is it important to you to know what I would do?' as this shifts the focus back on the relationship and gives an opportunity to explore what is happening between you, rather than expressly saying what you would do.

Self-disclosure should always be used 'sparingly'. While the client might appreciate your empathic understanding, he or she may not appreciate leaving the session knowing lots about your experience of grief, for instance, and very little about his or her own.

So, helpful self-disclosures are often short and infrequent, relevant to what the client is discussing, and appropriate to the phase of relationship development – more careful consideration about self-sharing should be given in the very early stages of development

> Culley and Bond (2004: 128) also set out some very good guidelines for self-disclosure:
>
> 1. *Understand your client first.* You will be in a position to self-disclose effectively if you have a clear understanding of how clients see their concerns and have considered what they may be implying or overlooking.
> 2. *Consider the impact.* Disclosure about your failures to cope may make you seem inexpert and unsafe to clients. Conversely, revealing your triumphs may daunt clients who are striving to make small changes.
> 3. *Be clear about your intentions.* Your aim is to assist the client. If you are disclosing to unburden yourself, gain sympathy or to relieve your own feelings, then it is more appropriately discussed either in supervision or in counselling for yourself (Hawkins and Shohet 2012).
> 4. *Be brief.* Talking at length about yourself takes the focus from clients and may burden or bore. It may also collude with avoidance behaviour, giving those who want to steer clear of talking about themselves a loophole.
> 5. *Tailor your self-disclosure.* By this, we mean use experiences with which clients can identify. Telling a client who is in debt and struggling that you understand what it is like to be short of money 'because £30,000 per year really doesn't go anywhere irrespective of what some people think' does not show much understanding of the client's world and is unhelpful.
> 6. *Be direct.* Use 'I' and describe the experience clearly and directly. End your statement by returning the focus to your client.

while you are building rapport and the working alliance. Self-disclosures need to be empathic to the client's experience, and genuine and real, but not 'expert'.

Unhelpful self-disclosures take up too much space and time; can sound as if you have minimised the client's experience by privileging your own story above theirs; and can lead to a client believing you are the expert therefore he or she must follow your example, or alternatively that you are not competent or well-adjusted enough to be his or her helper. Inappropriately used self-disclosure can change the working alliance to focus on the helper and lead the client to feel unsafe or burdened.

Self-disclosure should always be used within the best interests of the client and not as an opportunity for you to 'sound off' about your experiences – 'That's nothing, you should hear about my Saturday night' type responses, while tempting, need to be kept within friendship interactions rather than within this more formal helping relationship.

EXAMPLE

VIDEO CLIP 4a

WORKING WITH THE RELATIONSHIP

TABLE 4.1 Transcript of Video Clip 4a: Working with the relationship – use of immediacy and self-disclosure – Jacqui and Caz

Content	Process	Skills
J: Hi, Caz		
C: Hi, Jacqui		
J: Welcome back again, so we're going to start our third session now we've got 15 minutes, and your last session we were talking about some of the transitions that you are thinking about at the moment, and what you felt you'd achieved, and thinking about the eggs in the basket and your family and how important relationships and friendships were to you, and I thought you were just beginning to focus on where you thought you might be going in the future. So would that be a good place to start here?	Summarising the previous session and establishing time boundaries. The helper speaks slowly in a measured way, which gives the client a chance to feed back to the helper if she has summarised correctly. You may notice these summaries are tentative in a questioning manner. She returns to the client's metaphor	Summary The helper returns to the contract
C: That would be really useful I think, yeah		
J: OK, so . . . it's a big word, the future, isn't it?		
C: Um, very big (*shared laughter*)		Immediacy and challenge Moment of shared empathy and warmth
J: What does that do for you? It sounds like it's in capital letters at the moment, doesn't it?		Good open question and immediacy Use of metaphor Working with the relationship RSM
C: Yes, it's capital letters with a couple of exclamation marks at the end as well! It feels very . . .	The client has confirmed and joined with the helper's metaphor	
J: What are those exclamation marks meaning I wonder?	The helper makes stronger challenges here as the relationship is developing	Open and Socratic question Challenge Creativity and helping (Egan stage II)

table 4.1 continued

Content	Process	Skills
C: (*both C and J mirror taking a big sigh*) Oh what do they mean? Maybe that's a little bit of the fear, I think, the exclamation marks. What would the future look like? As I said in my last session, there's a definite sense of not wanting to go back and be so rigid in my thinking that only work and career can bring me *achievement* in any sense, but also at the same time recognising that I want to play a valid role in the workplace but maybe a little bit more on my terms so I can balance all my other interests, relationships a little bit more fruitfully	The helper visually responds here to the more serious tone. She reflects the client's more serious facial expressions	Mirroring Non-verbal communication Congruence Demonstrating good listening skills
J: So I wonder what your terms would mean?	The helper asks this open question with a smile, which the client responds to, both acknowledging that this is a strong and challenging question	Challenge
C: (*shared laughter*) My terms . . .	Empathic communication in the shared laughter	
J: Yes, it's a big one isn't it?	The helper acknowledges that she is being challenging	Empathy
C: It is a big one, because very much with me it's a process of having control, having a sense of the ability to use time effectively. To have time for all the different components of my life rather than just one and be absolutely focused in that. So having that control I think is really important to me		
J: So control about where and how you spend your time? And 'components', I was interested in that word, what does that mean to you? Have you thought about your components I suppose?	The helper picks up on the word 'control' and reflects this back, being transparent about her curiosity. She also picks up on the repeated word 'time'. She then clarifies what the client means about 'components'. The helper is working with the relationship to understand the client's perception of the meaning of these words	Closed questions Open questions Probing Empathy

table 4.1 continued

Content	Process	Skills
C: A little bit to do with what you were saying about the basket, with the friends, family, relationships but also activities that I . . . whether it's a simple walk in the park with the dog or going to the gym or going to a class or where I choose to a certain extent. I know it's not absolute free choice but I like the feeling I have at the minute that I have choice, that I have options and that's really important to me. So that's what control means to me . . . a phrase comes to mind, about dancing to someone else's tune. And I have a very strong sense at the minute. At the minute I'm partly self-employed and partly employed and I think increasingly I will probably move towards self-employment entirely. Maybe, don't know		Reassessing Attending and listening skills Good eye contact
J: So moving towards self-employment would be an option that you would like to fulfil in some way?	This is a closed question that could have been asked as an open question but it is a focus on what the client appears to be saying	Closed question Leading client down one path? Probing
C: Yes, I think so	The client confirms this but with 'I think so'. Maybe she does not agree with the helper's assumption	
J: Is that – this could be a personal response, but scary comes to mind, I don't know if that . . .	The helper again probes but owns this statement around the word 'scary' as her own perception. She offers this up to the client as a possibility that she can accept or reject	Immediacy/self-disclosure Challenge
C: Oh yes, absolutely, especially coming from a background where I've worked in either a school, or a local authority within a public sector institution, I don't know. That's the thing I don't know at the minute, I just don't know . . .	'Absolutely' confirms this	
J: Yes, yes		
C: I'm really in a – oh, I can really see the benefits of both and . . .		
J: But then I suppose that's what's useful about here, it's about thinking and exploring this space for you if you like (pondering yes), and it feels like it is a challenge this exploration in itself maybe?	The helper is acknowledging the challenge the client is facing. The helper is very real at this moment	Immediacy Empathy Giving feedback
C: Yes it is		

table 4.1 continued

Content	Process	Skills
J: Pinpointing exactly		Non-verbal indicator
C: Absolutely. Something that this session is raising for me is there needs to be more of that. There needs to be, well, pinning down, well, what is this fear over here and what am I hanging on to and what are the components, the elements that maybe stop me moving on or that I have to consider a little bit. They seem to be in a little bit of a *soup* maybe at the minute with it all. But it's OK, it's OK to be like that as well. It's a funny thing as I'm talking I'm saying to myself it's actually OK not to make a decision as yet cos that's taking me a long time to get to actually, to say it's OK to think about things, it's OK to try things out, it's OK to not by Monday 12 o'clock to have that diarised and scheduled and that's the thing you are going to do. Cos that's actually quite important to me that I've done that		
J: But that feels like it's a real achievement	Empathic response. Shared laughter. Eye contact. Exchange of smiles	Core conditions – empathy, acceptance, prizing the client
C: That's another egg in that basket (J: Yes, yes) it is (J: Absolutely) it is actually in itself and that's really important. That is really important to have done that	Both the helper and the client are continually picking up the original metaphor and expanding on it	
J: Are you the sort of person, Caz, that can feel quite, *(pondering)* um, I feel like 'chuffed' is the word I'm looking for, pleased with yourself, for reaching that point if you like? Recognizing it as a real positive for you?	The helper is picking up on the client's body language and tentatively exploring. The helper's gesture of the hand on her chest indicates that this is her feeling and she wonders if this is the client's feeling	Probing Non-verbal communication Use of immediacy – what is going on for me as the helper?
C: Absolutely. Because I think for so much time I would have seen that as maybe a self-indulgent way to think. How terribly indulgent for you to think in that way. And I would have criticised probably and made judgements either on myself or other people for, for goodness sake get on with it if you are going to do something – go and do it. There's real impatience to myself. That I really feel has been really important in my life to control, and use in a different way and use that energy differently	The client confirms the helper's hunch (this demonstrates that the relationship has become established, with the helper having an empathic knowing)	

USE OF SILENCE

> Silence, it seems, can communicate a whole range of feelings and reactions and being able to 'tune in' to what a persons silence may be saying is a very valuable aspect of active listening. Being able to respond appropriately to silence is equally important.
>
> (Aldridge and Rigby 2001: 103)

Within the English language, there are numerous metaphors relating to silence, such as 'silence is golden', 'pregnant pause', 'awkward silence', 'silent as the grave' and so on. Often, these sound negative, and we are sure you have all been in a situation when someone has said or done something and the room falls silent. These moments can be highly embarrassing and uncomfortable. Often, therefore, we are tuned to feeling anxious or awkward during these moments of silence and feel a need to say or do something to fill that gap. However, during a helping conversation, silence can be really useful for the client to pause, reflect, feel and show emotion and take stock of where he or she is. The skill is for the helper to remain active in his or her listening and gauge the situation through empathic eyes. Sometimes, it is useful to allow the silence for a moment and then ask a question about what is going on for the client at that moment. For example:

> 'I am wondering what you are thinking/feeling at this moment.'
>
> 'I notice you seem really tearful. What is going on for you now?'
>
> 'You look thoughtful – would you like to share your thoughts?'

At other times, it is better to just hold the silence and allow the client space and time to consider his or her next response. Interrupting the silence can disrupt this process. It is really important at this point to notice the client's body language – are his or her eyes looking upwards and not focusing, is his or her head down, does he or she look as if he or she is thinking? Is he or she too tearful to be able to respond at this point? It is a fine judgement to gauge when to break the silence or to allow space. The skill is to pay particular attention to the non-verbal communication and learn to trust the reflective space that is developing between you.

It is a very human response to want to reach out and touch someone who is crying. However, this could have the effect of shutting down the tears and stopping someone exploring his or her meaning. Sometimes, it is better to just hold the silence and maybe verbally check out he or she is OK. Passing a box of tissues might show an empathic response without the need to touch or interrupt the moment.

Cultural variations

> **In their paper 'Barriers to effective cross-cultural counseling', Sue and Sue (1977: 420) state: 'Misunderstandings that arise from cultural variations in verbal and nonverbal communication may lead to alienation and/or an inability to develop trust and rapport'.**

Different rules about when to 'speak or yield to another person' (ibid.: 427) can contribute to that loss of rapport. Silence may mean many different things in different cultures – it could be a sign of respect, politeness, may be viewed as a negative interruption or a desire for the other to take up the conversation, and it could be a place of privacy and reflection. While it is impossible to know and understand every cultural rule regarding the use of silence, we should not assume or second-guess what is meant by the silence, but wait for the client to give you some indication – often through his or her non-verbal communication – that he or she is ready to continue speaking. Self-awareness of your own cultural views around conversation conventions will enable you to put those aside and think more about what the silence might mean for the client.

EXAMPLE

This next clip comes towards the end of the second session, Jacqui having spent time over the last two sessions developing the relationship with Caz. Here, you can observe a good example of Jacqui holding a silence while Caz connects with an emotional realisation. Watch how Jacqui does this.

VIDEO CLIP 4b

WORKING WITH THE RELATIONSHIP – USE OF SILENCE: Jacqui and Caz

---

REFLECTIVE LEARNING JOURNAL EXERCISE

With your learning partner, take it in turns for 10 minutes to discuss a change you would like to make in your lives.

During the 10 minutes, in the helper role, see if you can leave pauses and silences at appropriate moments.

Monitor whether you feel the need to fill the silences but avoid doing it – how comfortable did that feel?

Take time after the session to watch back the video clip and see if there is anything you could have done differently regarding the use of silence.

Video your skills session

TABLE 4.2 Transcript of Video Clip 4b: Working with the relationship – use of silence – Jacqui and Caz

Content	Process	Skills
J: So would it be important here to think about what you have achieved as well as what you might look forward to? I was thinking about those two different places and maybe does there need to be a perspective if you like?	The helper gives the client an option of looking at achievements and future objectives	Creating new meaning (working with the relationship RSM) What solutions make sense for me? (Egan stage II) Reviewing possibilities
C: That would be really nice actually to do that. Because I think that's where I am in sort of, I'm aware of that, of that sort of process going on but I haven't clarified or put it together in any form. For me that would probably be very useful		
J: So would it be useful to think about what you have achieved and maybe even your take on it if you like? Does that make sense?	The helper makes this intervention quite tentatively. She is speaking quite slowly, thoughtfully and expressing warmth with a smile and eye contact. She is exploring different possibilities and perspectives (working with the relationship)	Clarifying and reassessing (working with the relationship RSM) What do you want? (Egan stage II-A)
C: Yeah		
J: Where would you like to start with that?	There appears to be deepening rapport between them	Open question Building rapport
C: Oooh! (*mutual laughter*) Yeah, starting is the difficult bit. I think what I've (*pause*) I think what I've learned most about in the recent past is that word achievement and what it means. Previously I think the word achievement was academic qualification, it was university, it was getting a job, it was moving into management. I had all my eggs in one basket	The helper holds the silence as the client pauses. The client introduces a metaphor	

table 4.2 continued

Content	Process	Skills
J: Big basket	The helper picks up on the client's metaphor. Tentative challenge	Paraphrase Challenge
C: Very big basket. Very big. Um, and I didn't recognise what achievement was elsewhere and I think I put so much of my time and soul really into that, and I think when I had my children, which was 12/13 years ago now, my first one. I started to really reassess that but not in a positive way. It was, how am I still going to achieve over here and be the perfect mother and be the perfect wife and have a perfect home, and I can give you a big list of what I thought I had to do to be an achiever	Notice the client's body language is becoming more agitated, lots of movement in her legs and her hand movements	Attending and listening Allowing client to tell the story (Egan stage I-A)
J: So, perfection. Part of the package?	The helper has picked up on the repeated word 'perfect' as an empathic response working within the developing relationship	Challenging paraphrase
C: Yeah. Absolutely, can't do anything just so, it's all got to be absolutely right. Um, didn't take very long for me to be very tired in that situation and to become psychologically exhausted as well as mentally and physically exhausted		
J: And anxious? I am just very aware I'm just (pats own chest)	The helper has an embodied response here to the client's visual and verbal clues around anxiety	Immediacy and self-disclosure Empathy Congruence Rogers core conditions
C: Anxiety was huge. Absolutely huge	The client has some verbal clues of discomfort here	
J: Um	The helper is affirming but also allowing space and moments of reflective silence	Use of silence Egan stage II Culley and Bond middle stage

table 4.2 continued

Content	Process	Skills
C: Um, and I look back at that time with a real sense of . . . I can't remember a great deal of it when my children were very little but I have an abiding memory of being so in love with my children and so happy with my family. But so anxious and crying all the time because I couldn't; that's where I wanted to be and I'd set myself these goals to be somewhere else and do these things as well as do that, as well as do everything perfectly and I have a huge memory of that time being very, very anxious . . . (*silence*)	The client's facial expressions are showing slight signs of distress as she describes this, and notice the sigh and hand movements	
C: Very anxious indeed . . . (*long silence*)		
J: OK? Just stay with this	The helper holds this moment and the relationship in a safe space. She shows empathy, her face is serious and she maintains eye contact, nodding and affirming	Unconditional positive regard Empathy Rogers core conditions
C: And I think as I have a . . . a really clear sense of that anxiety that just came back to me then		
J: I can see it	A small but very empathic response. The helper places her hands on the arms of the chair and the client mirrors this grounding gesture	Self-disclosure and immediacy Use of silence Non-verbal communication
C: . . . just took over, I think what I associate with moving forward is bringing that anxiety back because I think I have begun a process of learning that has crystallised in the last two or three years about what's important to me, what I really want to spend time doing and work is only now part of that. Um. It's still important but it's not my main driver any more. And I think it brings back the anxiety thinking. Oh, am I going to change again? Am I going to get it wrong? Am I going to be anxious like that again? Am I going to be running around and I can feel. I am feeling it in my head now and in my body that I'm racing		

table 4.2 continued

Content	Process	Skills
J: Yes, so just being aware of this situation we're in and I can see that this anxiety is rising through you like a barometer, OK. I am wondering how I might just help you feel a little bit more grounded here, that's all, and would it be useful to just maybe move a little bit away from the anxiety, and I am not ignoring it, I am just wanting to move away from it a little because I am just seeing that it is beginning to just	The helper returns to the contractual agreement and checks that the client is OK with the rising emotion. She demonstrates that she has listened to what the client is saying but has been grounding her through immediacy and non-verbal communication	Paraphrase and immediacy Re-establishing the contract Attending and listening
C: That's very good of you to do that		
J: . . . have a hold on you. Would that be useful to do that?		
C: Very useful		
J: OK		
J: . . . have a little bit of a hold on you. So let's think. Would it be all right if I took you back a bit then? We were thinking about your achievements. And when I heard you talk about your basket, I thought gosh, that's a really brilliantly full basket. Um, if you just took something out of the . . . if you looked at your basket full of your little eggs if you like of achievement. Which is the one, which is the biggest egg in there for you?	Lovely evidence of working with the relationship – the helper is allowing the client to choose the direction of the next session by 'choosing her egg'. Challenging and creating new meaning (working with the relationship)	
C: My family		
J: Family, yes . . .		

CLARIFYING

People share their stories in different ways. Some clients may speak quite freely and have a lot to say about their situation and others may be more tentative or reticent about sharing with you and need quite a lot of encouragement and prompting to describe their situation. Both these relationships hold challenges, and the skill of clarifying with the client is helpful to explore and understand his or her story and value system, as well as any conflicts that arise from this.

New students often report that they are really anxious about using their counselling skills but are then really surprised with some clients, where it was 'hard to get a word in edgeways!' Some clients get sidetracked on to a different subject or start their story halfway through, and it is hard to follow their train of thought or focus on what they are saying. While we avoid interrupting our clients, we do need to understand and follow them so helping them to clarify their story is an essential part of challenging skills.

> Clarity opens the door to more creative options for living. Vague stories lead to vague options and actions.
>
> (Egan 2002: 140)

Some skills we might use for this are summarising or even direct questions. These have the effect of drawing together the meaning and focus for both client and helper. We can do this tentatively through phrases such as:

> 'Can I just stop you for a minute to check that I really understand what you have just told me?'

> 'There are a lot of things you have told me today, can I just go through the main points to make sure I heard them all correctly?'

Or we can check through questions or facts with short reflections or summaries.

> Client: And then my husband left me, the kids went to university just after that and my mum died just before my dad and that was when I started this job.

> Helper: That sounds like an awful lot happening in a short space of time. Would you mind if we just go through that again so I really understand the situation and the timing of all this?

With the story clarified between you, this then opens the door to exploring options for change.

Even with the best intentions, it is sometimes hard to follow the client's train of thought or story, so admitting we are lost or have not understood helps the client to feel that he or she is being listened to and that what he or she is saying is important to the helper. It is much better to clarify than muddle through with a half understanding of the conversation. However, a mixture of skills here is better than a barrage of questions. We can use summaries, reflections or paraphrases to check our understanding.

Challenging and clarifying values

We discussed earlier that part of our role as a helper is not to impose our values on our clients, but equally we acknowledge that, as human beings, we all have our own value system. Clarifying our client's value system is a skill that can lead us to challenge any identifiable blind spots. Respect is essential, and we avoid judging our client's actions or attitudes; we are there to support him or her, he or she needs to know that we are on his or her side. If a client feels judged, he or she may resist our help, and this could potentially break down the relationship or contract. However, this does not mean that we need to be passive on important moral issues. We would not condone issues such as domestic violence, child abuse or strongly held principles concerning racism or homophobia, and we are entitled to state our values on these important aspects. However, we can do this in a gentle, non-judgemental way – 'I'm afraid I don't hold the same views about that' or 'You need to know that I can't condone violence of any form'.

But we remember that the session belongs to the client, and we keep the client's agenda in focus rather than our own. It is not our place to get on a soapbox; we do not judge, but neither are we a silent recipient. If something truly offends our moral principles, it would be appropriate to say this rather than the client assuming that we agree with him or her.

When we want to help our clients, it can be challenging not to jump in with advice. We might hold a personal opinion, for example, that our client might be better off leaving his or her current relationship, but this decision is not ours to make. We are there to support our clients to make whatever changes they decide to make, or not make, after helping them to review the possibilities and options.

It may be very apparent to us where our clients' value systems are hindering their progress. We avoid jumping in with a value judgement, but rather clarify first what our client's viewpoint is and then we may follow this up with a challenge if it feels appropriate.

> Client: My mother thought a woman's place was in the home, to be there for the kids and to look after your husband when he came home. I told my daughter that she wants to have her cake and eat it, she wants a career and children!
>
> Helper: Your mother's ideas seem to have been important to you and now your daughter has a different viewpoint. What was your experience as a wife and mum? Is there anything you would have liked to do differently?
>
> Client: Well actually I might have liked to have a medical career like my husband because I was really good at science at school but it was much harder for girls to be doctors in those days. It just wasn't done then.
>
> Helper: So if you imagine you were born in this generation today, how do you think it might have been for you?

EXAMPLE

VIDEO CLIP 4c

WORKING WITH THE RELATIONSHIP – CLARIFYING: Jacqui and Caz

TABLE 4.3 Transcript of Video Clip 4c: Working with the relationship – clarifying – Jacqui and Caz

Content	Process	Skills
J: I supposed I was wondering, and in a way this might be a bit of a challenge actually, because I was thinking although you've come from an origin, a history if you like of being quite structured and goal-driven and focused on something out there ahead of you, I'm trying to think if there were elements of that part of you that actually could be incredibly useful still and wouldn't necessarily serve you well to forget about all together. Do you see what I mean? (C: Absolutely) So thinking about how you combine the bits of that, that part of you that are actually quite useful, without being overtaken and driven by her. Does that make sense?	The helper summarises what she has heard and offers a potential goal to work with. This is tentatively offered, stated as a challenge	Challenge
Summary
Giving feedback
Clarifying and developing goals (the established relationship RSM)
Shaping goals (Egan stage II-C)
Deciding on appropriate change (Culley and Bond ending stage)
C: Absolutely. And I think that is certainly the process I've gone through in the last couple of months is actually thinking. When the anxiety arises at that time that's all I can think of is the negativity. But actually you are absolutely right, there are elements of that that I don't want to completely reject actually because it's served me very, very well, on lots of different levels whether it was materially, intellectually or whatever. And I think that's the process of that exploration is 'What do I take, what do I take and what do I leave?' actually		
J: What would you like to leave?	Open question has an effect of slowing the client down into a thoughtful place	Challenging open question
Holding of silence
Non-verbal communication
C: I'd like to leave (*long pause and pondering*) the absolute feeling of when I've got my teeth into something that I can't put it down, I can't put it down to the detriment of everybody and everything around me sometimes that I get so focused		

REASSESSING

In the previous example, you will see that the helper is exploring the value system that the client grew up with and going on to help her explore whether this value system remains helpful today. When we have clarified and followed our client's story, we may help to identify unhelpful and unproductive thinking by pointing out discrepancies between the past and the present. This can be a useful form of challenge, particularly to illuminate blind spots or inconsistencies.

> Client: I have never been able to assert myself. I am just hopeless at expressing my opinion. People just walk all over me.
>
> Helper: So it feels like you are constantly a doormat. Earlier you told me that your mum was going to book that family holiday in Devon and you said you wanted to go somewhere warmer and you all went to Spain instead. That sounded like you expressing your opinion and people listening to it.
>
> Client: Gosh I never thought about something like that because that is just my family. But they did listen to what I wanted then, didn't they?

Summarising progress, even in a short one-off session, is another form of reassessing that can take the form of a challenge.

> Helper: When you came here this morning you wanted to explore your difficult relationship with your boss and since we have talked we have realised that other people have a difficult relationship with him too.
>
> Client: Yes, I am beginning to realise it's not just me.
>
> Helper: So would it be helpful to think about how your colleagues manage to work with him?

In these examples of reassessing, you will see that the helper is prompting the client to consider a different viewpoint. The examples of the client response show that he or she is having small 'light bulb' moments as he or she is offered an alternative perspective. If your client does not respond in this way, you should not feel that this intervention was wrong. We work towards 'offering' these perspectives, and it is then up to the client whether it is useful for him or her in his or her circumstance. We are not advice giving, but rather we are laying out different perspectives to better enable the client to make informed choices.

PROBING

The helper can use probes to gain better understanding and definition of the client's issue or problem. Probes can clarify and go deeper into the issue or circumstance in the form of statements, summaries or questions. We try to use questions that are open and Socratic, with the intention to stimulate a deeper understanding for the client. Some examples might be:

> 'What's the worst thing that could happen?'
>
> 'What would you tell a friend to do in this situation?'
>
> 'How does that fit with what you just said?'

A form of probing is where we ask the client a question that he or she already knows the answer to. We are probing deeper into his or her perceptions, often through our observation of the verbal or non-verbal clues that the client provides.

> 'I noticed when you talked about visiting New Zealand to see your family, you said it "felt like home". I wonder what you meant by that? I am curious whether the UK feels like home?'

This open question enables the client to explore his or her feelings at a deeper level through reflecting on prompts that the helper has picked up on. As helpers, we learn to develop our awareness around the sentences of gestures that 'don't quite fit'. Handing these back to the client is a gentle but effective form of challenge that can lead to a fuller explanation and exploration.

As we discussed in Chapter 3, the overuse of questions can be irritating to the client and, when probing, it is better to vary our use of skills rather than follow one question on with another. We are now beginning to develop a toolbox of skills and we can explore other probing skills such as non-verbal prompts, leaving silences, short statements or single-word reflections.

> Client: When I am in New Zealand with my folks, it really feels like home.
>
> Helper: (*head leaning to one side in an inquisitive gesture and pausing*) Home?
>
> Client: Yes, I really belong there.
>
> Helper: And you now live in the UK.
>
> Client: Yes, it's funny that my permanent home is here but it doesn't feel like it.
>
> Helper: Can you say more about those feelings?

The above prompts, pauses and final open question show the client that the helper is curious and interested, but also probing the meaning beneath the statement around 'home'.

GIVING FEEDBACK AND SHARING INFORMATION

> I've learned that people will forget what you said, people will forget what you did, but people will never forget how you made them feel.
>
> (Maya Angelou, in Kelly 2003: 263)

We begin this section with this quotation as to us it really illustrates how important it is to give feedback and impart information or news in a way that people will remember in a positive way. We have included how to give feedback in Chapter 2 as part of the learning partner agreement, and we feel it is important to reiterate the 'art' of giving feedback and sharing information within this 'section on challenging' as we consider it can be very challenging for a helper to give honest and clear feedback or to share information in an honest and 'owned' way. Receiving feedback helps us to become more aware of what we do, and why and how we do it. It gives us an opportunity to change and modify our behaviour, and it helps endorse the more positive aspects of our behaviour. As helpers, it may be useful to give feedback to a client about how *you* experience *him or her* within the relationship, either through the use of immediacy or by thinking carefully about what you are going to feed back and introducing feedback at a point in the relationship where it feels right to bring it up. This has the effect of increasing the client's self-awareness and deepening understanding of how others, outside of the helper relationship, might also be experiencing him or her.

> '*I experience* you as a strong, independent woman who finds it difficult to ask for help and support from me.'

> 'When you express anger, *I notice* you go very quiet and monosyllabic in your responses to me.'

> '*I feel frustrated* when you arrive 10 minutes late for each session.'

Often, as health professionals, part of the helper role is to share information or 'news' with the client. Our work within this field has shown us how difficult and ambiguous the role can become when you have to combine giving important, factual and necessary information to the client and 'care for and listen to' the client at the same time.

In their paper on the shared treatment decision-making model, Charles *et al.* (1999) talk of three different models of sharing information:

- *Paternalistic*: The professional is seen as the expert and patients agree to the professional's decision and choice by passively acquiescing.
- *Informed*: The sole responsibility of the professional is to transfer the information. Patients do all the deliberating and decision-making with no professional steer.
- *Shared*: Patients and professionals share information two-way and both agree on decisions. Both ask and answer questions and build consensus. This approach is characterised by listening – on both sides.

While this model is more directly related to a patient/professional medical intervention, its principles are true within the helping model. Sharing of information, where there is time to discuss and listen to the client's experiences and responses, is far more preferable to telling or transferring the information in a one-way exchange.

When sharing information, it is important not to pre-judge or anticipate the response.

> it is not our job to tell them the news is 'bad' ... we tell them the facts and try to empathise; they decide how they feel about it.
>
> (Feirn 2013)

Each individual client will receive news differently – sometimes, if someone is experiencing difficult health symptoms, it is good news for him or her to receive a medical diagnosis as symptoms can then be explained and acknowledged. Often, we surprise ourselves with our reactions – when I (Becky) received my redundancy notice, I found myself leaping around the room in excitement – the anxiety and sadness came at different times in the process. The key is to share the information from a neutral stance and not to make assumptions that the client will react in the same way as you (or even the same way as a majority of people might react). Every client is an individual, and his or her responses will be individual. A really good example of this is of an audiologist giving the news to a deaf mother that her baby's hearing test was 'fine' – the mother thought that 'fine' meant the baby was deaf like her, and the audiologist meant 'fine' – the baby is hearing like her (West 2012).

As helpers, we might share information that we feel will be of benefit to the client – names of support groups/normalising situations/refererences to guidelines and literature, and so on. Information should also be offered tentatively and with an open mind as it may or may not be useful to the client. Information sharing, offering treatment, referrals to other agencies and so on must always be offered as a choice, thereby allowing the client to make his or her own decisions about what is right for him or her, or not.

EXAMPLE

VIDEO CLIP 4d

WORKING WITH THE RELATIONSHIP:
Glyn and Rob

Now is the time to see if you can identify the Process and the Skills, as we have done in previous transcripts. As you watch the next video clip consider and note down examples of Process and Skills on the blank transcript (Appendix 4). In particular:

- Which skills does the counsellor use to challenge the client?
- How does the client respond?
- Can you identify examples of creating new meaning and perspectives with the client?

TABLE 4.4 Transcript of Video Clip 4d: Working with the relationship – Glyn and Rob

Content	Process	Skills
G: Rob, just so I'm sure I understand everything that's going on here. Your mum and brother have just recently moved. You've got some very mixed feelings about that we've talked about. Just wondered where you are with it all. Where does it feel it is for you now?		
R: Yeah, I feel more isolated now and, um, as I said, I moved to Reading, which isn't too far away, and it was nice being close to them. Not too close, they can't turn up for a cup of tea every five minutes but it was nice being close to them, you know. Cos I've been away for a long time so I guess I'm kind of used to that, um, and it was nice to get some of it back because when I moved away I also felt like I sort of lost something with my mum and the rest of my family, you know		
G: What do you feel you lost?		
R: Just growing up with them, spending time in the same rooms, just doing everyday stuff. I don't know what that is, in a way I do know what that is with my brother but I don't know what it is with all of us. And I will never know because it's gone. Um. And it didn't happen. We saw each other but it's not the same as coming home from school and stuff. So it was nice being back near and even though I'm used to being away from my mum and my brother and my family it was just nice to have it. So now it's a bit, yeah, I know this feeling		
G: Yeah		
R: So I can cope with it. Doesn't mean I like it		
G: OK, can you tell me about what the feeling does to you?		
R: What it does?		
G: What does it present to you?		
R: Um		

table 4.4 continued

Content	Process	Skills
G: Cos you said you felt isolated		
R: Yeah, um, it makes things a bit hard to do, it's difficult to explain but it's like a . . . I just want to go 'umph'		
G: OK		
R: You know, and . . . yeah, I feel heavier and I feel a bit sort of more tired. It's not quite hopeless, it's not that bad, but it's just like . . . you know, I miss them		
G: You miss them		
R: Miss them, yeah. I felt like I had . . . as much as we argue all the bloody time, it's like I had a bit of support, you know, it's like, you know, it's that thing about family are a pain but at the same time you love them. And I, er, I didn't know until I just said it but I guess I feel like that		
G: So you feel that you miss them and that makes you feel heavy		
R: Yeah, bit of a struggle		
G: So what do you want to do about that?		
R: (deep breath) Phew. That's a big question. Um		
G: What do you think will reduce some of that for you?		
R: Um, I was going to say to see them and in a way that would but it's more that I want to be happier without that, if you see what I mean. Where I kind of, where I don't rely on them. Although I can kind of feel myself getting tied up in knots here because it's not that I don't want to be with them and it's not that I want to dismiss how I am feeling, but I want to be OK. I mean I am OK but I want to be just anyway		
G: So it sounds like you need some autonomy but you still want to be close to your family		

table 4.4 continued

Content	Process	Skills
R: Well that's the thing. I have loads of autonomy I have loads of it, you know it's . . . I'm very used to being on my own and doing things on my own and, you know, if something needs doing I'll do it. And it's nice to be close to them but I . . . what I want is the autonomy plus . . . plus the closeness just for the sake of us being who we are. My family being who we are, you know. I guess, and this is when I start tearing up and feeling sad again, it's like, when I talk about, when I talk about them now . . . and it's getting really difficult to say, um. It's almost nostalgic whereas when we are living day to day I can kind of see why I don't, um. Why I don't see them all the time. You know, there's a kind of a . . . not that we argue with each other but . . .		
R: . . . the way that we talk is pretty straightforward really. My mum can be quite, um. I kind of see it as quite critical. She tells me I'm being too sensitive and it's just like kind of – OK! *(laughs)* But that's kind of the way we get on, um. Sorry, I don't know whether I'm getting a bit lost but I've kind of forgotten		
G: So what do you want here? What is it you want? So you say you've got your autonomy but you say you want your autonomy and closeness, so what is it you want?		
R: I want to feel happy in myself so that I can go and do what I want to do without the feeling that I'm missing out on something, the feeling that I owe somebody something, that I owe my family something while I'm at it. Part of the thing about moving away is . . . is I always kind of had a sense in some way of what I'd lost. It's like every time I do something it's a choice, you know, and there's only so much time. There's only so much life that I have and that sounds quite . . . like it might be a bit much but it's not. Literally, there's only so long that we live and I really feel it when I choose to spend my time with my family or alone. I really wonder what else could be you know. When they move away and I have that kind of emptiness, that hole, it really hurts		

table 4.4 continued

Content	Process	Skills

G: So how can we simplify that? How can we put that into something that you want that's going to make things better for you?

R: I think for me what would really work is, you know, like I've just said about life being short to kind of break that down a bit instead of having some kind of abstract idea that kind of life is short it's actually about day to day stuff and about actually just accepting that bit and rather than just dwelling on the fact that actually time is just slipping away. It's a case of actually time is slipping away, time is slipping away for everybody, you know, we are all here but I can use it to do what I want, that's it, I can use it to do what I want and that's the bit about not owing other people something

G: OK

R: Does that make sense?

G: Yeah. Can I? Just to make sure I understand what you were looking for. You have this loss here that it feels like you're working with and you want to be able to have your autonomy that you've got but also still have the ability to sort of move on in your life by some sort of acceptance of that

R: It's that acceptance that really hits me when you were telling me that

G: OK

R: You know cos the autonomy and the things I can do for myself since I've grown up. I can do all of that and I know I have done for ages but it's the, it's the acceptance and the being comfortable in myself that actually this is my time and I can spend it how I want and that might mean an afternoon in front of the telly, that might mean that I can choose what I do and that's OK and it doesn't have to be anything huge but it's OK to want something just because I want it

G: OK

R: You know?

G: Yeah

WORKING WITH THE RELATIONSHIP

> **REFLECTIVE LEARNING JOURNAL EXERCISE**
>
> Were you able to fill out the process box and the skills box?
>
> How easy or difficult was it to identify the different skills and process?
>
> Compare your observations with the completed transcript at the back of the book (Appendix 4b).
>
> Reflect on the areas you found it difficult to identify. Why do you think that was?
>
> Because this is an unscripted video clip, it is not possible to demonstrate all the different skills of challenging but hopefully this video clip demonstrated a flavour of how you might work with the relationship to help your client to create new meaning, different possibilities and perspective.

REFLECT, PRACTISE AND EVALUATE

With your learning partner:

In the role of client, describe something that you find difficult to do – for example:

- returning a purchase to a store;
- complaining about a meal in a restaurant; or
- asking for a pay rise.

Take it in turns to be the helper and client for 10 minutes each.

As the helper, try to use challenging skills to work through the difficulty with the client.

Video the session to watch back and reflect on and evaluate the skills you have used.

Video your skills session

MODEL BOX

> In this chapter, we have referred to:
>
> - The Relational Skills Model – working with the relationship (Midwinter and Dickson 2015)
> - Types of immediacy (Egan 2002: 210)
> - Blind spots (Egan 2002: 177)
> - Guidelines for using immediacy (Culley and Bond 2004: 133)
> - Guidelines for using self-disclosure (Culley and Bond 2004: 128)
> - Models of sharing information (Charles et al. 1999)
> - Depressogenic assumptions (dysfunctional assumptions or maladaptive rules) (Beck et al. 1979: 244)

SUMMARY

- When working with the relationship, we are using enhanced skills to create new meaning, different possibilities and perspectives.
- The use of silence is a skill in itself and a valuable aspect of active listening.
- Challenging needs to be tentative, appropriate and sensitive. There are different types of challenges depending on the context within which we use them.
- Self-disclosure should be used sparingly and it needs to be relevant to what the client is discussing and appropriate to the phase of relationship development.
- Immediacy, as a form of challenge, can be a spontaneous and highly effective intervention. It is based on empathic understanding, mutuality, and the sharing of hunches, thoughts and ideas.
- Giving feedback to clients should always be for their benefit. Receiving feedback helps us to become more aware of what we do, and why and how we do it.

Chapter 5
The established relationship

At this phase, the helper and client are able to clarify and focus on likely changes and work collaboratively to make plans, set goals and consider and evaluate possible strategies and directions. The focus within this phase is on goal setting and evaluation. Intuitive and learned skills within this phase are:

- Working empathically
- Focusing
- Use of metaphor and hunches
- Drawing together themes
- Clarifying and developing goals
- Action planning

TEACHING

WORKING EMPATHICALLY

In Chapter 1, we looked at Roger's core conditions and defined empathy as the ability to step into another's shoes and imagine life from his or her perspective. Empathy is more than sympathetic understanding; friends can give us that – in showing empathy as a helper, we situate ourselves alongside our client and we demonstrate our empathy to him or her through our verbal and non-verbal responses.

Mearns and Cooper (2005: 36) write that empathy combined with unconditional positive regard and congruence need to all be present in order to work at 'relational depth'. While our book is not aimed at training therapists, we consider that this also applies in the helper role. If we want to demonstrate a *deeper* empathy in our helping role, it is important that we hold all these 'core conditions' by being respectful and real at the same time as demonstrating our understanding and empathy for our client's feelings.

We also avoid over-identifying with our client's issues. We are there to help and 'me too' responses are not always helpful, even if we can relate to what he or she is telling us. Relationship requires difference (Schmid 2002), even if there are similarities and identification with each other. In our 'differences', we are meeting and connecting with the client through our demonstration of empathic understanding.

Empathy can be demonstrated through the skill of immediacy or self-disclosure:

Helper: When you tell me that, I feel quite sad.

Client: Actually, no one really understood how I felt then.

Or through affirmations:

Helper: And it seems to me that you were really strong to deal with that.

Client: Yes, I suppose I did deal with that OK, didn't I?

These *deeper*, more relational empathic responses will come when we understand a little about our client and what he or she is bringing, and after we have established the working alliance so the expression of deeper empathy is an appropriate skill to use in the intuitive *established relationship* phase. At the same time as we empathise, we need to be aware of our client's responses. We check for clues that we are understanding and tracking our client through his or her verbal and non-verbal responses. We might look for signs that the client is disturbed by, or resisting, our response and then check whether this is because we have not understood or because we were *too accurate* in our response (Egan 2002: 114). Empathy can be given as a warm demonstration of fellow feeling or take the form of empathic challenge where we might highlight a phrase or action.

Helper: When you tell me that, I feel quite sad.

Client: No it was fine.

Helper: Fine?

Client: Well, it was quite a tough time actually.

The helper has decided to respond with a reflective challenge. As helpers, we need to gauge whether and when to empathically challenge and we need to be congruent when we do not seem to be tracking or understanding our client.

Helper: When you tell me that, I feel quite sad.

Client: Yes it was sad but that is not what I was talking about.

Helper: OK, let's make sure I am understanding. Tell me what it is that you were really talking about.

In this example, the helper has decided to go with the client's response and acknowledge that he or she might not have understood. The helper here might have had a hunch that the client is indeed sad but he or she has decided this is not the time to challenge it. We can take prompts from our client's responses to our empathy in order to decide whether we follow up on it. Being empathic is not the same as colluding with the client, but we avoid a situation where our client feels threatened by being 'put on the spot'; this could be detrimental to our relationship and have the effect of shutting it down. With the core conditions in place, we remain sensitive to his or her needs. However, neither do we shy away from our empathic challenge if we think it will help our client to focus or clarify. At this phase of having established the relationship, we will have a better sense of whether to pursue our empathic challenge or hold back.

Expressing empathy through body language

Sometimes a non-verbal response can more effectively convey empathy as we allow the client to continue to relate his or her story. This can be a very powerful response for your client. You can observe this in the video clips with the helper and client.

> **REFLECTIVE LEARNING JOURNAL EXERCISE**
>
> Turn off the sound and re-watch the last video clip (you can do this with your own video exercises too).
>
> What non-verbal prompts does the helper use to convey empathy?
>
> How does the client respond to this?
>
> How do you think you demonstrate empathy in your role as a helper?

Non-verbal empathic response can be quite subtle, and we all have our individual ways of demonstrating it. We should try to feel normal, relaxed and comfortable with our responses. We are aiming for a congruent relationship, and we need to be real and avoid play-acting.

> **Non-verbal empathy might take the form of:**
> - a slight inclination of the head that indicates we are listening;
> - mirroring of body language by the way we sit opposite each other;
> - eye contact – even for a short moment;
> - shared laughter; or
> - a look of concern when our client discloses a difficulty.

Empathy is a feeling and we can learn to tune in to our 'felt sense' when we are with a client. If we feel saddened by what he or she is telling us, would it be helpful to share this? We ask ourselves whether this is our feeling or a reflection of how the client is feeling? Could we be picking up on a feeling – for instance, sadness or anger – that the client is not recognising or acknowledging in him or herself? If we suspect this is the case, would it be helpful if we share our feeling? Our aim in this phase is to help the client clarify and work towards possible changes and this empathic congruence may help him or her towards this goal.

FOCUSING

When we ask a client to describe his or her issue or problem, often he or she may respond with a generalisation or express a really big 'worry'. For example:

> 'I just want to be happy.'
>
> 'Life seems just too much at the moment.'

In our wish to help our client, it can be tempting to want to cover everything that the client has brought, but helping our client to focus more specifically can move towards goal setting and we can always return to other issues later if time allows. We may also decide to signpost him or her on to other helping professionals if we do not feel qualified to help. We remember our role as a helper and what is realistically achievable within our relationship, and ensure that the client understands this too.

Sometimes our client will be in the middle of a crisis, in which case this is likely to be our focus, but at other times we may need to help our client to centre on a particular concern. Egan (2002) helps us to prioritise this with *leverage*, working on issues that make a difference.

> Egan's guidelines for choosing issues to be worked on are:
> - If there is a crisis, first help the client manage the crisis.
> - Begin with the problem that seems to be causing most pain for the client.
> - Begin with issues the client sees as important and is willing to work on.
> - Begin with some manageable sub-problem of a larger problem situation.
> - Begin with a problem that, if handled, will lead to some kind of general improvement in the client's condition.
> - Focus on a problem for which the benefits outweigh the costs.
>
> *(Egan 2002: 233)*

We may use these leverage guidelines when we are initially identifying problems and assessing our client's needs in the *developing relationship* but they are equally useful at this stage of the *established relationship* where we are helping our client to focus on a specific area of concern in preparation for implementing change. As practitioners, we may be confined to time constraints or managerial roles that will dictate what is possible to work on, so it is useful to help the client to focus.

There are a number of ways to help a client to focus and Socratic questions (see Chapter 3) are useful here.

> 'We have discussed a number of things that are troubling you at the moment. If you can imagine that you made a pile of those problems, which one do you think would be at the top?'

It might be useful to think of a number of questions that we can use to help our clients focus and we can watch how the helper in the next video clip does this.

We could ask our clients to visually draw or write a list of issues to numerically prioritise, remaining mindful and realistic about what is achievable within the context of this relationship.

We can also use paraphrases, reflections or summaries to highlight and focus. Or ask our client one word that would describe his or her problem and then put that word into a phrase or sentence (Lazarus 1976).

Helper: Could you use one word that describes your problem?

Client: Stuck.

Helper: Stuck? Now can you put this word stuck into a sentence?

Client: I am stuck being overweight and I can never change.

USE OF METAPHOR AND HUNCHES

Some of us find it useful to work with metaphor or imagery. Working with a client's images can be a powerful way of identifying meanings. We often use metaphor in everyday life, almost without awareness.

> 'I will cross that bridge when I come to it.'
>
> 'I'm in between a rock and a hard place.'
>
> 'Now the boot's on the other foot.'

It is important that the metaphor *feels* comfortable to use. Use of metaphor is a personal preference and not everyone gains from it. We need to be aware that metaphors are cultural; they may have different or no meaning to us, particularly if English is not our first language. Take a look at the following examples:

French
'Je parle français comme une vache espagnole.'
Translates
'I speak French like a Spanish cow.'
Meaning
'I speak French really badly.'

German
'Ohrwurm.'
Translates
'Ear worm.'
Meaning
'A piece of music that keeps running around in our head.'

If we have not heard these metaphors before, they might feel a little strange to us, but in our own language metaphor may be a useful way of sharing meaning and feeling.

For some people, visual mental imagery is a powerful tool to explore meaning. We can investigate whether this would be helpful for our client by offering the use of metaphor in an open question:

'Do you have an image that comes into your head when you think of that?'

'Can you tell me what that looks like?'

Sometimes we have a strong image coming into our head from something our client said and we can offer that image to explore shared meaning.

Client: I feel so stuck with this.

Helper: I had an image that came into my head when you said that of a row of doors in a building – all closed.

Client: Yes, that's it, it's like there are all these doors I could walk through but it's really scary because I can't see what is behind them all!

Helper: Can you see what is behind any of them?

Client: Well, yes . . . one of them means changing my job.

Helper: What would it be like to stand outside that door and imagine walking through it?

We offer metaphor and hunches tentatively. As we track our client, we become aware of hunches around possible blind spots or negative self-defeating thinking. If we have a strong thought or image that comes into our head, we notice it and consider whether it would be helpful to share it.

We might have a strong sense that fear of failure or lack of confidence might be holding our client back from making choices. Rather than ask a direct question from this hunch, we might explore this more carefully using the skills that we have learned. We are aware that this is our *hunch* and it may or may not fit for our client. We define the word hunch as a *feeling*, *guess* or *idea*. Phrasing our hunch in a tentative way will give our client the option to pick up on our hunch or not. For example:

'I have a sense that . . .'

'I wonder if . . .'

'I had a thought/image just then when you said that, and I wonder whether it would be helpful to share it?'

Rather than:

'I think you are . . .'

'You should do . . .'

These could make our client feel judged and defensive.

It is helpful to remember that our client needs to find his or her own solution and perspective, and while we can empathise with our client, our solutions and ideas may not be right for him or her.

However, our hunches are a useful tool in the helping relationship. We can offer our clients multiple outlooks where they may seem to have had a single viewpoint. We can invite them to consider different ways to recognise their strengths, which they can then utilise.

EXAMPLE

VIDEO CLIP 5a

THE ESTABLISHED RELATIONSHIP – USE OF METAPHOR: Jacqui and Becky

TABLE 5.1 Transcript of Video Clip 5a: The established relationship – use of metaphor – Jacqui and Becky

Content	Process	Skills
J: So Becky, is now a good moment for you to think about what you want to say in this session here?	Revisiting the contract	Leading questions to clarify
B: Yeah, um, I think the thing that I have been thinking about for a while, and it is coming closer and closer, is a big transition that I am going to make professionally in my working life over the next 12 months. And there are a number of factors that contribute to the decision-making, um, and I kinda don't know where I am with it. I don't think I have swung from one end of a spectrum to the other quite so quickly and so often, so I would just like to explore what that might be about, and that factors maybe that are contributing to my confusion about it		Problem identification (developing the relationship) Telling the story (Egan stage I: what's going on?)
J: Um, swinging about		Short paraphrase Attending and listening Culley and Bond foundation skills
B: Yeah		
J: Sounds . . . unstable (*laughs*)		One-word paraphrase
B: Yeah. Really unstable, and on the one hand exciting, and on the other hand terrifying. And it's like I don't know the difference at the moment with this subject. Am I terrified or am I just overexcited? I don't know, I'm both and neither, it's a weird feeling		
J: It sounds like the spectrum feels quite wide at the moment and the feelings have some similarity for you? Or not, in a way?	Seems like the helper got a little lost here by checking out her assumption and then withdrawing it so as not to lead the client	Summarising and closed question Identifying feeling Using an open question such as 'How does it feel to you?' might have been a more useful intervention

table 5.1 continued

Content	Process	Skills
B: I don't think I have ever felt them so similar. I think in the past, when I have been terrified, I have known that I'm terrified, and it is like I know what I am terrified of and I know the sensation. And when I am really excited, I know what really excited is, and at the moment it's like I am both of them together. And that's how it feels		
J: And maybe this hasn't happened to you before?	The helper is making an assumption and checking this out with the question	Closed question, but tentatively asked Identifying content
B: Not so closely linked. I might have been excited and terrified if I've been on, um. the only thing I can think of is like a ride, you know, like one of these really terrifying rides. You are really, really excited and then you get on the ride, and then you are just about to go down, and then (*sharp intake of breath*) and then the terror hits me, and then I come out the end of the ride. Actually, that's a really good metaphor, that's what it feels like. I feel like I am at the top of a ride and I've gone up the (*gestures the steps*) and I am at that bit, and I know that any moment now I'm going down. Yeah, that's quite a good metaphor	Even though the last intervention ended with a closed question, it enabled the client to explore what is really going on for her	Introduces metaphor
J: You explained it so well to me, I really, really understood that. And also, not knowing where that ride is going to take you. Are you going down or are you going along? Are you going that way or that way? Or have you given it some sort of thought?	Demonstrating understanding and that the client has been heard, but using closed questions, which might have evoked a 'yes/no' answer. A better intervention might have been to give a fuller summary – that is, 'It sounds as though you've lost your direction. I'm wondering what your thoughts are about that?'	Immediacy Reflecting content and meaning summary Identifying actions Closed questions Attending and listening Picks up on metaphor

table 5.1 continued

Content	Process	Skills
B: Do you know, I think just sitting here realising the most terrifying bit is I don't know when I'm going to go, I don't know when the ride is going to start. I've gone to the top, I know it's going to go at any moment and maybe there will be a bell and then I'll go, or maybe there won't be a bell and I will just go and I won't even know I've gone. That's how it feels. And then that's . . . I haven't even thought about the twists and turns, it's just the where am I going to go?	The helper's exploration of where the ride is going to take the client has enabled the client to clarify what the most terrifying bit is for her, and it is not where it is going to take her, but when it is going to start. An important realisation for the client	Identifying feelings, content and meaning Identifying blind spots (Egan stage I: what's really going on?)
J: Yeah, when is it going to take off?	The helper then continues with the thread about when it is going to start	Paraphrase
B: When is it going to go? When is the ride going to start?		
J: Do you have any idea? I mean, is there any indication?		Open question
B: I've got this time boundary, yeah, but I don't know. I've got that time boundary of when that's going to happen but I don't know if that's the beginning of the ride. Or whether I'll be in a queue for . . . 20 minutes or . . . you know, keeping on with that metaphor, it's something about I know when I've got to start it in some way, and I don't know if I've got to get on the ride. I don't know if I'll choose not to get on the ride		
J: Um, you might not choose to get on the ride? Would that depend on the ride? Choosing not to get on it, or is it dependent on other factors?	The helper is working collaboratively with the client to consider and evaluate possible strategies and directions (the established relationship)	Closed questions for clarifying Egan stage I: what's going on? Culley and Bond middle stage
B: Oh, that's interesting. I don't know. And maybe that's the excitement and the fear. I actually don't know . . . yeah . . . I don't know whether I can choose or whether I will be forced to get on the ride maybe	The client is interested in exploring her element of choice – moving on	Clarifying and focusing on likely changes (the established relationship) Egan stage I–C

table 5.1 continued

Content	Process	Skills
J: Do you imagine a ride that you would like to take? Do you go with that ever?		Closed question for clarifying
B: Yeah. Which ride would I take? I would like one with enough fear and excitement in it, with enough risk in it to be exciting, but that I knew that all the bolts were screwed up and somebody hadn't just put it together overnight. You know, that a great huge team of builders had built the ride and it had been safety checked. You know. (*laughs*) That's what I want, that would be the ride, and then it wouldn't matter how many twists and turns were in the actual ride, as long as I know that it was definitely going to be safe		
J: So the safety element is really important. But it needs to be also an area where you can feel challenged		Paraphrase linking the safety with the 'twists and turns' and rephrasing that as 'challenge'
B: Yes		

DRAWING TOGETHER THEMES

Only when we have identified choices can we move towards goal setting. We draw together themes with the aim of helping our client *consider and evaluate possible strategies and directions*. Imagining these possibilities can help our clients with motivation to change, moving them away from the problem and towards the solution.

> 'You have said that you want to lose weight and we have looked at all the ways people do that, such as joining a programme online, attending a weight-loss class or joining the gym, and getting a personal trainer. When you think about those possibilities, do you have an idea what might work for you?'

In this example, the helper has highlighted strategies that have been discussed, opening up the possibility for the client that he or she might work towards his or her goal. In order to do this, he or she needs to develop inspiration that it is *'do-able'* because others have done it. Egan refers to this as 'possible selves', and says that 'hope' is a key preliminary to change (Egan 2002: 262). Often, we will find that our clients hold themselves back because of fear of change, and if we are really honest with ourselves, we might admit that many of us avoid change unless it feels really necessary or we can see that it holds potential benefits.

In the previous section on introducing hunches, we discussed how we might explore multiple viewpoints with our clients. Here, we can use the skill of brainstorming, often these days referred to as 'blue-sky thinking'.

One way we can do this might be to make a list with our client. We start with the proviso that he or she remains open-minded. If we come up with ideas for our clients, we can often be met with a 'yes, but' response. It is important that the client is proactive in this list, and one of the ways we might encourage this is in a more light-hearted way.

> *Helper:* If, as you say you want to, you were to change your job, what could you imagine yourself doing?
>
> *Client:* That's it really, I don't know what else I could possibly do.
>
> *Helper:* OK, if you remember, we have agreed to stay open to any possibility. What would be your dream job?
>
> *Client:* (*laughs*) Well that's easy. I always wanted to be an airline pilot so I could travel the world.
>
> *Helper:* OK, let's add that one to the list. If travel is important, what other jobs might involve travel?
>
> *Client:* Well, actually, my cousin works in the airport and he gets cheap flights, there might be something there and I suppose that might happen working in a travel agency.
>
> *Helper:* Airline pilot, airport work and travel agency. That's a good start – anything else?

> Miracle imagery questions can also help with exploring blue-sky thinking:
>
> 'If you woke up tomorrow morning and everything was how you would like it to be, how would it be?'
>
> 'What would be different from how it is now?'
>
> 'If you were visited by a fairy godmother and given a magic wish, what would you wish for?'
>
> 'What would you need in order to be able to do this?'
>
> *(adapted from De Shazer 1988)*

Some clients can be held back from visualising this with 'black-and-white thinking' (where it is either all good or all bad) or 'catastrophising' (thinking failure or the worst is inevitable) (Beck *et al.* 1979: 26). In this case, we may need to support them in challenging these assumptions through clarifying and developing goals or action planning.

EXAMPLE

VIDEO CLIP 5b

THE ESTABLISHED RELATIONSHIP – DRAWING TOGETHER THEMES: Jacqui and Becky

TABLE 5.2 Transcript of Video Clip 5b: The established relationship – drawing together themes– Jacqui and Becky

Content	Process	Skills
J: Listening to you, it seems you've got three separate areas of success. You've got the financial success, earning money that gives you the freedom to do what you like to do. There's the academic success that is structured within some sort of organisation and then there's the success that I think you were talking about – about family life, about the core values, um, contentment. So at the moment, I mean, do you think that you are ticking quite a lot of boxes for yourself at the moment? And you're facing big change, and how are you going to still feel successful in all three areas?	The helper is drawing together the themes be reflecting back to the client everything she has heard and clarifying the possible choices that she has discussed	Paraphrasing and summarising follow by closed question Choosing/leverage
B: You've hit the nail on the head. At the moment, I have achieved that level of success, um, and I want that to change		
J: You do want it to change		Reflection
B: Yes, I want that to. I want to use this next 12 months to put in place a change. I want that to, not that I'm not happy with what I've got at the moment. I am. But I just don't think it's what I want in the future. The one I don't want is the middle professional one. I still want the financial. And, you know, I'm aware I will make some adjustments for that cos I'm not fussed at all about making some changes in the future financially to make sure . . . you can't always get what you want in life, that's fine. Home life and content is going to change anyway with the kids leaving home and doing their own thing, so that's going to be a change which is natural. The one in the middle is the one I want to change. I want success in a different way		
J: Umm . . . and it feels like that might be a really big subject (both laugh) for the next session	Gentle way of bringing the session to a close	Deeper empathy What will you take forward to work on? (Egan stage I-C)
B: Another time!		
J: Cos I think we've pretty much done our 20 minutes. Is that OK with you?		Working within the boundaries of the contract
B: Yeah, brilliant, thank you. Food for thought		
J: Thank you, Becky		
B: Thank you		

CLARIFYING AND DEVELOPING GOALS

When people embark on change, or begin to integrate new learning, they can become 'consciously incompetent'.

> Robinson's competence cycle (Robinson 1974) lists four levels of competence:
>
> - unconsciously incompetent;
> - consciously incompetent;
> - consciously competent; and
> - unconsciously competent.

The helper role can often have a 'psycho-educative' element, where the helper may help clients 'uncover information which they would be unlikely to find out or understand on their own' (Wilson and McMahon 2006: 57). We believe this educative element is particularly helpful when considering the 'competence cycle' in relation to clarifying and developing goals.

In our *unconsciously incompetent* state, we can happily go about our daily business, having no understanding or knowledge that we 'don't know how to do something'. We have never tried to do it and it does not bother us to know that we are incompetent at it. People often use the metaphor of driving a car to explain this. Before learning to drive, we have no idea whether we will be good at it or not. However, once you begin to learn, you quickly become aware that it is not as easy as you might have thought; it takes a certain technique to be able to accelerate and change gear at the same time, look in the mirror, signal and manoeuvre, and so on. At this stage, we become *consciously incompetent* and it can be a very uncomfortable place to be. It is often at this stage that people decide to return to the place of comfort and decide that meeting a new, perhaps daunting, goal is not so important after all.

In clarifying and developing goals, it is important, therefore, to support the client to become *consciously competent* — to reflect upon his or her strengths and weaknesses, to set goals that are realistic yet creative and that are both short- and long-term goals so that they are not too daunting or too far away to seem achievable. And hopefully, some time in the future, the client will look and realise that she has achieved her goal and, without realising it, she is *unconsciously competent* at what she does and is ready to make new changes again.

There are many different models that relate to goal setting and action planning. Within our counselling training, we have relied on the following models.

SMART goals

I (Becky) first came across SMART goals when I worked in the civil service back in the 1980s. It was something that we had to do as part of our annual review process. SMART goals, as I used them in the workplace back then, were:

- Specific
- Measurable
- Achievable
- Realistic
- Timebound

Doran (1981) now uses the same acronym, but he uses the A as Agreed, as opposed to Achievable.

Setting goals that are SMART gives a more focused, realistic plan to work towards. SMART goals can be used to define short-term or long-term goals (although it is useful to review the timing at regular intervals if the goal is to be achieved in the longer term). The suggested way of working is to have three defined goals to work on, at any one time – a short-term goal, a medium-term goal and a long-term goal. Goals can relate to an internal action ('I am going to think about the changes I want to make in my life') or an external action ('I have decided to speak to my boss about my workload').

People may come with a clear, defined goal – for example, 'I've joined a weight-loss plan as I would like to lose weight by Christmas'. The more defined goals are easier to place within the SMART process, as in this example, the Specific is to lose weight, the Measurable is how much weight, the weight-loss plan states it is Achievable, half a stone is Realistic and there is a cut-off period for Christmas, by which Time the client would have achieved the goal.

The more vague ideas, however, need more exploration. A more general goal I (Becky) decided to work on was that I thought I drank too much alcohol. I did not really have a clear idea why, just that I thought I 'should' drink less. My helper initially looked at my value base and explored with me why it was important that I achieve my goal and did I really want to, or was I doing it because I thought I should? We also looked at the benefits of what I achieved by drinking alcohol – for example, relaxation, social benefits and so on. I realised through the discussion that I did not want to exclude alcohol completely so we set up a Specific goal, which was that I would cut down on my alcohol intake. Next, we discussed what 'cutting down' meant, and I decided I would not drink during the week (my goal became Measurable). We looked at my habits and activities during the week and I decided that the only pitfall I could see was on a Wednesday evening, which was the only evening in the week when I could sit down and relax and the time when I was most likely to have a glass of wine. I made a decision that on a Wednesday evening, I would find an alternative behaviour that still enabled me to feel 'treated' but did not involve alcohol. I thought this would be Achievable and Realistic. I said I would like to give it a go until Christmas and see how I got on, so my goal was Timebound.

In clarifying and developing goals, it is important to think about the reason for choosing them. At the time of choosing the goal of reducing alcohol, I had not realised the link between having a glass of wine and relaxation. Exploring this further enabled me to think about how manic my life had become – having a glass of wine in the evening ensured I would not answer any work emails and I would not drive so I could sit back and relax. So at an unconscious level, I was preserving some relaxation time, which was very important to me. Working collaboratively with my helper, I was able to rethink my attitude towards alcohol and turn it into a positive goal, without feeling deprived of my important 'me time'.

Asking the question 'Do these goals reflect my core values?' can be really useful.

> There are silent forces behind many of your actions and decisions. The goal of 'values clarification' is for their influence to become fully conscious, for you to explore and honestly acknowledge what you truly value at this time in your life. You can be more self-directed and effective when you know which values you really choose to keep and live by as an adult, and which ones will get priority over others.
> (Sichel 1993, section III: 48, cited in Neenan and Dryden 2002: 58)

Rogers (1964) believes that, as infants, we are born with an 'organismic valuing process' that enables us to weigh up our experiences, and that these experiences are 'selected or rejected, depending on whether, at that moment, it tends to actualize the organism or not' (Rogers 1964: 161).

As infants, we only have our own internal frame of reference – we know what we need and the things that we like or dislike, and we are not influenced by those values external to us. Yet, as we grow up, this changes very quickly as we learn that our behaviour influences whether we get our needs met and that our behaviour leads to a determined behaviour by others. We begin to assimilate conditions of worth – for example, 'I am only loved if I behave in a certain way'.

Introjected values become part of a pattern by which we live. Carver and Baird (1998: 289) describe this pattern as:

> External pressures are eventually internalized, giving rise to introjected self-regulation. Introjected behaviours are guided by internal forces, but these forces consists of pressures, such as guilt or anxiety, or a desire to please.

As we mature, more and more of these introjected values become '*truths*'. These truths can become 'scripts' by which we live our life: 'I must do everything right to achieve', 'I must get a proper job', 'I am only successful if I earn large amounts of money' and so on.

It can be really useful, therefore, to identify some of these introjected values with a client. To begin unpicking and challenging these values, it is essential that you have built up a good relationship and rapport with the client, that you communicate with him or her that his or her values are acceptable, and that he or she 'is prized as a person' (Rogers 1964: 163). This can be achieved through using good counselling skills and providing the client with the core conditions.

EXAMPLE

VIDEO CLIP 5c

THE ESTABLISHED RELATIONSHIP: Glyn and Rob

TABLE 5.3 Transcript of Video Clip 5c: The established relationship – Glyn and Rob

Content	Process	Skills
G: Rob, great to see you again. You remember last time we met, you were talking about the move of your brother and mum to the new place and some of the stuff that was coming up, and when we finished speaking you were talking about some of the choices that you wanted to make. Can you remember that?	The relationship appears more collaborative here, suggesting a more established relationship	Summary
R: A little bit, yeah. I mean, I think I just wanted a bit of just being settled in my freedom and to be comfortable. I think I said that I was kind of OK with making the choices I was making and that I was quite used to that, but I always felt like I kind of owed my family something, and I wanted to not feel like that so that I could actually enjoy the time that I've got rather than feel like I kind of had to spend it with them or miss out	The helper's summary enables the client to synthesise his thoughts	
G: So can we spend a bit of time talking about how we can try and achieve that for you?	Working collaboratively to make plans	Open question
R: Yeah, OK		
G: Are you able to tell me what you want here? What exactly you want us to work on to enable that?		Action planning Developing goals
R: Well, I don't know exactly what would help really. I think in some way, I could do something very practical and it could be like, well, I could spend my evenings doing this or that or the other. Somehow I don't think that would stick with me. It's more about my kind of attitude I think, and if I'm kind of settled in that and I'm happier in that, then the rest then kind of comes with it		
G: When you've tried to achieve something like this before, how have you done it? Can you think of an example when you have worked on something like this before and come to a successful conclusion with it?		Drawing together themes

table 5.3 continued

Content	Process	Skills
R: Um, I can't think of a specific example, though I suppose driving comes to mind for some reason. Um, it's like when I first learned to drive, I was really, really scared about getting in a car. I mean, literally, it might sound silly I suppose, but I thought I could actually really hurt myself for a long time and now I get in a car and most of the time . . . I mean, I'm not talking about rush hour traffic or anything . . . most of the time, I really enjoy it. It's kind of had the opposite effect, it chills me out, and there was a certain amount of having to just sit through it and . . . but there was also . . . I think that's what I mean about the attitude, it's like I can look at things in two different ways. I can look at the pessimistic possibility that . . . you know, like I was talking about making a choice and I was kind of . . . I have some time here and some time there, it's like what am I missing out on or actually what have I got and why have I chosen to do this, and just to, um, to believe in myself. Oh, hang on. What happened there? To believe that the choices I make are OK for me at the time. And that's all right	The client describes, through his use of the 'driving' metaphor, how his intuitive and learned skills developed from fear to confidence. The client is having a number of insights about his ability to make choices, and considering and evaluating possible strategies and directions	
G: Yes . . . OK		
R: I don't need anyone else to tell me that when it works		
G: So it's about being allowed to make those choices for you		Paraphrase
R: It's about *me* letting myself make those choices for you		
G: OK. So how are we going to achieve that? What's stopping you at the moment from . . . what's stopping you from being able to make those choices?	The helper is exploring potential blocks and working out what is hindering the client from making progress	Challenging questions
R: You know I've got this. It was my mum's voice in my head as soon as you said that. These are my words but it's like 'you've let me down', and she never said that to me, those are mine, but that's kind of how I feel	Important insight for the client of factors that may be hindering his choices	
G: And is that what you are hearing now? That you've let her down if you make some choices that are yours?		Reflection Challenging and empathic

table 5.3 continued

Content	Process	Skills
R: It's when I moved away		
G: OK	Very affirming	
R: That's when I did. You know I've never said that out loud. Um . . .		
G: Can you tell me a little bit more about that?		Open question
R: Well, you know that kind of last time I was saying that I moved away when I was 13?		
G: Yeah		
R: And, um, things were pretty horrible for me around that time, um. There were lots of arguments, I mean there were lots of arguments between my dad and my mum, but there were lots of arguments between my mum's new partner and us, and he was a new guy and thing were different, you know he had a different way of doing things and things felt safe, and at that time dad was here and he was so nice to me, nice to us, when we came to Bristol it was somewhere that was far away from all the crap that was going on and he helped us move, you know, I grew up in a place where there was lots of arguing but it's actually adults getting at each other so, um, I think . . . it's being settled with that bit of me really helps, and that's where it all comes from, but if I can get to a place where . . . sounds funny to say, but I realise that I have grown up, that I'm not doing too badly. No, I'll rephrase that actually, I'm doing pretty well! But it's been a struggle, and that I've worked for what I've got, and there's always something else that I want. I don't mean like physical stuff, I mean some of that too, but that's easy, you know. You throw money at it and it works, but that I, that I'm all right, that I, that being happy is not wrong. That being happy is not something bad. If I can hold on to that somehow	Through the use of the helper's open question, 'Can you tell me a little bit more about that?', the client has begun to look for and create new meaning and alternative perspectives	
G: And is that what's happening at the moment, you know? Is there a feeling that being happy is bad? Because of this move?		

table 5.3 continued

Content	Process	Skills
R: No, it's … no, no, it's not that. Right now, I just feel sad, I have no idea where any of this came from, um …	As an established relationship, the client is comfortable in rejecting the helper's assumption	
G: Well, we'll just sit with that for a moment		Deeper empathy
R: All right. (shared silence) I keep thinking of a flower, I don't know why but it's almost like a yellow daffodil and it's like I've spent a lot of my time being closed up and in the shade	Client uses a metaphor to make sense of his emotions	
G: OK		
R: And occasionally I kind of poke my head out and spread leaves and petals, and it's safe and it's OK. And the thing is I know this! You know, I know this, but it's like I have to wade through something. It's like I have to dig through something to get to it		
G: And this wading through something, to dig through something, is this something we need to work towards to help you get through that?	The helper picks up on the client's metaphor, using it to work collaboratively and make plans	
R: Try it. …		
G: To improve where you are with this		
R: Try it, yeah, I'd be up for that	Working very collaboratively	
G: So how are we going to achieve that? (silence) What needs to change? (silence)	The helper is working empathically, and this can be seen through his non-verbal communication	Clarifying and developing goals
R: I think it's just nice to say it out loud, you know, and I don't think … in one sense it's little stuff. It's … it sounds like a silly example but if I want a cup of tea I can have a cup of tea. But there's a part of me that doesn't believe that. If I need to sleep, all really basic stuff. Get some sleep rather than carry on working. You know, I work pretty hard and I tend to think, oh, I'll just do this next bit, I'll just do the next bit then I can switch off		

Force field analysis

Kurt Lewin (1951) developed the concept of *force field analysis* as a tool for change. He described any current level of performance or being 'as a state of equilibrium between the driving forces that encourage upward movement and the restraining forces that discourage it'.

In other words, there are a number of forces that are influencing our desire to change – those forces that are *for* the change and those forces that are *against* the change. So there are forces that are driving the change – the positive forces – and those that are restraining the change – the obstacles to the change.

Restraining Forces

Forces resisting change

EQUILIBRIUM

Forces for change

Driving forces

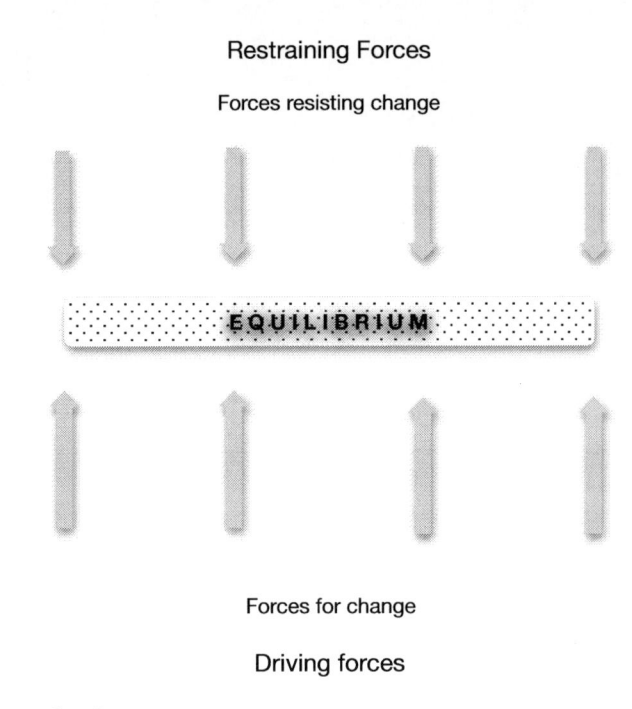

FIGURE 5.1 Forces for change
Source: Taken from the original ideas of Lewin (1951)

VIDEO CLIP 5d
THE ESTABLISHED RELATIONSHIP – FORCE FIELD ANALYSIS EXAMPLE: Becky and Janie

It seems that for movement to happen, work needs to be done to identify and increase the forces that are helping and enabling change to happen, and to identify and decrease the forces that are hindering the process. These forces can be internal forces, such as values/feelings/cognitions/strengths and weaknesses/resilience, and external forces, such as people/resources/time boundaries/societal rules and regulations/health and fitness.

EXAMPLE

TABLE 5.4 Transcript of Video Clip 5d: The established relationship – force field analysis example – Becky and Janie

Content	Process	Skills
B: OK Janie, so we've talked about an issue that you have where you have difficulty taking that issue forward, and we are going to be looking at the things that are holding you back and doing an exercise that is called force field analysis. So what that is, is that we are going to be looking at all the helpful factors, things that are helpful to you moving forward with your issue, and all the hindering factors, things that are blocking you and stopping you from moving forward. And once we have done that, we are then going to see if we can look at some strategies, ways of strengthening the helpful ones and weakening the hindering ones. Does that sound all right?	The helper begins to work collaboratively to consider the helpful and hindering forces that affect the client's goals	Introducing the model
J: That would be great		
B: OK, so if you could give me a really brief outline of the issue that you have		Focusing
J: Well, as we were talking about it, what I notice is, that a really important part of my work is that I take time to myself in terms of my looking after my health or doing things that are interesting that are not to do with work. You know, there's the gym, there is art, there is music and what I notice is, that I find it really difficult to give myself permission to take time in my week to do those things		
B: OK, so the thing that we are looking at then, is you looking after yourself and taking time to look after yourself. So what helpful things do you do, or people, or anything that is helpful to you taking time out to look after yourself? Can you think of the things that are helpful to that process?		Open question and probing
J: Um, sometimes it is helpful, for things . . . say that I do go singing, that it's a commitment, because I go off because I'm with a choir so that's a certain night that I do that, so when that's there, that is helpful		

table 5.4 continued

Content	Process	Skills
B: OK, so a singing commitment. And on a scale of 1 to 10, where 0 is not helpful at all and 10 being a really helpful thing, where would you put your singing commitment?		Using scaling as a tool to measure the impact of the commitment (CBT)
J: Probably a 6 or a 7		
B: A 6 or 7. So we've got a singing commitment. Anything else that you think is helpful?		Continues to evaluate each helpful factor
J: OK, I've got a gym membership		
B: Gym membership, so on a 1 to 10		
J: Um, I don't know if it's up on a high, cos that's the problem, it's not using the gym and it becomes a guilt thing. Probably that's lower, that's probably a 4		
B: OK, so we've got gym membership, yep		
J: What are the other things that are helpful? Um, it's helpful if I can allocate time		
B: OK, and how easy is that?		
J: It's not so easy, that's the bit that is down the lower end, it would be helpful but I don't do it		
B: You don't do it, so allocating time. I'm wondering if there are any people that are helpful to this, or relationships?		The helper helps the client to recognise any existing resources
J: Yes, my partner is helpful with that, if we would go to the gym together or do a creative thing with er being an artist and doing some art stuff with her, and yes, encouraging		
B: So on a 1 to 10?		
J: She's probably up there on a 7 to 8		
B: OK, so it looks like we have a number of helpful things, ranging from . . . what would you say the allocating time is? I've put it down the lower end		
J: It is the lower end because sometimes it's not helpful because it doesn't work		
B: So a number . . .		Clarifying

table 5.4 continued

Content	Process	Skills
J: Yeah, probably about a 1		
B: About a 1		
J: A 1 to 2		
B: 1 to 2. So we have the allocating time that would be helpful if you were able to do that. You've got the gym membership, which is relatively helpful as it helps you to look after yourself. We've got your singing commitment, which is quite high and you are committed to, and that is a way of looking after yourself and your partner who shares ideas with you and is creative and goes to the gym with you, up the higher end		Summary
J: Yeah		
B: And all of those things are helping you to move forward to spending more time looking after yourself. What are the things that hinder you, or hold you back?		Open question to begin to consider hindering factors
J: Er, work		
B: Work, and one the 1 to 10 . . .		
J: That's right up high on the 8 or 9		
B: So 8 or 9 is work that hinders you		
J: Yeah, and some kind of, I don't know if that would go into it, but some kind of guilty conscious		
B: Yeah, definitely, if that's a block and holding you back and that's a value		
J: Yeah, about spending time		
B: So a guilty conscious, where would you put that?		
J: That's probably up on a 7 or 8		
B: So about 7 or 8, you've got guilt		
J: And the time commitment because time is just too full, it holds me back		
B: So the allocating time is a helpful thing but actual time isn't so helpful, so is that up high again?		Balancing helpful and hindering factors

table 5.4 continued

Content	Process	Skills
J: Probably. I do make time, so it's probably not as high, it's maybe up in the 6 and 7		
B: OK, yeah, so can you think of any other things that block, things that hold you back?		
J: Yeah, I think the . . . I ought to be doing this and the guilt thing seems to be about that, that seems to be a big one		
B: OK, so we've got a number of things that are holding you back. In the main, the lack of time, the feelings I ought to be doing this, I ought to be doing that, feelings of guilt and your work commitments, which are really high. So what we are going to look at now are ways of strengthening the things that you do find helpful and ways of weakening the things that aren't so helpful. The things that are holding you back. For the purposes of this exercise, we haven't got time to look at all of them, so do you have one that you might pick that we might work on to look at some strategies?		Summary Drawing together themes Clarifying and developing a goal
J: Strategies, do you want a strong one?		
B: It's entirely up to you, you choose which one you would like to work on		
J: The one to work on is the guilt because I feel that is a big thing		
B: OK, so what we can do is think about where that guilt evolves from, what is that about? Why does the guilt stop you from looking after yourself? And that sounds like there is quite a lot in that, just in that one issue, so what we will do in our next session is think about the strategies that might be useful in helping to kind of weaken those guilt feelings, make them a lot less and much more helpful things that might work so that you can take forward that aim that you have to be able to spending more time looking after yourself		Identifying feelings and meaning Focusing
J: That would be really useful, if you can unlock that, that would be fantastic, great thank you		Contracting for future session

> **REFLECTIVE LEARNING JOURNAL EXERCISE**
>
> With your learning partner:
>
> Take 10 minutes each to identify a goal. Spend equal time in the session to list all the forces that are helpful to the change and all the forces that are hindering the change.

Video your skills session

ACTION PLANNING

> Change is disturbing when it is done to us, exhilarating when it is done by us.
> (Moss Kanter, cited in Holman *et al.* 2008: preface)

We have now clarified and developed our goals, and we are thinking about putting them into action. On the face of it, this sounds like a fairly easy and achievable part of the process. If only this was the case! There are a number of factors that get in the way of us planning and achieving our goals. In the next chapter, we will be looking at change models, in order for us, as helpers, to facilitate change with our clients, through being able to identify and understand where our clients might be within the change process. But even before that stage, there are habits and behaviours that can get in the way of us turning our *ideas into action*.

There may be blocks to change, such as unhealthy cognitions and behaviours, procrastinating and resistance to change, and part of the helper's role might be to explore these blocks with the client. It might also be that the client would like to be more assertive to gain the confidence to implement or challenge areas of his or her life that need to change, and good helper skills using the core conditions of empathy, respect and genuineness to explore the factors that hinder development of confidence can be useful.

Here are some of the common blocks to learning (adapted from Centre for Coaching 2011).

Having a closed mind (or, as we term it, the 'yes, but' client)

Often, clients come for help as they want something about their life to change, but somehow change never seems to happen. Working with the client, you can get a sense of him having a single train of thought – with lots of 'shoulds' and 'oughts' in his language. He does not seem open to challenge or even tentative suggestions, and can often respond with a 'yes, but' reply. Exploring with the client both the feelings and thoughts that lead to this response can be a way of opening up his mind to another way of responding. It is also about being realistic – a client may know deep down that he has not got the skills required to meet the demands of his goals, and the 'yes, but' response might be a 'cover' for this:

> Helper: You've talked a lot about how bored and fed up you are with your existing job.
>
> Client: Yes, I want to move into a different career but I haven't got the skills as this job is all I've ever known.

Working with the client first to identify generally what new skills he might need to learn in order to move into a new career, and then to determine whether the 'pay-off' will match the effort to learn the new skills, may help open the client's mind to various new possibilities, as opposed to focusing on a specific example.

Impatience (or, I want change to happen and I want it to happen now)

I (Becky) can really resonate with this block! If I want to paint a wall, I do not want to wait for the preparation to be done, for the furniture to be moved or the masking tape to be placed. I want to just paint the wall! For others with this block, it can be very difficult to spend time action planning or thinking about whether something is measurable or achievable – they just want to get on. One strategy might be help the client to devise a 'priority of daily tasks list', setting out what *has* to be done today, what is *preferable* to do today and what *might* be done today, to enable the client to get a sense of what her priorities are and what might have to be left until a later time.

Expected to use a non-preferred learning style (or, I don't do creativity!)

We can often get stuck in our most comfortable learning style.

> Convergent, outcome-directed thinking is processed in one hemisphere of the brain – the left – while associative (linking, creative) thinking is processed in the other – the right.
>
> (McDermott and Jago 2005: 165)

However, there is no reason why we need to stay in our comfort zones, and, as helpers, we can support our clients to try a different way of learning (and accept and acknowledge their failures if it does not work). It is often better to explore with the client his or her preferred way of learning and, as the relationship develops, to encourage a new and different way of learning.

Fear (or, I just can't)

Being afraid to try out something new or different can be a real block to learning. A helper will need to use counselling skills to listen to the client's fears, reflecting back his or her feelings and thoughts and using Socratic questions to deepen the client's awareness about what might be underpinning the fear.

> Failure and rejection are probably the two main reasons why people avoid taking risks.
>
> (Neenan and Dryden 2002: 120)

One of the most useful aspects is to define and assess the risks of change. Often, it is the fear of failure that stops us from making changes in our life. While the role of the helper is not to direct their client to take risks, encouraging clients to take small risks, to experience what it is like to fail or to achieve, is an important skill that a client can learn through experience, and a helper can facilitate and support a client through that learning process.

We have worked with many people who are very committed to the things that they know they will succeed in, but avoid taking on anything where they assess the risk of failure is too high. They become very successful in their field but often have a sense of their lives being unfulfilled. An example of this is when working with a very successful professional businessman, who had financed his children through university, had a lovely home and settled lifestyle, and yet talked of feeling empty and unfulfilled. When this was explored, he explained how he had always wanted to be a musician but had decided that it would not lead to a 'proper' job and that his father would think he had failed to achieve in life. In these latter years of his life, he wished he had at least tried to become a successful musician and had faced the setbacks and the failures and enjoyed the process. In not taking the risk, the client denied himself the opportunity of fulfilling his desires, as well as the experience of 'picking himself up and starting over again' when there were setbacks.

> Achieving real personal growth can start with you learning to take the 'horror' (emotional disturbance) out of risk-taking.
>
> (Neenan and Dryden 2002: 120)

Often, it is through taking a risk and experiencing the sense of failure that the learning takes place, and you can see that your world has not fallen to pieces because you were not able to be successful in the task you have undertaken. Taking a risk to do something differently also enables you to experience a different result – 'if you always do what you always do, you always get what you always get'.

We believe people often transpose failure of a task into 'I am a failure' and to avoid the emotional disturbances linked to the 'I am a failure' thought, they avoid doing things that might lead to this response. Encouraging clients to experience small setbacks and experience and explore their 'I am a failure' responses to these setbacks can lead to deep, insightful connections that enable them to understand and appreciate their own worth (and not rely solely on external validation to feel worthy). However, if these responses relate to deep-rooted self-esteem issues, it may be advisable to encourage the client to seek professional counselling before any further work is undertaken.

Embracing both success and failure is enriching and life enhancing. Gaining confidence to take risks opens up new opportunities to enhance your everyday life and take control of the changes you would like to make, and being alongside a client as he or she achieves this personal growth can be extremely rewarding for the helper.

Writing an action plan

It is important to think about one goal at a time, and to concentrate on any sub-goals within that main goal, before moving on to the next goal. In the table below, we have referred to those sub-goals as 'milestones'. To enable you to achieve your main goals, there may be a number of milestones you need to achieve. Writing a milestone timetable can be one way of tracking your success in meeting your main goal, as it allows you to reassess at regular intervals and to notice when you might be procrastinating or when your time management needs more attention. It is a way of setting realistic deadlines. This can be particularly helpful when setting a long-term goal as it breaks the goal down into small and achievable milestones. The most important things to think about when deciding upon the milestones are:

> 'How will I know when I've accomplished my goal?'
>
> 'What did I need to do to get there?'
>
> 'Have I got the necessary skills/resources to achieve my goal?'
>
> 'Is there enough challenge/flexibility/risk/creativity/sustainability in the steps?'

This enables you to have a retrospective look at what enabled you to be successful and to be really specific in identifying each step of the process.

REFLECT, PRACTISE AND EVALUATE

With your learning partner, take 10 minutes each to think about the goal you discussed during the force field analysis exercise and, using the helpful forces that were identified, fill in the blank milestone timetable (Appendix 5), focusing on two main goals and seeing if you can break it down into achievable milestones.

Watch back and reflect on and evaluate the skills you have used.

Video your skills session

MODEL BOX

In this chapter, we have referred to:

- The Relational Skills Model – the established relationship (Midwinter and Dickson 2015)
- Sharing empathic highlights (Egan 2002)
- Robinson's competence cycle (Robinson 1974)
- SMART goals (Doran 1981)
- Force field analysis (Lewin 1951)
- Common blocks to learning (Centre for Coaching 2011)

TABLE 5.5 Timetable of milestones – example from force field analysis in Video Clip 5d

Main goal	Milestones	Action by	Completion date	Comments
Spending more time on self-care	Spend more time at the gym	Janie	Next week	
	Allocate time within the week for regular personal time	Janie	End of the month	Diary really busy until end of month, so allocated personal time not realistic until then
	Make more time with partner to do things together	Janie/partner	End of the week	To look through diaries and make joint plans
	To cut work hours to four days per week	Janie/work	End of October	Need to arrange a meeting to discuss with my line manager

Goal number 2

SUMMARY

- Embedding our intuitive and learned skills into the relationship can develop deeper, more relational, empathic responses.
- Empathy is often expressed through our non-verbal communication. Being aware of what our body is portraying to the client is an important aspect of empathic communication.
- If your client is in crisis, it is important to help the client to work through the crisis by focusing on the issues that are causing the most distress or that the client feels are the most important.
- Use of metaphor is a personal preference and not everyone gains from it. Metaphors are cultural and may have different or no meaning to others.
- Once clients have identified choices, they can move towards goal setting.
- Understanding the competence cycle will enable helpers to support clients in becoming *consciously competent*.
- Force field analysis is a useful tool to help clients to look at helpful and hindering forces in moving forward to achieve their goals.
- It is important to think about one goal at a time. Sub-goals can be placed within a milestone document to help work through them more strategically.

Chapter 6
Maintaining the relationship

The helper and client are now ready to consider how the client's goals could be implemented. It is useful here for the helper to hold an awareness and understanding of the theory of change and transitions. The focus is on supporting and encouraging the client to implement and maintain change and support self-management strategies. We will also discuss the ongoing relationship where we might continue to review, monitor and evaluate the client's progress with them, to facilitate an ending or signpost on:

- The nature of change
- Theory of change and change models
- Resistance to change and systems awareness
- Maintaining change and ending the relationship

TEACHING

THE NATURE OF CHANGE

The nature of change is dependent upon two factors – the *rate* of the change and the *extent* of the change. The extent of change can be transformational or simply a realignment or readjustment. The rate of change can be sudden and fast, or incremental and slow. These factors can have a real impact on the way that we respond to change. For example, parents live with their growing children, anticipating that one day in the future they will leave home, maybe to go to university, to share a home with friends, to travel or to set up home with a partner. And while that move away from home may be emotional for the parents, it is less distressing, as the change has occurred incrementally over a number of years and is anticipated. However, if you go into work one morning, you are all called into a meeting and you are told the shop that you are working in has gone into receivership and that it will be closed with immediate effect, that change can feel devastating – the rate of change is too fast and the extent of change is too great.

Changes can be simultaneous, too; often people seek help when they have a number of changes all occurring at the same time and the extent and rate of the changes are too much to handle at the same time.

When looking at the nature of change, it is important to consider the effect of change on an individual. One of the most important factors in determining the effects of change is the element of choice in the transition.

With unemployment, for example, it may take someone a lot longer to think positively about what he or she might have gained from losing his or her employment, if that change is enforced upon him or her. If, on the other hand, someone makes a choice to leave employment, he or she may, prior to leaving or immediately thereafter, think about how he or she might replace some of the losses of being outside of employment by anticipating the gains, setting up alternative plans and sorting out financial affairs. Therefore, the effects of the transition, such as shock and denial, anxiety, depression and searching for meaning (Hopson and Adams 1976), may be lessened if there is choice. However, in our experience, people still tend to go through the stages of transition, even when change is expected.

Another important factor is how individual the extent of the change is. What can be transformational for one individual can be devastating for another. An individual who has perhaps only been employed by a company for a short period of time, has not invested a huge amount of time or commitment to that company and is given a notice period and a financial incentive to accept redundancy may experience less distress than an individual who has been employed for over 20 years. The long-term worker may have a final salary pension that is going to be affected, may have developed a wide professional and social network within the organisation, may be financially dependent on a salary that he or she is unlikely to match outside of that company, and have qualifications that are outdated and unacceptable in the professional climate within which he or she is going to have to compete for jobs. The impact of a redundancy on this individual is likely to be profound and could lead to physical and emotional decline.

The other type of change is an anticipated change that does not happen. Schlossberg et al. (1995: 156) describe this as a 'non-event' or absence of something that was anticipated. They describe the transitional stage as *moving in, moving through and moving out*, and events as anticipated transitions, unanticipated transitions, and non-events (transitions that are anticipated, but do not occur) – for example, broken engagements that result in not getting married, or the couple who plan to have children but cannot conceive. These non-events can move through the same transition cycle or symptoms of loss, even though they are not an actual change but were an anticipated change.

REFLECTIVE LEARNING JOURNAL EXERCISE

Think about the changes you have gone through over the last two years.

Reflect on the rate and extent of these changes.

How might change feel for you in the four different quadrants?

FIGURE 6.1 The four quadrants of change

Reconstruction	Radical
Changing the whole or parts into something else. This type of change can be fast or slow, and the results can be minimal or transformational. Reconstruction can be predictable and voluntary, but it can also be unpredictable and involuntary, such as a reconstruction in the workplace or rebuilding a home after flood damage	Once made, they change that person's life forever. These changes can be revolutionary, challenging, creative, rebellious and political. Usually occurs fast with lots of simultaneous changes happening at the same time. The result is usually transformational. Change is often unpredictable and, whether it happens voluntarily or involuntarily, it can be very stressful – for example, emigrating
Adaption	**Evolution**
Adjusting and modifying to be more practical, useful and to fit in with something else. Although 'having to adapt' can often be involuntary, the results are usually small and the adaption can take place incrementally over a long period of time. The end result is usually predicted, such as children leaving home, working towards retirement and recovering from ill health	Change that happens slowly over time and is voluntary and predictable. The results are transformational but often less impacting as they happen over long periods of time. Through these changes, we grow, we develop, we gain experience, we mature and we move on through our lives

THEORY OF CHANGE AND CHANGE MODELS

As we discussed in Chapter 5, many of us have a natural resistance to change. Not all changes cause transition, but if we have an understanding of some of the theories of transitions, we can help our clients explore and identify their position and work alongside them to explore any 'stuck places' they may find themselves in.

Psychosynthesis theory (Feltham and Horton 2000: 332) describes two different orientations to change:

- *Regressive* – where we stay with a behaviour or view that is no longer benefiting us, which we have outgrown or impacts on us negatively. Staying with this regressive view causes us more pain.
- *Progressive* – where we change a pattern or behaviour, let go of previous ways of being or situations, meet challenges and make tough choices we would prefer to avoid. This can also be painful and disruptive, but it has the potential to be transformative and liberating.

These views also apply to non-voluntary transitions that we have no control over – for example, illness and ageing – but where we can choose how we respond to our feelings of powerlessness.

There are a number of transition models, and you may want to explore more of these in your further studies (see the model box for further information), but here we will explore a couple of the transition models that we feel are helpful to understand the change process more fully. Hopson and Adams (1976) focus on the changes to the level of self-esteem over time, and the Prochaska and DiClemente (1986) model focuses on the experience and maintenance of change. With information on the nature and theory of change, you can start to look for clues towards your client's 'position of transition' – for example, denial, depression, numbness – as these may be a response to change.

Some examples of life transitions could be:

- bereavement;
- redundancy;
- job change;
- marital separation;
- major changes in lifestyle;
- midlife crisis;
- children leaving home;
- move to residential accommodation;
- addiction recovery;
- culture shock;
- geographical transitions; and
- spiritual realisations.

In this chapter, we will explore some of the positions of change that might be applied to these life transitions, but we will mainly use the example of redundancy to explore this in more depth.

Hopson and Adams seven-stage model of transition

This model outlines the changes in self-esteem during transitions, and this is a good basis for many other models of change.

1 *Numbness*: There may be a lack of any identifiable feeling at all or a frozenness and inability to act. When asked, your client will probably be unable to tell you how he or she is feeling or be unable to name/describe his or her emotions.

2 *Denial*: The crisis can feel too big to react to and there may be a minimising or denial. A parody of a famous quote from Kipling reads, 'If you can keep your head, when all around you are losing theirs, then you are not fully aware of the situation'. Another way of explaining this could be that your client is in the stage of denial where, despite the change being challenging or difficult, he or she is responding as if it does not have any consequences for him or her, or as if nothing has happened. A typical example of this in redundancy is the common occurrence of people who continue to pretend to 'go to work' after they have lost their job and where their partners do not even know about the job loss until later.

3 *Depression*: This is when there is a developing awareness of the implications of change. The situation might feel too overwhelming, and we can see no way out or forward and have a sense of hopelessness. The implications of change are sinking in and can feel overwhelming. Loss of sleep, appetite, inertia, inactivity and tearfulness are common symptoms.

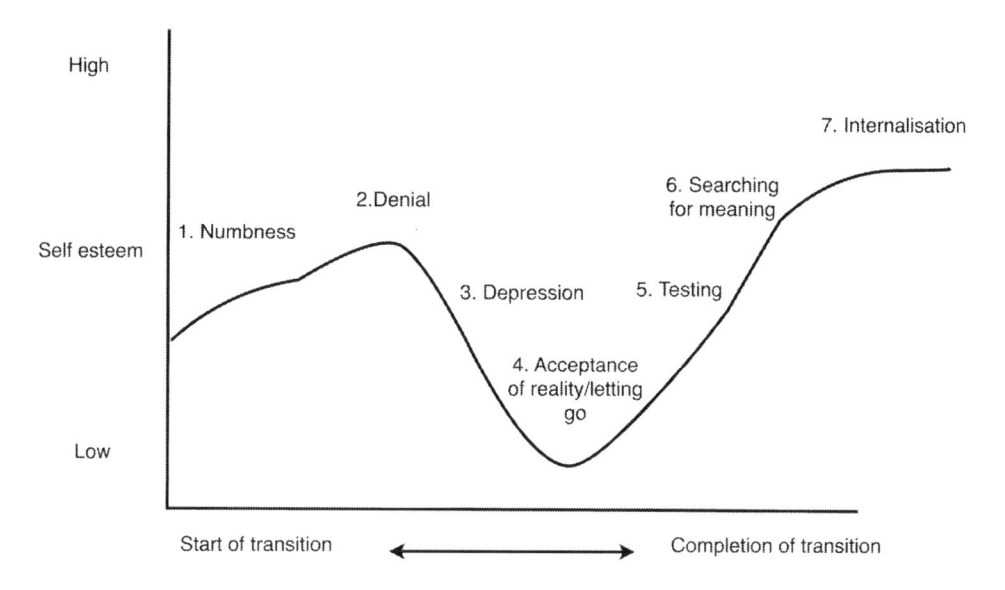

FIGURE 6.2 Hopson and Adams stages of transition
Source: Adapted from Hopson and Adams (1976)

If this is severe, or we fear that a client may be suicidal, we would be signposting on to medical professions.

4 Acceptance of reality/letting go: At this stage, our client may be moving through the emotions and feelings associated with change. Notice from Figure 6.2 that he or she is at his or her lowest point of self-esteem. At this point, there begins to be an acceptance of the inevitability of change and a letting go of previous situations. Loss is slowly beginning to move to consolidation or hope.

5 Testing: Having begun the process of acceptance, there is a trying out of the new situation. Here, your client may begin to resign him or herself to the transition and think about his or her potential or options.

6 Searching for meaning: This is the reflective stage where our client begins to seek out meaning for the new situation. This may be rationalising or looking for reason – 'every cloud has a silver lining' – and it is a further process of acceptance and moving through.

7 Internalisation: This is where we 'take on board' the new situation and internalise the meaning of the change. At this stage, we can observe that our client has moved through the transition and it may be internalised as an achievement or recognition in positive terminology – for example, 'cancer survivor'.

In our experience, this process is not linear, and clients move backwards and forwards between the various stages of transition. It is also unique to each individual how long he or she remains at one stage of the process. Even if the change is anticipated, clients still move through the stages, but they may move through them more quickly.

One area of change that is becoming more prevalent in our society is redundancy. Within our own social and family contexts, almost every family has been affected by redundancy.

The CIPD Work Audit in March 2013 stated that approximately one in ten employees will have directly experienced redundancy. Redundancy is therefore likely to be a major life transition for a number of people, now and in the future.

> Although it is generally, and correctly, acknowledged that the scale of redundancy during and since the recession of 2008–9 is much less than originally feared, it is evidence that the direct experience of redundancy has nonetheless been widespread.
>
> (Philpott 2012: 3)

An individual facing redundancy (or potential redundancy) will go through a process of transition and may remain at any one of the stages, or go backwards and forwards between these stages.

In the following fictional example of Jack's shock redundancy, we explore the stages of transition. Jack is looking at this retrospectively, and in all likelihood these stages will take time to move through and between:

Jack suffered an outbreak of severe eczema when was made redundant three months previously and he is describing his situation to his nurse.

Nurse: Your skin condition is definitely improving, Jack, can you tell me how it's been for you?

Jack: Gosh, it has been such a hard time. When I look back at when I had the shock of the redundancy, I couldn't feel anything *(numbness)*. It was bizarre, really, when I look back. I didn't tell my wife, I just couldn't. I actually pretended to go into work at the normal time and what I was doing was spending my whole day in the library and coming home at 5.30 as usual *(denial)*. Then this awful eczema started and she knew there was something really wrong and I had to tell her. She was really shocked that I hadn't told her as we normally have a very open and honest relationship. I couldn't explain to her why that was. That was when I lost my appetite couldn't go out and slept all day in front of the TV *(depression)*.

Nurse: And how are you today, Jack?

Jack: Well, now I realise that I am not going to get another job anything like that last one at my age *(acceptance of reality/letting go)*. Actually, that is not as bad as I thought, I have begun to realise that I have got some transferable skills *(testing)*. I know how to work with people and I have done some volunteering at the city farm with some youngsters. Do you know I am really enjoying it and there may even be some chance for some paid work *(searching for new meaning)*.

Nurse: You look really pleased about that.

Jack: Yes, I am. Sadly, I just heard about an ex-colleague, the same age as me, who has had a serious stroke. That was awful and I couldn't help feeling that could have happened to me. My job was very stressful, I can't help thinking that maybe I got out in time after all? Life's too short, isn't it *(internalisation)*?

Hopson and Adams (1976: 24) describe a transition as a 'discontinuity in a person's life space', and they suggest that people can experience similar feelings and patterns in various types of transitions as they adjust to change and internalise it. As a helper, we can find that the use of open questions, reflections and summaries may help identify areas of 'stuckness' within this process and help our clients to move forward.

Jahoda (1979) lists the following as symptoms following redundancy:

- bored;
- apathetic;
- inertia;
- helplessness;
- loss of sense of identity; and
- loss of self-respect.

In our experience as counsellors, these symptoms can appear anywhere within the first four stages of the transition. As described by Figure 6.2, individuals often feel at their worst during the acceptance of reality/letting go stage of the process. This is when the full reality of the situation hits home and there is a realisation of 'no going back'. My own experience of redundancy echoes this process (Becky). I was probably at my 'happiest' about the situation when in the denial stage. I still had hope and aspirations that it would not happen (even though I had been told categorically that the school within which I was working was closing). As I came out of the denial stage, I felt depressed and low about the situation but still had bouts of 'hopefulness'. It was only when I realised that there was no hope and that no one was fighting to keep the school open that the realisation hit, and I remember sitting in my office, sobbing uncontrollably. It was difficult to have any positive feelings or aspirations for the future at that stage. My employers offered counselling, and I found this helpful to enable me to discuss the situation and understand my reactions. However, a number of my colleagues who were experiencing the same situation did not find that counselling offered through the employer was helpful, and they found other ways to seek support, outside of the organisation.

Fink et al. (1971) describe a similar process of reaction to redundancy: shock/denial/acceptance/adaption. It is important to note that different support is necessary at the different stages. At the shock and denial stages, it is important to work with the individual to explore his or her social context, physiology, actions, cognitions and emotions (Williams et al. 2008). This may lead the individual challenging his or her negative core beliefs – for example, 'It's my fault, and they were just waiting for an opportunity to get rid of me'. Other consequences may be drinking heavily or suffering from insomnia; the individual may be experiencing shame and guilt or relief and excitement, and it may be helpful to support someone to explore this, hopefully enabling him or her to move into the adaption stage. Supporting someone through the different stages can enable him or her to test out the different scenarios available to him or her, to search for new meaning, set goals and generate alternative solutions.

We have used an example of redundancy to illustrate the change process, yet any transition can be impacting, and an awareness of the models of change can be really useful when working with someone in any transition.

Cycle of change model

Prochaska and DiClemente's (1986) model of the cycle of change can be applied not only to addiction, which was its primary aim, but also to other difficult transitions where change needs to be maintained. This model has stages relating to the experience of change, as in Hopson and Adams (1976), but the model sees the change process as cyclical rather than linear.

The stages of change are:

- *Precontemplation*: not yet acknowledging that there is a problem behaviour that needs to be changed.
- *Contemplation*: acknowledging that there is a problem but not yet ready or sure of wanting to make a change.
- *Preparation/Determination*: getting ready to change.
- *Action/Willpower*: changing behaviour.
- *Maintenance*: maintaining the behaviour change.
- *Relapse*: returning to older behaviours and abandoning the new changes.

The following two scenarios show where James (a fictional client) might be within this cycle of change:

In the past, James' work attendance had been poor but more recently it had improved for a few weeks. Now, however, he has a meeting with his manager because he has been absent for a number of Mondays and turning up late for work on other days looking ill and extremely tired.

Manager: James, we needed to arrange this meeting because we have been concerned about your work and particularly your absences. I am worried about you because

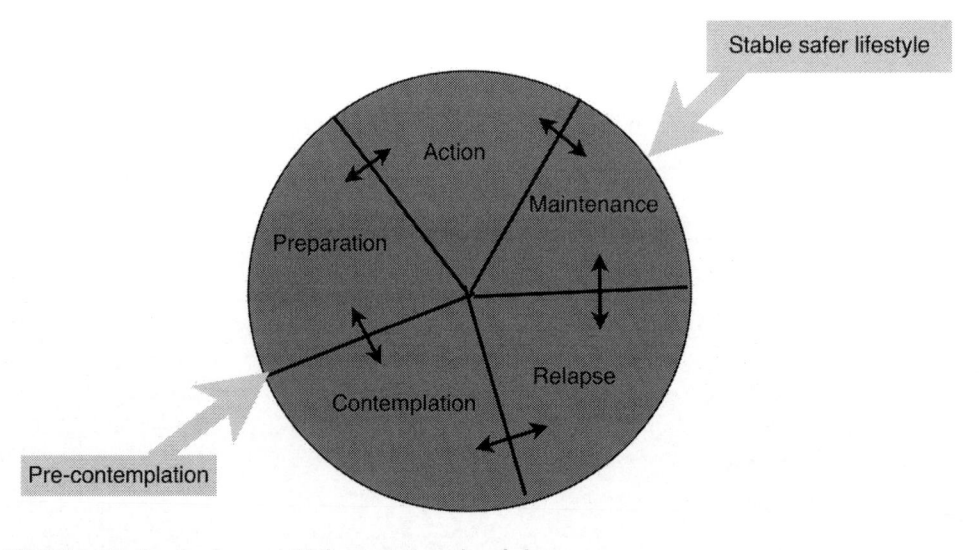

FIGURE 6.3 Prochaska and DiClemente's cycle of change
Source: Adapted from Prochaska and DiClemente (1983)

you have looked ill and stressed again lately. Are there any problems at home that you need to tell us about?

James: Well it has been very difficult at home lately, as I have been stressed with my relationship. My wife has been really unreasonable and seemed to have got it into her head that I have a drink problem. She got me to call these people from Alcoholics Anonymous and I did see them just to prove to her that it wasn't a problem, even went to a few meetings and stayed off the beer for a few weeks. But it is ridiculous really. She doesn't understand that I am just a normal bloke and just need a few drinks when I get home to relax from work.

In this next example, James has moved from the pre-contemplative stage of refuting that he has a problem with alcohol to the contemplation stage, where he agreed to attend AA meetings.

Manager: James, we needed to arrange this meeting because we have been concerned about your work and particularly your absences. I am worried about you because you have looked ill and stressed again lately. Are there any problems at home that you need to tell us about?

James: I was sort of expecting this meeting actually because it has been very difficult at home lately as my wife confronted me with how things were at home (*contemplation*) and I realised that I had an alcohol problem (*preparation*). I have contacted Alcoholics Anonymous (*action*) and gone to meetings for a few weeks (*maintenance*), but it is really hard and lately I have stopped going and slid back into the old ways of how it was before (*relapse*). I am at my wits' end and I just don't know how to stop.

So we can see how our clients might *step out* of the cycle of change at any stage or move between stages. In the first example, we can clearly see that James is experiencing a resistance to change, whereas in the second scenario he appears to want to make the change but is finding it too challenging.

In this next example, you will witness the helper taking the client through the cycle of change. We have intentionally not used material where a client is in the midst of a huge personal transition, as this would not have been ethical. So this is a subtler example, where you will be able to track the various stages of transition.

EXAMPLE

VIDEO CLIP 6a

MAINTAINING AND ENDING THE RELATIONSHIP – STAGES OF TRANSITION: Glyn and Rob

TABLE 6.1 Transcript of Video Clip 6a: Maintaining and ending the relationship – stages of transition – Glyn and Rob

Content	Process	Skills
G: So, if you want to achieve the fact that you are able to make decisions and choices without thinking that you owe somebody for making them when you think things like that	The helper's initial opening question is not clear	
R: Say that again		
G: If you want to be able to make choices here without being worried about what you owe other people … (R: Yeah, OK) … how are we going to put that into purpose, how are we going to measure that? What goals do we need to set?	As the relationship is well established, the client is able to ask for clarification	Clarifying and developing goals (Egan stage III-B – 'best fit strategies')
R: (*sighs*) Measure it would be … just how much time I give myself	The helper rephrases the question. Working collaboratively with the use of the word 'we'	
G: Yeah	Acceptance of reality and letting go (Hopson and Adams). The client sighs deeply as he slowly moves towards consolidation and hope	
R: Yeah, yeah, and what I do with that time is up to me		
G: So the choice of free allocation of your time	Testing (Hopson and Adams) beginning to try out the new situation	
R: It's like I'm good at kind of allocating my time, say I'll do this, then I'll do this, then I'll do this. But that's not the same to me as actually being free	Further testing of previous patterns versus future options (Hopson and Adams) (Prochaska and DiClemente)	
G: So would it be a 'me time' type thing for you?		Evaluating the strategies (Egan stage III-B)
R: Me time?		
G: Yes, time specifically set aside for you	Helping to raise the client's awareness	
R: See, I would really struggle with setting, at least to being with, with really setting it aside, but I think that would be a good start	Resistance to change	
G: What would you be more comfortable with then?	The helper is supporting the client to implement change	Focusing

table 6.1 continued

Content	Process	Skills
R: I don't know. I really don't know at the moment. I think it's that thing about, you know, I work until it's finished. There's something, it would be nice to feel that I can do a bit and OK, I may not have finished it off, but there's no point in pushing myself till I'm exhausted. Cos that's what I'll do sometimes	Contemplation and preparation (Prochaska and DiClemente)	
G: OK		
R: I can do a bit and it doesn't mean that there's any kind of threat or anything or that I owe anybody afterwards . . . and then I can do a bit more, then I can do a bit more but in between . . . it's OK to have a rest . . . sounds like really basic stuff!		
G: You're absolutely . . . I can understand where you're coming from with this, but how are we going to implement it, how are we going to . . . ?	The helper is supporting the client to maintain change (Prochaska and DiClemente)	Confronting and focusing
R: You mean like in my day?		
G: Yeah, how are we going to put something that we can allow you to plan and help you move along with this rather than later on starting to feel that 'actually I do owe somebody if I have a break and I shouldn't be doing this'? How do we put it in, how do we move forward with it?		Action planning (Egan stage III-C)
R: I get Fridays off and one of the things that I've been doing is going to the gym and going to the sauna and I find that really helps	These challenges have really helped the client to define actions (Prochaska and DiClemente)	
G: Fantastic		Encouragement and affirmations
R: You know, I sit there and it really relaxes me, it's great for my leg	Client is beginning to explore the benefits of future plans and searching for meaning (Hopson and Adams)	
G: Yeah		Affirming

table 6.1 continued

Content	Process	Skills
R: Um, and that time's really precious to me, you know, cos I get out of there and I feel good and so it's something like that	Searching for meaning (Hopson and Adams)	
G: So, OK, that would be on a regular basis?	Implementing change	Action planning
R: Um, yeah. How often I'm not sure, I was thinking every week or every couple of weeks. What I don't want is for this, sort of 'me time' to become a forced thing cos part of what I would do is turn it into work. I want to do things for the pleasure of it but that would be one thing	Future planning and maintaining change (Prochaska and DiClemente)	
G: So, just so I understand this. You would like the autonomy to choose when you need your own 'me time' to reinforce what you feel that's good for you	The helper is reflecting back to the previous session when autonomy was acknowledged as important to the client	Clarification
R: That's, yeah, that's really well put. It's like it is up to me but when it's up to me is as important as what I do	There is a shared understanding between the helper and the client in this response to the helper's reflection	
G: Oh right		
R: You know?		
G: Yeah		
R: And I take it when I need it. And it's OK to need it. And it might just be something as simple as actually going to a supermarket and saying, well, I could buy myself a pizza cos that would feed me, or I could, I could buy myself, I don't know the bits and pieces for a meal that I *really* want. That isn't so quick, it would take me longer but I love cooking and I realise when I'm stressed I don't cook, cos you know it's easier to bung something in the microwave but that, again that relaxes me	Continued non-verbal affirmations from the helper. Action (Prochaska and Di Clemente)	
G: So how could we improve that sort of awareness so you were able to do that when you need to do it?	Maintaining change	Open question
R: Um		

table 6.1 continued

Content	Process	Skills
G: What would help that? Because there's a possibility that if it's happened before, that you're not making these choices when you need them to help yourself feel better about yourself . . .	The helper is supporting the client to avoid relapse (Prochaska and DiClemente)	Drawing together themes
R: Yeah		
G: . . . it may happen again, so how can we build something in that's going to improve the awareness of when you need to do something like that?	Exploring relapse prevention (Prochaska and DiClemente)	Evaluating the change
R: (long pause) The first thing that comes to mind is like a bit of meditation or just take a breather for a minute and, you know, like I can feel the stress in my face, so just to kind of . . .	Action (Prochaska and DiClemente) and testing other strategies	
G: So there are kind of triggers there aren't there that tell you that things are not going as well as they should be?		Evaluating change
R: You know what would really help actually is to keep my leg comfortable because it's tense all the time but one of the things that really helps is when my legs are comfortable it's like the rest of me is more comfortable I have like a more fluid movement. Again, I've never really thought of that before, I've never said it out loud	Maintenance (Prochaska and DiClemente) The client continues to explore testing and meaning	
G: And how would you do that in your day-to-day work then?		Action planning
R: Stretch for 10 minutes in the morning or something like that. So that actually it just becomes part of what I do and it settles in and it relaxes me. Um, and it's good for me too	Action	
G: So let's talk. Let's reiterate some of those goals that we've just been talking about. Allowing your awareness between when you start getting tense, your leg, giving some time set aside for your leg, to enable you to make those choices	The helper draws together strategies in order to help the client to internalise changes	Reviewing and evaluating
R: Right		
G: When you feel it will help you to improve the whole situation about where you are		

table 6.1 continued

Content	Process	Skills
R: So I'm not quite sure I understand what you mean?		
G: What I am saying is if we were able to set some goals where you were able to put into motion some of these things so that when you leave here you are able to do that	Evaluating possible strategies and directions	Action planning
R: So say for instance that, um, yeah when I get up in the morning, you know like now it gets light really early . . . I wake up earlier than I need to really and just to have a stretch. I was going to say go for a walk but that sounds like a bit too much effort but just to sort of even when I'm sitting there just to stretch out or I even sort of, you know, when I'm standing up. And to kind of do it because I remember why I'm doing it, I think that's really important, to remember why I'm doing it and . . . that's . . . yeah, it's about, um. I think what really helps is when sort of things become simple like one thing flows into another, like when I'm going shopping and I could do it on the way home rather than think, 'God I've got to make an extra trip for that' or something. It's much easier just to pop in and go, well I'll pick some stuff up now and then I've got what I need with me and it's just. It's my basic level of happiness it's just a bit higher	The client is exploring action and maintenance (Prochaska and DiClemente)	
G: It sounds really good, Rob. It's a bit like, you know, when people say, you know, they 'live to work' rather than 'working to live', this is about working so you can live, so it's about putting things in to your work that allows you to live		Encouragement support and affirmations
Feedback and sharing information
R: You know what, when I started the new job it was a shock and there were a few weeks when I just got up and I thought is this what people do for 40 bloody years	The client reviews previous depression stage (Hopson and Adams)	
G: Um		
R: You know?		

table 6.1 continued

Content	Process	Skills
G: Yeah		
R: Get up, go to work, do my thing, come home. There's got to be more to life than that. You know, I've settled in now so it's better but that's it, you know. I want to, and this is where it goes back to the how time is precious. I want to spend my time well. I don't mean live up to something, I just mean to spend it how I want to spend it and I want to *live* rather than struggle. Rather than work cos the other thing I have always been told one way or another is that I could do better than I am. And I think that has a lot to do with, you know, living up to something and never quite being good enough. And ironically I was going to say it sounds arrogant but I, it doesn't, you know, I'm pretty good at it. If I do something I do it pretty well	The client is moving through testing and meaning to internalisation	
G: So yeah, that all sounds fantastic. So can we just consolidate those things that will help you and do you feel they will help you?	Working collaboratively	
R: I hope so. I hope so. I guess I don't know untill I try. You know, you asked me what had worked before and I think, I think they will. I hope they will		

> **REFLECTIVE LEARNING JOURNAL EXERCISE**
>
> With your learning partner:
>
> Take turns to discuss a transition that is happening or has happened to you in the last two years.
>
> In the helper role, try to determine the various stages of self-esteem (Hopson and Adams 1976) that the client may have gone through during this transition and where he or she might be now in the cycle of change (Prochaska and Di Clemente 1986).

Video your skills session

Grief and loss models

Grief is usually associated with death and bereavement, but we can equally apply the grief models to other forms of loss – for example, loss of relationship, loss of employment or status, or irreversible loss of a faculty such as sight or hearing.

Loss often challenges our assumptions about our world and situation, it can be sudden and unexpected, or, as in the case of chronic illness, protracted and anticipated – for example, a terminal prognosis, gradual loss of sight.

There are a number of models of grief (see the model box and further reading). Murray Parkes (1972) is well known for his theory of the grief process, looking at the phases of adult grief in relationship to the feelings and emotions that might be experienced. But he cautioned against simplification of the process, because 'every person and every grief is different' (Parkes 1972: 160). Often, grief and loss can be associated with an agenda that we *should* be feeling certain things at certain times. People can sometimes make well-meaning but unhelpful comments in their attempt to offer support:

> 'It has been two years, they should be getting over it by now.'
>
> 'It was his time to go.'
>
> 'The miscarriage is very sad, but you're young, you can have another child.'

As helpers, we can use the different phases that Parkes sets out to help to *normalise* the process for our clients, who may be baffled and disturbed by these distressing responses to their loss – anger, disbelief, despair or guilt.

> Nurse: Hello, Jenny. It has been a while since we have met and I am wondering how it has been for you lately?
>
> Jenny: Well, my sight has deteriorated quite a lot since last time, like you said it would, and I am having an assessment to be registered partially sighted.

Nurse: How is that feeling?

Jenny: It's really weird because I am not really feeling anything. I suppose I should be angry or sad or something, but I just feel numb.

Nurse: Well, I don't know if this is helpful or not, but a lot of people tell me they feel like that initially, sort of numb and not feeling anything.

Jenny: Yes, that's it. Like it's happening to someone else but I know it's not, it's happening to me.

Grief responses can vary greatly between cultures. In the UK, we may appear quite reserved about our responses to grief, whereas in other countries there can be a verbal outpouring of emotions at funerals.

Stroebe and Schut (1995) studied cultural aspects of grief where they compared responses that seemed culturally acceptable – such as a shrine to dead ancestors in Japan – pointing out that a Western response to this shrine might be to see it as unresolved grief and an 'unhealthy' response. This led them to a dual-process model of both a loss orientation (as in Parkes 1972) and a restoration orientation. Stroebe and Schut's study related to how people both experienced and *coped* with loss in consideration of the variety of cultural norms and strategies around the bereavement process. They saw the 'experiencing' and 'adapting' to grief as being processes that go on at the same time.

Grief models

Murray Parkes (1972) model of grief:

- *Numbness*: shock and disbelief.
- *Pining*: anger, guilt and physical restlessness.
- *Disorganisation and despair*: depression, loneliness and anxiety.
- *Reorganisation*: recovery and acceptance.

Worden (2009) suggests *tasks* of loss:

- *Accept* the reality of the loss.
- *Process* the pain of grief.
- *Adjust* to the world without the deceased.
- *Relocate* the deceased emotionally and move on with life.

Tonkin (1996) suggests:

- That the bereaved person's life grows around the loss rather than 'recovers' from it.
- That the bereaved person may have an expectation from self and others that he or she will eventually 'get over it' or 'recover', but in fact he or she will adapt and extend life around the loss, which will 'remain' but will become more manageable.

> Stroebe and Schut (1995) dual-process model:
>
> - Feelings and activities following a bereavement are divided into loss and restoration, both being seen as equally important.
> - *Loss* activities would include the grief process and denial or resistance to restoration activities.
> - *Restoration* activities would include integrating the changes resulting from the loss, doing new things, new roles and identity.

Other useful models

There are a number of models drawn from CBT that could be helpful to people suffering adverse effects of change. Here are brief outlines of two models, but further sources can be found in the model box.

ABCDE model developed from Ellis (1962)

The model is made up of the five sections:

TABLE 6.2 ABCDE model

Target problem	Performance-interfering thoughts	Emotional/behavioural and physiological reaction	Performance-enhancing thoughts	Effective and new approach to problem
A (activating event)	B (beliefs)	C (consequences)	D (dispute)	E (effective outcome)

For instance, someone losing a long-term relationship may be struggling with a lot of unhelpful beliefs about him or herself ('I should have been a better partner then she wouldn't have left me' or 'I'll never get another partner'). This model is useful in challenging those beliefs, testing the accuracy of the statements and replacing them with more preferential statements.

SPACE model (Edgerton and Palmer 2005)

The acronym SPACE refers to:

- Social context
- Physiology
- Action
- Cognition
- Emotion

The client may find him or herself withdrawing from his or her friends and family and become isolated (S).

He or she may be struggling with symptoms such as insomnia, illness and stress-related headaches (P).

He or she may develop habits such as overeating/drinking, watching TV excessively, obsessive compulsive actions such as cleaning or hand washing. He or she may stop socialising (A).

Following this loss, a person may have thoughts such as 'I'm not good enough', 'I'll always be alone', 'I always knew I was no good, they were waiting for an opportunity to leave me' (C).

He or she may feel anger, rejection, shame and anxiety (E).

Working through this model enables the client to draw links between his or her thoughts, actions, physical symptoms and emotions, and explore what is within his or her influence to control, to think about any specific context where his or her issues are worse or better and to understand his or her cultural beliefs and values.

RESISTANCE TO CHANGE AND SYSTEMS AWARENESS

None of us exist in total isolation from others, and most of us are part of many 'systems'. Our 'primary' system is usually family and partners, but the family system connects with other systems, such as our work, education, culture, religion and social groups. Individuals within these systems are interdependent and interconnected. It is easy to feel that there are just the two of us in the room and we are trying to work within confidentiality boundaries, but we all come with outside influences, life experiences, views and opinions that form part of the influence of our 'systems'. This is true for our clients and also for us; we are all part of various systems throughout our lives, and it is important for helpers to be aware that these systems can *help* or *hinder* the helping process.

A general understanding of systems theory can provide a useful insight into our client's relationship with change or transition, especially if he or she is coming up against blocks or resistances.

Systems have a tendency to want to regulate and maintain themselves in order to stay as they are. This is known as *homeostasis*. Families, in particular, can have family 'rules', communication patterns or blaming patterns that reinforce the maintenance of the family system.

> *Helper*: So, Kevin, you are saying that you would like to leave your wife because she has had lots of affairs and you know that you don't love each other any more. I am curious to know what is holding you back from moving out?
>
> *Client*: Well, what would people think? Divorce has never been done in our family!

Changes in one of our systems can affect other systems in our lives; what is going on in our home life will often affect our work, and vice versa.

It is important to look at the *life cycle* of a system (McLeod 1998). Stress is more likely to occur around life-cycle transition points (Carter and McGoldrick 1989). How people react to these transitions can dictate how well their system continues to function. Guttman (1991) sees events as having the potential to affect life in one of two ways: either they can keep the system frozen and unable to move on, or they can take life forward with a new set of rules and a rearrangement of roles.

In the previous example, 'Kevin' might decide not to divorce because the family pressure feels too strong and influential, so the system remains the same, or he might decide to divorce and the family does or does not adapt to the new experience. Another example of this can be when a family member comes out as gay. Initial reactions can often be negative (Fisher *et al.* 2010) if the family norm has been heterosexual or there are strong cultural beliefs about gay relationships, but in some cases the family can adapt to the 'change' and a new same-sex partner and integrate them into the family. In other examples, families can struggle to adapt to gay children and the system breaks down.

REFLECTIVE LEARNING JOURNAL EXERCISE

With your learning partner:

Both your learning partner and yourself make a list of the systems you or your family belong to. You can start with reference to the questions below but can expand on any more you can think of:

- What is your ethnic background?
- Are you a parent? If so, what kind of school do your children attend? What kind of school did you attend?
- Do you have or are you a parent, grandparent, brother, sister, aunt or uncle?
- What type of employment do you have?
- Do you have any political or religious affiliations that you are comfortable to share?
- Are you a member of a social group?

When you have finished your list, compare notes for similarities/differences.

In your learning journal, reflect further upon how your systems have influenced or hindered you.

What do you think may be the impact of these on the helper relationship?

Cultural influence

We, as social beings, have created cultures encompassing all of the values, attitudes and behaviours common to our different groups that dictate the way in which we live our lives. These cultures determine the way that we react in certain situations and shape our ways of behaving and thinking (Feltham and Horton 2000). They define which rules or mechanisms we follow and whether we choose to live within open or closed systems. These mechanisms can keep us safe and boundaried, and yet they can also keep us frozen or stifled and unable to evolve. Some clients experience difficulties in changing their lives, because there is an expectation that they continue to function in a particular way because it has become established by their culture. By changing a cultural or traditional belief, clients will be involved in initiating both internal and external changes in their lives (D'Ardenne and Mahtani 1999). They are not only altering their internal thoughts, feelings and attitudes, but also their external world, which will impact on their relationships and personal circumstances. If a client comes from a culture that places greater emphasis on a system remaining homeostatic, any change that alters traditional beliefs or values will have a significant impact on all of the individuals within it. Any change can therefore be daunting for the client and could be resisted.

> **Our role is to help clients to look at any aspects that are resisting the change, internally and within their systems, and to support the client, not only while he or she is making the decision to change, but also in the time following.**

MAINTAINING CHANGE AND ENDING THE RELATIONSHIP

Maintaining positive change can involve a lifetime commitment. Once we have initiated the change, resisting the urge to return to old patterns of behaviour or familiar ways of being can be very hard. Part of our role as helper is to support the client to develop ways to help him or herself. The client should be encouraged to look at his or her existing strategies for problem-solving and to look for new ways to help sustain change. It is useful to explore the pitfalls:

- In what circumstances is he or she likely to revert to his or her 'old ways'?
- Does he or she need to avoid situations where this might happen?
- Is her or she able to identify early warning signs?
- What are the self-defeating beliefs that he or she holds about him or herself, and how might he or she change these into more positive beliefs?
- Is he or she confident that if relapse happens, he or she has a strategy in place to overcome his or her difficulties?

A client may like to be more assertive in order to gain the confidence to implement or challenge areas of his or her life where change needs to happen, and good counselling skills, using the core conditions of empathy, respect and genuineness to explore the factors that hinder development of confidence, would be useful.

It can be frustrating for a helper to see his or her client regress or return to old patterns that he or she had at the beginning of your work together. One way of avoiding these frustrations is to 'not have too much desire for the client's outcome'. Maintaining the relationship will be more beneficial to the client than directing an outcome or trying to lead the client down your 'garden path'. Staying alongside the client on his or her journey and encouraging and facilitating his or her growth, in particular at times when the client is struggling to achieve or maintain his or her goals, is an important part of the maintenance of the relationship, and it is important to embrace both the successes and failures along the way.

Helping the client to explore and acknowledge potential difficulties and encouraging the client if and when relapse does occur can be beneficial in keeping the client on track and helping him or her to develop strategies that become useful to him or her for life, not just for that particular change.

Every helping relationship will differ in terms of intensity and time allocation. However, how you end each relationship is important, and the client needs to be clear about the ending – for example, whether he or she will be able to return for support or where he or she might access other support. It is the helper's role to be clear about your role in the future and, if necessary, to signpost the client to other opportunities outside of the helper/client relationship that you have developed.

Always allow time either towards the end of the session, or allow a final session, for the client to ask any questions about the whole process and to give and receive feedback.

EXAMPLE

VIDEO CLIP 6d

MAINTAINING AND ENDING THE RELATIONSHIP – FINAL STAGES OF TRANSITION:
Glyn and Rob

TABLE 6.3 Transcript of Video Clip 6b: Maintaining and ending the relationship – final stages of transition – Glyn and Rob

Content	Process	Skills
G: Now we've looked at some of those goals, Rob, can we just look at them again and see what's the best way for you to achieve them if that's the way you want to work with this?	The relationship is now at a phase where the skills are embedded	Reviewing goals
R: Yeah, OK		
G: So just let's talk through them individually. You talked about when you were out buying better meals for yourself, so ….	Implementing change. The helper is guiding the client through goals	
R: Yeah, and enjoying cooking them rather than cooking something quick	The client seems attuned with the helper	
G: So what would enable that for you?	Looking at the client's self-supporting strategies	Challenge
R: Um, I don't know, I don't know exactly, I mean there's obviously turning up at the shop and like I said, sort of building it into my routine that I pick it up on the way home rather than have to go out of my way in order to do something special although I would do that if I was in the mood to, um and er. You know what I tend to like is a bit of variety so I think that would keep it going. You know, where I shop or what I buy. It's just, it's about being free with what I can do. You know, rather than making it feel like a chore, I think	Action and willpower (Prochaska and DiClemente) and internalisation (Hopson and Adams)	
G: And when you make the choice – cos this is what this is about, making a choice – what would be the trigger for that do you feel? When you needed to do something like that if you felt you needed to do something like that	Exploring existing strategies	Raising awareness
R: How would I know that it was time to go and do something that I wanted to do?	Maintenance (Prochaska and DiClemente)	
G: Yeah		

table 6.3 continued

Content	Process	Skills
R: *(long sigh)* There's probably a few, there's probably a few. I mean it might be that I've had a particularly tough day at work. It might be that actually I have some time to myself and you know what I really fancy doing something with it, you know, um. It might be that I got friends round. It could be all sorts of different things I think		
G: And what about the gym side of it? Because you mentioned sometimes you like to go to the gym		Reviewing and evaluating goals
R: Yeah, I think what really helps with the gym is, it's one of those funny ones where having a bit of a set routine with the gym does help		
G: OK		
R: Like, going on a Friday, partly because it is a bit of hard work so there is a bit of, if I have a bit of structure then it's great, to keep me going. And if I kind of see some difference in me, if I feel better	The client is reflecting on existing strategies and how these have worked in the past	
G: Yeah		
R: You know, and then on top of that sometimes what I could do is go to the sauna in between. So say like when I go on a Friday, I could go on a Tuesday but not to feel like I had to go on a Tuesday but to have it in mind that actually I can go again if I want to	Integration (Hopson and Adams) Maintenance (Prochaska and DiClemente) The client is thinking about new and different ways to maintain the change	
G: That king of freedom of choice we've talked about throughout, haven't we? And finally we also talked about the third option	The helper seems ambiguous about the third option and the client helps him out Very collaborative relationship, indicating that the phase of the relationship is now secure	
R: Um, was it my legs and, um?		
G: Yes, the exercising		

table 6.3 continued

Content	Process	Skills
R: Yeah that one is . . . in a way it's kind of one of the really important ones. Well, they're all really important but it's the longest serving one. Cos I've kind of had it from whenever I was this high that it's a stretch. And it's actually painful to do but I think, I think with that it's a case of putting it together with, um, you know, going to the gym		
G: OK		
R: Because of how it feels and it just feels right and it feels better for me to be able to walk around loosely, if that, I don't know whether that makes sense to you?		
G: It makes perfect sense, yeah, makes perfect sense		Encouraging and affirming Core conditions evident
R: Yeah, um, so what would help me keep that going is if I had the other stuff going as well		
G: So they are all connected with each other?		
R: Yeah, I think, I think so	The client is becoming much clearer about his goals and his strategies for success	
G: Sounds a really good idea, particularly because you said earlier on that, that if you were more comfortable throughout the day with your leg, then things would feel better for you	You might see a connection here to Stroebe and Schut's dual-process model of loss and restoration	Encouragement and supportive by reminding the client of previous wishes
R: It's, you know, I'd never really thought about it but it's amazing how much of what I'm talking about, my . . . I think what I am really talking about is the struggle that I have and what I'm just realising is it's actually a physical struggle but it's also like an emotional and a psychological struggle, um, and what I really want is to not have to struggle so much		

table 6.3 continued

Content	Process	Skills
G: OK. So it sounds like your saying that by having some of these goals set for you to manage this that it could improve your physical position as well		
R: Well, everything, everything. I guess I've just realised that I didn't know they were all connected and they are. Um, yeah, yeah (pause), yeah. I'm just thinking there is bound to be days when I don't fancy going down the gym or I think, well actually I've got enough food in the fridge and I can cobble something together from what I've got and . . . I don't want to lose that either	The client is making clear connections and realisations. Moving towards a stable, more healthy lifestyle (Prochaska and DiClemente). Supporting self-management strategies (Midwinter and Dickson)	Good use of silence
G: Yeah, yeah		
R: You know, and it's about being easier on myself, you know . . . yeah		
G: That sounds really good, Rob, it sounds, you know, how you've worked on that choice, that autonomy of choice to improve things for you. Sounds like a really good way ahead for yourself	The helper returns to the word 'autonomy' to tie up the threads of the story	Encouragement Deeper empathy
R: It's good of you to say that, you know, I've . . . at the same time it's kind of odd for me to hear cos I've never really had that. You know, as I was saying, well there's this bit, well yeah, but what's missing. Yeah but what are you not doing. To have you sit with me and say 'yes that's a good thing you go for it'. That's what it sounds like to me. That, that means a lot	Supporting self-management strategies (Midwinter and Dickson)	
G: Thank you, and it's been really good working with you. I've enjoyed spending some time to help you move some way with this. So thank you for that as well, and in future maybe we could get together again and see how it's going?		Signposting and ending the relationship
R: Yeah, I think that would be good, I'd like that		
G: Thank you		
R: Cool		

REFLECT, PRACTISE AND EVALUATE

With your learning partner, take turns to reflect on a change or transition you have made within your life.

How have you maintained that change?

What has enabled or hindered you with maintaining the change?

After the session, reflect on your practice session and evaluate the skills used.

MODEL BOX

In this chapter, we have referred to:

- The Relational Skills Model – maintaining the relationship (Midwinter and Dickson 2015)
- The seven stages of transition (adapted from Hopson and Adams 1976)
- The ABC model (Ellis 1962)
- The model of cognitive therapy (Beck *at al.* 1979)
- Cycle of change (Prochaska and DiClemente 1986)
- Model of grief (Parkes 1972)
- Tasks of loss (Worden 2009)
- Growing around grief (Tonkin 1996)
- Dual-process model (Stroebe and Schut 1995)
- Non-event (Schlossberg 1995)

SUMMARY

- The nature of change depends on the rate and extent of change.
- Change can be anticipated or unanticipated, voluntary or involuntary.
- There are seven stages of transition where self-esteem is affected over a period of time.
- The cycle of change models identify a person's position within the cycle of change.
- Grief models can be applied to support clients through other examples of loss.
- We are all part of various systems throughout our lives, and it is important for helpers to be aware that these systems can *help* or *hinder* the helping process.

Chapter 7
Deepening your understanding

You have now worked through the Relational Skills Model, applying the model with your learning partner and potentially integrating and embedding counselling skills into your work settings. This chapter will help to deepen your understanding of the value of the use of these skills, and will cover some of the common issues or situations that may arise as you work more formally with them. In this chapter, we will explore:

- The powerful tool of counselling skills
- Working within your competencies
- Working across difference and diversity
- Introduction to transactional analysis and the ego-state model
- Dealing with difficult clients
- Getting it wrong and accountability

TEACHING

THE POWERFUL TOOL OF COUNSELLING SKILLS

Having completed a short two-day introduction to counselling skills course, a student told us about her experience of practising her new counselling skills with her hairdresser:

> It was amazing and really scary at the same time. I had been going to my hairdresser for about four years. I knew very little about her personal life, we had the usual conversations – Where are you going on holiday? And that sort of thing. This time I just reflected back, paraphrased, summarised, etc. and practised the skills I had learnt on the course. By the end of the haircut she had told me really intimate details about her life. All about her relationship, family and sadness about the miscarriages she had had. I hadn't said anything really, it was extraordinary the way that she opened up to me and quite frightening as I suddenly realised what a powerful tool counselling skills were. It felt like a big responsibility.
>
> (Barr 2000)

In Chapter 3 of this book, we referred to the BACP Ethical Framework for Counselling and Psychotherapy (BACP 2013) as being a useful reference for the use of counselling skills. Now that you have been practising your skills with your learning partner, we imagine that you have also become aware of the power of counselling skills. It is often said that 'with power comes responsibility', so with this understanding, it seems a good time to revisit those ethical considerations and reconsider their importance through fresh eyes.

> *Being trustworthy*: the helpers are honest and act in good faith.
>
> *Autonomy*: the client's right to have and make choices of his or her own free will.
>
> *Beneficence*: to work in the best interest of the client and others.
>
> *Non-maleficence*: to do no harm to the client.
>
> *Justice*: to offer services fairly and equally to all.
>
> *Self-respect*: to acknowledge your strengths and have an appreciation of your limitations.

There are many good things about developing our communication and listening skills through the use of counselling skills. We can help people explore their difficulties without undue influence and we can provide a supportive environment to enable positive change. We have explored many of these aspects throughout this book, but we always need to be mindful that our clients are making their own choices of their own free will. We ensure they are fully informed and that the contract and the boundaries of this relationship are mutually agreed. At the time of this book going to press (summer 2014), the BACP was in the process of reviewing the ethical framework, and so we suggest that you visit the website (www.bacp.co.uk) for updates on this.

REFLECTIVE LEARNING JOURNAL EXERCISE

With your learning partner, consider these questions:

What safeguards have you learned that need to be in place to ensure the ethical framework is applied?

Where do you think you might use counselling skills, and can you think of examples of where it might not be appropriate?

WORKING WITHIN YOUR COMPETENCIES

Having worked through the handbook, you can now begin to reflect on where you are now and what stage you are with your learning. You may feel more confident than when you started out or you may still have concerns or anxieties about how competent you feel. A reminder of the competence model is useful to see where we are with our learning.

> *Unconscious incompetence* – this is the stage where you are not even aware that you do not have a particular competence. *Conscious incompetence* – this is when you know that you want to learn how to do something but you are incompetent at doing it. *Conscious competence* – this is when you can achieve this particular task but you are very conscious about everything you do. *Unconscious competence* – this is when you finally master it and you do not even think about what you have such as when you have learned to ride a bike very successfully.
>
> (Howell 1982: 29–33)

When you began to work with this handbook, you will have had some motivation to pick it up either as part of a course or with an aim to learn more and embed your counselling and communication skills within your work setting. At this stage, you may have been in a stage of *conscious incompetence*. As you have worked through this book, you will have moved from this stage into more *conscious competence*, where you are using your core counselling skills effectively alongside a developing ability to choose how you are using them – for example, 'I can paraphrase now' or 'I might ask an open question'.

Now we are moving towards developing an *unconscious competence*. As we continue to practise and embed our counselling skills, we will think less obviously about the skills and they will become more naturally integrated into our work. Alongside this, we can begin to develop an ability to identify those situations that may be beyond our competence as a helper and decide when it may be appropriate and ethical to signpost our client on to a relevant professional. This is the stage where, alongside our *conscious competence*, we develop and tune in to our own *internal supervisor*. We will discuss this and how we work reflexively in more detail in Chapter 8, but in this chapter we will consider what we might do when obstacles arise within the helping relationship and when we might consider signposting to or consulting a professional in the situations where we are aware that we feel *consciously incompetent*. Additionally, we may need to expand our learning or awareness to better meet our client's needs.

Some areas to consider when thinking about working within your competency are as follows.

Dual roles

Many people using this book to develop their communication skills will have more than one relationship with their clients. For example, you may be a colleague to your client, or his or her line manager, his or her medical practitioner, welfare officer and so on. Managing these dual roles can be difficult and conflicting as there may be different influences and agendas from each role. We introduced this concept in Chapter 2, but now that we have embedded some of these skills we will revisit this to examine these issues in more depth.

Clarity of role is essential from the outset in order for a trust to be developed between you and your client. In each relationship, it is important to try to envisage how your client might experience and respond to you. Consider what dual roles might impact the following relationships:

1   A nurse practitioner that is working with a patient diagnosed with diabetes. The client has dressings that need to be changed on sores on her legs.
2   The audiologist who is working with a patient with progressive deafness who chooses not to use his hearing aids.
3   The line manager of a charitable service whose employee is separating from her long-term partner and suspected of embezzling funds from the charity.
4   The military welfare officer who is working with an injured officer who is contesting his pension rights.

When touch is a necessary part of the relationship

Medical practitioners often have to touch and examine their patients. Sometimes this more intimate relationship can be a time where issues can be discussed. The nurse in example 1 might find it an opportune moment to use communication and listening skills while applying dressings to his or her patient. It might support a sense of caring and empathy. For other patients, touch might be challenging, and this would have the opposite effect of closing them down, particularly if the treatment was painful. Medical practitioners can take time to consider this with each individual client, reflecting on the situation and looking for signs that the client is relaxed and inviting communication during this physical contact or whether the two roles of physical care and using counselling skills are better dealt with separately.

In Chapter 3, we explored the use of touch 'in general', and you will remember that we tended towards caution with using touch because clients can easily misconstrue it. A hand on the shoulder can feel affirming or it can feel condescending. We are now so much more aware of the *power* of the relationship, and so can understand and envisage that our client may feel *disempowered* to reject our offer of physical touch.

It is important to consider why we are using touch. The most important question we ask ourselves is: is it for us or for the client?

Wearing our 'expert hat'

An important aspect to consider is whether our clients see us as 'an expert'. Perhaps this could induce a response of awe and inability to question us or put their views forward? We need to consider whether our dual role with our clients puts them at a disadvantage, preventing them from responding from a place of equality. They might also be confused by our response and have different expectations from us, having anticipated that they had come only to consult an expert and now the relationship has changed to a helping role where they are making the decisions for themselves. The patient who consults the audiologist in example 2 could potentially have difficulty discussing his personal circumstances and instead feel in awe of a medical 'expert' who will make the decisions for him. Some patients feel that they should not take up the doctor or practitioner's time, or see their worries as being irrelevant. We have all met people who have a seemingly unquestioning belief in those in 'expert' roles, such as medical or legal experts. We often describe it as *consulting* lawyers and doctors and acknowledging their *superior* knowledge. We need to stand outside this professional dual relationship and consider what impact this might have in our interactions with our clients.

It is our responsibility to ask ourselves whether our clients are contracting into this relationship willingly, or are they deferring to our 'superior' knowledge? The line manager and military welfare officer in examples 3 and 4 may have professional responsibilities towards their clients' competency in their work settings. Managers' roles frequently involve evaluating their employees' work, monitoring competence and reporting back to the organisation. While a helper might have empathy for his or her client's situation, conflict can arise in roles within the organisations if there are boundary or work ethic issues.

Can our clients give their 'informed consent' to share their issues with us, or do they feel they have no choice because of the professional relationship that already exists?

With your learning partner, take turns to consider the following questions, applying them to the role in which you might practise your counselling skills.

REFLECTIVE LEARNING JOURNAL EXERCISE

Reflect on the following:

- Could my client see me as an expert or specialist?
- Do I have a potential position of 'authority' over my client?
- Could there be a situation where my work relationship with my client may mean I need to make decisions on his or her behalf, or about him or her?
- What implications do these considerations have about the contract and relationship that I make with my client?

Dual relationships and outside contact

Some dual relationships, such as the ones we have discussed earlier, are more obvious, but some are less so. If we were professional counsellors, we would have a strict ethical framework around dual relationships – for example, not counselling friends or work colleagues – and in this situation dual roles are perhaps easier to navigate and more clear-cut. Return to Chapter 1, and the table set out by Culley and Bond (2004) differentiating the difference between counselling and counselling skills (Figure 1.1). You will find that this provides a good checklist to explore the potential dual relationships that you might experience within your own work.

However, when we consider the example of the student at the beginning of the chapter, and the impact of her use of counselling skills with her hairdresser, who is more of an acquaintance, we can see how easily our client may share personal details and information with us. So how might we respond to that if, for example, we meet at a work party, have children who share the same school, or find we have joined the same book club or salsa class?

The initial contract that we established when we were setting up the relationship can include establishing a 'what if' scenario. We can establish what preferred response our client would like from us should we bump into him or her in a different setting. Useful questions to ask might be:

> 'What if we meet outside/in another role? How would you like it to be?'
>
> 'Would you like me to acknowledge you and say hello or prefer me not to?'
>
> 'If people ask how we know each other, what would you like us to say?'

We are very aware that we may have been privy to a lot of personal information about our client. Respecting and maintaining those boundaries is an integral part of our contract and is easier to set up from the outset rather than create awkwardness when we might meet in a different situation.

WORKING ACROSS DIFFERENCE AND DIVERSITY

This is a good time to repeat what we wrote earlier about cultural expectations and diversity. Diversity is about more than race and culture – it is also about gender, age, sexual orientation, beliefs and disability. Diversity is about the human qualities that are different to our own and may be outside of our own experiences or cultural norms, but are present in other individuals or groups. Recognising and having acceptance of these differences is crucial within the helping relationship. We need to educate ourselves about diversity and equality and have knowledge about different client cultures to provide a culturally appropriate service and to ensure we do not rely on our clients to inform and educate us.

It is important to be self-reflexive and aware of your own culture and values and to consider the impact of these on the helping relationship. To broaden your knowledge and awareness of your own and others' cultural differences and identity, you need to have a diverse social network, read widely, attend diversity and equality training, and discuss issues that arise with peers. It is important to have an awareness of language and communications issues (in particular when working with a client where English is not his or her first language) and to be insightful of the cultural differences in non-verbal responses and discuss meaning with clients.

It is important that helpers do not fall into the trap of 'stereotyping' clients or making assumptions that clients share the same values and cultural norms as them. There is a huge diversity of experience of people who might come from the 'same social group', and it should not be assumed that they share similar personal qualities, skills, experiences or cultural values.

It is important in a therapeutic encounter to honour the trust of clients, through being attentive of their individual needs, communicating in culturally appropriate ways, remaining in contact with the client and empathic to his or her understanding of the helping relationship and his or her world outside, and to be respectful of his or her views, ideas and ways of being. It is important to value each client's uniqueness.

Let us have a look at what difference mean to us.

REFLECTIVE LEARNING JOURNAL EXERCISE 1

List all of the different groups that you consider might experience discrimination.

Do you fall within any of those listed categories? If so, have you experienced discrimination?

Reflect on what that experience was like.

Has that experience changed the way that you are with others?

Thinking back to the first reflective exercise in the introduction – 'who am I?' – take this exercise further, thinking more about who you are in *different contexts*.

REFLECTIVE LEARNING JOURNAL EXERCISE 2

How do you define yourself in different contexts?

How do you imagine others define you?

How do you act/appear differently based on those definitions of yourself/defined by others?

Now ask yourself the following questions that will inform you more about your own prejudices and judgements (Appendix 6). The answers to these questions will not be discussed, so be as honest as you can be.

DEEPENING YOUR UNDERSTANDING

a Think of three things, off the top of your head, which might bias you *towards* someone.

i _____

ii _____

iii _____

b Think of three things, off the top of your head, which might bias you *against* someone.

i _____

ii _____

iii _____

c Do any of these fall into categories that you have listed above (Appendix 6)?

d Think of what you do when you are biased towards or away from someone? How do you act/appear differently based on your definitions and assumptions of others?

FIGURE 7.1 Prejudices and judgements

As a helper, you need to be aware of what the legal, professional and organisation requirements regarding equal opportunities, diversity and anti-discrimination are.

Who within your organisation might be able to help you with this?

INTRODUCTION TO TRANSACTIONAL ANALYSIS AND THE EGO-STATE MODEL

Sometimes it is not easy to understand why a relationship is not working. As a helper, you have every intention to like the client and to give him or her appropriate help and support. However, sometimes a relationship goes wrong, for no obvious reason, and this can feel confusing, and you may begin to lack confidence. One theory we refer our students to in all the training that we do on counselling skills is that of transactional analysis (TA). An awareness of our 'ego-states' and how we respond under stress can have a profound effect on our 'transactions' with others, and when we become consciously aware of our behaviours, thoughts and feelings, we can make a choice about how we might need to change or alter them to improve the relationship. While this theory is based on interactions between others, TA is also useful as a tool for the 'conversations' we have internally. Once we become aware of our ego-states, we can shift the way that we interact within ourselves too.

> Transactional analysis is a theory of personality and a systematic psychotherapy for personal growth and personal change.
>
> (Stewart and Joines 1987: 3)

Transactional analysis (TA) was founded by psychiatrist Eric Berne (1919–70). TA acknowledges and integrates the three main theoretical modes of psychology – psychoanalysis, CBT and humanistic.

Its emphasis is on communication and interactions between people: 'a transaction may be of spoken words, expressed feelings, physical behaviours, shared thoughts, stated opinions or beliefs' (Lapworth and Sills 2011: 1).

Its *philosophical assumptions* are:

- That people are OK – the 'I'm OK, you're OK' principle.
- That everyone has the capacity to think.
- That people decide their own destiny and these decisions can be changed.

(Stewart 2000: 13)

These beliefs mean that, in principle, everyone has 'a fundamental worth and as such should be valued and respected' (Lapworth and Sills 2011: 5).

Berne believed that each of us has within us three ego-states – the parent, adult and child ego-states. The *parent* ego-state holds the behaviours, thoughts and feelings derived from parents or authoritative figures; the *adult* ego-state holds the behaviours, thoughts and feelings that are responses to the reality in the present; and the *child* ego-state holds the behaviours, thoughts and feelings experienced in our childhood.

Berne defined an ego-state as a:

> consistent pattern of feeling and experience directly related to a corresponding consistent pattern of behaviour.
>
> (Stewart and Joines 1987: 15)

Therefore, we are able to look for clues in words, in behaviour and non-verbally, which will give us an indication of which ego-state we might be in ourselves and to acknowledge the ego-states of those we interact with.

DEEPENING YOUR UNDERSTANDING

PARENT EGO-STATE
Behaviours, thoughts and feelings derived from parents or parental figures.

ADULT EGO-STATE
Behaviours, thoughts and feelings which are responses to reality in the here and now

CHILD EGO-STATE
Behaviours, thoughts and feelings experienced in our childhood

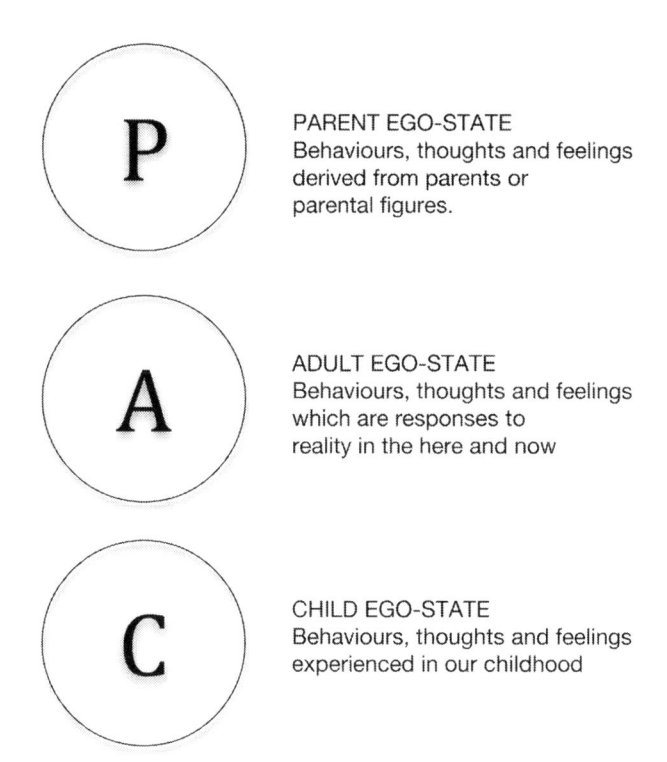

FIGURE 7.2 TA ego-states

> It is a way in which the person experiences herself and the world at any given moment, and in which she manifests that experience externally in her behaviour.
>
> (Stewart 2000: 3)

This can be so helpful when we are working with and supporting others. Knowing which ego-state we go into under stress can help us to change the direction of some of the difficult interactions we have with those we are helping.

The ego-state model further divides the ego-states to show us the process of how we use them (Stewart and Joines 1987). The parent ego-state is divided into the nurturing parent and the controlling parent (also referred to as the critical parent), and the child ego-state is divided into the adapted child and the natural child (also referred to as the free child). Each of these ego-states has a positive and a negative influence. You do not have to be child or 'childish' to have behaviours, thoughts and feelings in the child ego-state, and likewise you do not have to be a parent to experience the parent ego-state.

Nurturing parent: Caring and nurturing with a positive regard for the other. The negative influences can be the 'overprotective, smothering' behaviours.

Controlling parent (also referred to as *critical parent*): The positive influences can be guidance and setting of rules – 'you must meet the 12 o'clock deadline'. The negative influences often involve a 'put-down' or diminishing the other with the intention of the other feeling

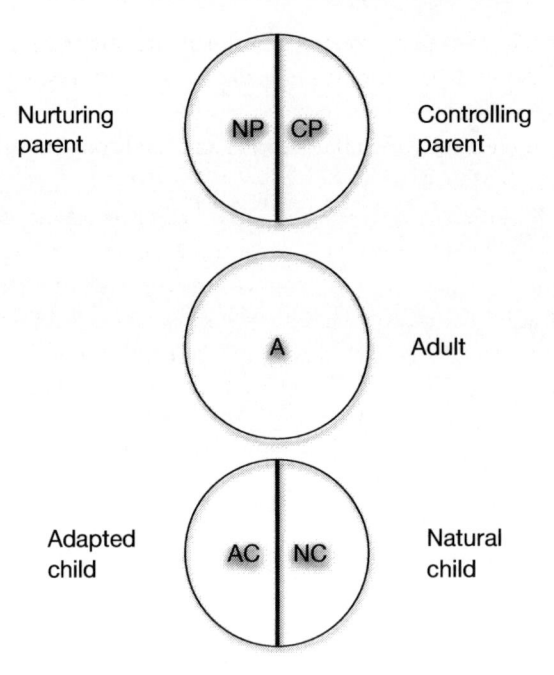

FIGURE 7.3 TA parent and child ego-states

negative about the interaction – 'you must meet the 12 o'clock deadline but that's unlikely as you're usually so slow'.

Adult: In the here and now, going about the daily business, dealing with things as they arise. This is the state in which we plan things, consider the situation, and make decisions and act on them. The negative influences can be that creativity is restricted, and actions and behaviours can be routine and feelings rationalised.

> The Adult Ego-State is the only state in which we can learn something new about ourselves.
>
> (Board 1998: 84)

Adapted child: Can be vulnerable or rebellious. Applying the rules that you learned to get by as a child to fit with the demands of parent/parent-figures. The positive influences are that we are able to keep ourselves safe and not have to set new rules by which to live our everyday lives: 'By following these rule-following patters we often get what we want comfortably for ourselves and other people' (Stewart and Joines 1987: 23). The less positive influences are that when we are in our adapted child ego-state, we are displaying behaviours, thoughts and feelings from the past, and these may no longer be appropriate in our current situation.

Natural child (also referred to as *free child*): Doing or feeling what you wish, without paying attention to parental rules or limits. Freely expressing authentic emotions and feelings. Can be seen as negative if these behaviours do not conform to social or cultural norms and can be unsafe if behaviours are totally unboundaried.

There is no hierarchy in the ego-states – all of them are important and we unconsciously flip between them many times in a day. However, if, under stress, we use and rely heavily on one ego-state more than the others (especially if the negative influences are paramount), then we need to consciously redress the balance and focus our energy in raising the ego-state that we use less frequently.

Communication and interactions between individuals can be enhanced by the knowledge of Berne's ego-state model. Once we have an awareness of the three ego-states, individuals can make a conscious decision to shift position to improve the communication. We might choose to take action to raise our own adult ego-state, acknowledge when it is appropriate to use our nurturing parent ego-state and, to improve creativity and energy levels, we can release our natural child ego-state.

> **A day in the life of Becky and her ego-states**
>
> The alarm goes off at 7.45. I stretch languidly and lie there for a moment, feeling content. The moment of panic hits me – today is the day that I am running the trauma workshop for the counsellors who work for a very reputable charity group. I begin to feel really anxious – I'm not feeling prepared for it. I kept meaning to spend more time on the workshop preparation but other tasks kept taking over. My anxiety rises and I begin to feel sick. A very familiar feeling from childhood when I felt nervous or anxious about anything (*adapted child*). The voice inside my head begins to sound critical.
>
> 'You are going to make a complete mess of this. It's Saturday morning and everyone is giving up their precious time to come and listen to you and they are all going to think it's a waste of their time and money. What made you think you were good enough to take on this course?' (*negative controlling parent*)
>
> I begin to feel tearful and really wish I hadn't agreed to do the training. The door opens and my partner enters with a cup of tea and a buttered crumpet.
>
> 'I thought you might need a treat', he says, 'as I know you are going to be really worried about today' (*nurturing parent*).
>
> 'I'm petrified', I say, 'I'm not sure I can do this, I might have to call in sick' (*adapted child – avoidant behaviour*).
>
> 'Don't be daft', he says, 'you can do this with your eyes closed. You've been teaching this stuff for years and you work much better on the hoof than you do when you over-prepare (*nurturing parent*). Come on, eat your breakfast and sort yourself out else you are going to be late' (*positive controlling parent*).
>
> An hour later, I am dressed and on the train. I read through my notes, check I have my PowerPoint on a pen and check my handouts (*adult*). I feel much more in control and very present.

When I arrive at the venue, I am greeted by the organiser and shown to the room.

'We were expecting about 20 today but word has got around that you were presenting this subject, so it might be nearer 30!'

Once again, I feel the surge of sickness hit my throat. What are they expecting? Why am I feeling so much pressure to perform well? What if I don't tell them anything new or interesting (*adapted child*)? My internal *nurturing parent* kicks in and I tell myself that it's an interesting subject, very relevant to the work that these counsellors do and of course they are going to be interested. I bring myself back to the here and now (*adult*) and set up the equipment, grab myself a tea and focus on the room and the people within it.

Once I started teaching, everything fell into place. The group were great and really interested in the subject so listened well (*adult*). At one point, a group member shared a very personal example of working with trauma and for a brief moment her distress became apparent. The 'counsellor' in me gave an appropriately empathic response and the group member found she was able to contain her distress and we were able to continue with the session (*nurturing parent*).

At the end of the session, there was time for questions. One person in the room seemed to want to take more time than the group allowed by repeatedly asking questions and then not accepting my answer but wanting to give her own examples. I tried very hard to remain in my *adult* but after a while I could hear irritation creep into my voice. In a very childish, rebellious way, in my head I wanted to say, 'Perhaps you would like to come up and address the group if you think you are so clever' (*adapted child*).

Realising that response would be totally inappropriate, I consciously shifted my energy back into my *adult* and explained that the session was very short and I was sorry that we didn't have time for that level of discussion, and asked if there was anyone else in the group who had a question. We moved on much more comfortably after that.

Feedback from the group at the end of the session was really positive (their *nurturing parent*). The group had thoroughly enjoyed the session and most of them commented that they had learned a lot. I metaphorically gave myself a pat on the back (*nurturing parent*).

Instead of immediately going back on the train, I decided to take a look around the beautiful surroundings, feeling excited that the presentation had gone so well and allowing myself the time to reflect upon the day and bask in the success of it (*natural child*).

You can see from the above example that some behaviours, thoughts and feelings are outside of our conscious awareness. These are responses that we have embedded into our lives from a very young age. We are not aware that we respond from a certain ego-state as they are automatic. How many times have you heard someone say 'I sounded just like my mother then' when he or she is addressing issues (usually critically) with his or her own children? I (Becky) know I have said it many a time! That is because we have internalised those responses from our parental or authoritative 'voices' and, under stress, we 'act them out'. Imagine attending a staff meeting. Prior to the meeting, you have been content and getting on with your daily business. Your boss is frustrated and irritable. He begins the meeting by telling everyone how deadlines have not been met and that certain people have not been 'pulling their weight' and how everyone has to 'buck up their ideas'. Or words to that effect! How have you begun to feel? My hunch is not very good. My guess is that you either feel really vulnerable – 'I wonder if he is talking about me? Am I the one who is not pulling their weight?' – or very rebellious – 'I can't believe he is saying that, he is the one who is always taking long lunches and is never around. He should buck up his ideas before he starts shooting his mouth off'. You have moved unconsciously into your adapted child ego-state as a result of your boss having moved into his controlling parent ego-state. Once you have awareness of this, you have a choice in how you respond. You might choose to give the rebellious adapted child response (however, I am not sure you would get very far with that response in the meeting), or you could respond from your adult, perhaps by asking for evidence of the deadlines that have not been made and ideas about how you could improve your productivity.

As a helper, an awareness of the ego-states can be so useful. It is unlikely that someone seeking help or support for an issue that he or she is finding difficult to handle will present in his or her adult ego-state. It is much more likely that he or she will present either in his or her parent or adapted child ego-state. A client in his or her negative controlling parent ego-state might seem frustrated or angry – 'You are the third person I have been referred to today, I hope you are not going to waste my time as well'. If you, as a helper, feel threatened or the comment is unjustified, you might feel like responding from your own internalised controlling parent voice, or you might respond from familiar scripts in adapted child. However, making a conscious choice to shift into your nurturing parent ego-state and respond empathically, 'I'm so sorry you have had a difficulty getting to see me but lets see how I might be able to help you now you are here', could change the dynamics of the interaction immediately.

Looking out for clues as to what ego-state your client might be in, and analysing your own behaviours, thoughts and feelings to look for clues as to your own ego-state, can help you become more aware of the transactions between you and which ego-states might be influencing the relationship.

> **REFLECTIVE LEARNING JOURNAL EXERCISE**
>
> See if you can identify the ego-state that a person might be in from the interactions below:
>
> *Boss*: I'm really fed up with you, you promised you would let me read that paper by the end of the week and it's already lunchtime on Friday and I haven't seen it, you never do what I ask.
> *Employee*: (*tearfully*) I don't know how you can say that, I've been rushing around all week and you haven't done anything to help at all, all you ever do is moan at me.
>
> *Tutor*: It's important that you all read Chapter 7 before the class tomorrow, as we will be analysing it during the session.
> *Student*: (*thinks to herself*) I've got a lovely evening planned tonight so I'm not going to read that paper.
>
> *Client*: I'm sorry to bother you with my problems, I'm sure you have loads of patients who have problems far worse than mine, I'm sure I shouldn't be taking up your time.
> *Helper*: Of course you are not taking up my time, that is what I am here for. You are not a bother at all. Tell me what is worrying you.
>
> *Helper*: We have discussed how we are going to work together. Would you like to meet me next Tuesday for our first session?
> *Client*: Yes, everything seems right and I would really like to start working together, thank you.

DEALING WITH DIFFICULT CLIENTS

Sometimes we will come across difficult challenging situations that are beyond our capabilities and training as a helper, in which case we will need to refer to a relevant helping professional. In Chapter 8, we will cover how we might recognise this through our reflexive practice. As we embed our skills into our work, we may find ourselves in the 'conscious incompetence' phase, and anxieties can arise about how to respond to difficult situations. In our skills practice, our learning partner will probably have supported us in practising our counselling skills by being an 'ideal' client, but in reality some clients can be less ideal and present more of a challenge.

In this section, we consider working with less responsive clients. We ask ourselves if or how we might work with a client who is under the influence of alcohol or drugs. What if a client gets angry with us? What if a client is passive, says very little, or appears reluctant to engage with us at all?

Professional counsellors working with the core conditions would consider whether their client was in sufficient '*psychological contact*' with them to engage with a counselling relationship and that the 'communication to the client of the therapists empathic understanding

TABLE 7.1 Clues to identifying ego-states

	Nurturing parent	Controlling parent	Adult	Adapted child	Natural child
Behaviour	Warm and comforting Smiling Inviting Tactile Empathic body mirroring Caring Leaning forward	Frowning Finger-stabbing movements Thumping on table Non-verbal body responses – red face/neck Pulsating veins in neck Shaking Authoritative body language – crossed arms Impatient tapping of foot Tight-lipped and tense	Quiet and thoughtful Measured responses Alert/wide-eyed Sitting erect Looking interested	Tearful Closed body language Shouting Withdrawn Shaking Sniggering Childlike behaviours such as thumb sucking Sulking Demanding	Relaxed body language Fast movements Laughing Agile Giggling Spontaneous Creative cuddling toys Looking startled
Words	Well done I love you Great Good Let me do that for you You can do this	Should Ought You're useless Why can't you do this? Ridiculous Must Always Disapproving	How? What? Why? Absolutely Why not? Can you . . . ? I think . . . Seeking information Reasoned argument	I can't I'm scared I try Please Thank you I feel . . . Can I? Should I? I must/must not	WOW! This is fun I want I am happy I won't . . .
Voice	Soft Loving Comforting Concerned Over-sympathetic	Harsh Critical Patronising Disgusted Firm Condescending Cold	Monotone Precise Static Even tone	Whingey Quiet/introverted Defiant Placating Demanding Baby talk	Loud Excitable Energetic Happy Angry Sad
Feelings	Loving Empathic Sympathetic Joyful Maternal/paternal	Irritable Anger Judgemental Frustrated Protective	When in adult state, often no feelings are present	Frightened Anxious Angry Shame Guilt Warm, pleasant childhood feelings flooding back Feeling 'bad' Nervous	Elated Sad Excited Curious Delight Anger

Source: Developed from the original ideas of Berne (2010)

and unconditional positive regard is to a minimal degree achieved' (Rogers 1957: 96). We think that this applies equally to helping relationships.

As helpers, we will be keen to provide support and help to our clients, but this enthusiasm always needs to be balanced with an awareness of the limitations of this role. This is part of the development of our conscious competency.

Clients under the influence of alcohol or drugs

Your organisation may have clear guidelines and directives about whether you work with clients who are under the influence of alcohol or drugs. But if your client is heavily under the influence, you should consider whether he or she is able to engage in the helper/client relationship as it may mean that it is not be possible to set up and develop the relationship. If he or she is in a state of distress and his or her drinking or drug use is a reaction to this, we might gently suggest that we postpone the work until he or she feels better able to talk to us. We try to be empathic and non-judgemental, but equally we need to be in psychological contact with our clients in order for the helping role to be effective. It might become apparent that his or her intoxication may be part of a bigger problem, in which case we might consider signposting him or her to appropriate professional help. We need to make a judgement on this as soon as we realise the situation, as 'ploughing on' with our counselling skills and ignoring the situation is likely to cause further problems and misunderstandings. Those of us who work with addiction will know that how the addict experiences an initial awareness that there is a problem could very well be a life-saving experience. So our 'challenges' are both tentative and supportive.

Angry clients

Many of our students worry about working with a client who is angry. Of course, sometimes it may be helpful for a client to get in touch with some anger when he or she is examining his or her issues and difficult circumstances. We might even feel encouraged by this as an appropriate response to a difficult historical event or previous blind spots. It may be *appropriate anger*. However, it is *inappropriate* is when the anger is strongly directed at us. In our enthusiasm to help, we should not become a 'doormat' for our clients' feelings. However, it is our experience that 'angry' clients may be unaware about how intimidating their anger is. If it feels OK, we may consider giving this feedback in the form of self-disclosure. We can consider the client's anger within the TA ego states: is he or she in his or her *adapted child* or *controlling parent*? In which case, it may be helpful to the client to disclose how intimidating or difficult it is to be on the receiving end of his or her anger, and this often has the effect of defusing the situation. From our nurturing parent ego-state, we may respond by saying something such as 'I understand how angry you are at the moment, but shouting at me is not helpful. Shall we quietly explore what is making you so angry?'

We should not put up with unacceptable behaviour, and we always need to consider both ourselves and the client in the situation where we feel intimidated or threatened.

'Passive' or 'sent' clients

Some clients appear reluctant to engage in the helping relationship. These clients can respond with one-word answers, even to our open questions – 'Yes', 'No' or 'I don't know'. Again, a reflection on their ego-states and ours may help us to explore this block in the relationship. Are they in *adapted child* and, in response to this, are we feeling in *controlling parent*? It is often useful to return to the original contract. Is our client here willingly or is he or she there as a response to pressure from a manager or spouse? Clients who feel *sent* to see us may need to explore their feelings about this before continuing. They need to feel that they have entered into the helping relationship willingly or it is unlikely to be successful.

Dealing with our own strong emotions

We have talked a lot about the importance of empathy and being able to put ourselves into the other person's shoes. In some circumstances, listening to another person's sorrow and allowing ourselves to really connect with that person's sadness can be tough for the helper to sit alongside. For example, most of us would feel extremely sad as we hear a young mother talk of her life-limiting illness and how her greatest regret is leaving her two young children and not being able to see them grow up. As we incorporate the core conditions into our helping skills, we have learned to attune ourselves to our own feelings *and* have an understanding of what it might be like for that mother, even though we may not have had that experience ourselves. As caring helpers, we may connect with our emotions, either verbally or non-verbally, and our aim is that the client can see that he or she has been listened to and understood. We may also have experienced helpers who have let us know in different ways that they have been moved by what we have said and it can feel like an extremely respectful and rewarding experience.

However, when thinking more about our own self-care, it is important to be aware of our '*resonance*' when listening to and sharing clients' material. Resonance is when we hear a story and echoes of that story resonate with our world, our understanding and our emotions. It is different from empathy because with resonance we are connecting and identifying with our own stories, as opposed to seeing it or experiencing it from the other's perspectives. When we resonate with a client's story, we have a sense that it belongs to us, but we have yet to place either the cognitive thoughts or the emotional feelings that surround it to what we are hearing. It is often a bodily sensation that feels familiar but we do not know why. There can be a moment of identification ('I remember feeling this way when my dad died'), or it can be more of a vague sense or feeling ('As I listen to you telling me this, I am aware that I am feeling really shaky'). Quite often, resonance takes us by surprise – one moment you are listening to the client, the next you are overwhelmed by feelings and sensations that somehow feel too strong to be empathy. Resonance is a very interactive experience; it is not necessary for you to have shared the same experience as your client, rather something about the story that the client is telling connects with you on a very deep level and you are reminded of feelings from your own past experience(s). The importance of recognising resonance 'in the moment' is that we can make a conscious decision to put those feelings to one side, recognising them as our own, and focus back on the client. Once we have a better understanding of resonance and how it can crop up, we are better prepared to respond to it. There is nothing wrong with experiencing resonance with a client; it seems to be a very natural experience when it occurs, yet it is something that has to be managed within the session. It is also important to be reflective after a session where resonance has occurred and see if you can make any cognitive connections to the feelings you have felt. We can make use of our *internal supervisor* to try to recognise whether we are feeling resonance rather than empathy, and we can also discuss this with our learning partner as he or she may have had similar experiences to share. There could be occasions, however, when the resonance can be overwhelming and really affect us. We find ourselves thinking about our client's situation a lot of the time outside our helping relationship and feel very affected by it. A professional counsellor would take this to clinical supervision or personal therapy, and you may consider whether you have a similar resource available to you. Is this something you would discuss with your line manager? Do you have external supervision in your work situation? Is this problem beyond your expertise and do you need to refer this client on to an appropriate professional? (See Chapter 8 for more on this.)

GETTING IT WRONG AND ACCOUNTABILITY

There is a saying that 'we learn by our mistakes'. When we start to use our skills, we can worry about doing it wrong as we feel that making mistakes will have a detrimental effect on our client. We can feel 'consciously incompetent' and fear that we will upset or 'damage' our client in some way through our own lack of skills. If we recognise we have made a mistake through not understanding our client or responding with the 'wrong' skill, we can get back on track by saying just that, apologising to our client and asking him or her to repeat or explain what he or she said. Often, this has the effect of our client feeling more valued and listened to rather than if we lose the thread and pretend we are following him or her.

The following example is of an apparently well-meaning helper who is not actively listening or using her counselling skills appropriately. The helper appears friendly and empathic, but she is relating to her client as a friend and advice giver, imposing her values and not identifying the problem from the client's point of view. Consequently, the new meaning and possibilities are from the helper's perspective and the work is not collaborative.

EXAMPLE

You will now watch the video clip of this short session, paying particular attention to the helper and client's non-verbal communications, as well as what they say to each other. The following transcript includes our observations of the process and potential TA ego-states.

In the following exercise, we would like you to critique the session you have just watched. Using the transcript (Appendix 7), write comments on what you have observed. Then go on to consider the following questions and discuss with your learning partner.

VIDEO CLIP 7a

SESSION TO CRITIQUE:
Janie and Becky

> ### REFLECTIVE LEARNING JOURNAL EXERCISE
>
> What constructive feedback would you give the helper as the observer of this session?
>
> What do you understand about the client's process in this, and how would you have responded to her as a helper?
>
> Consider what skills you might have used in this scenario.
>
> Now compare your comments and observations with the transcript below.

TABLE 7.2 Transcript of Video Clip 7a: Session to critique – Janie and Becky

Content	Process	Skills
J: So, Becky, hi		
B: Hi		
J: So you were going to be talking about something you talked about before in counselling?	There is no evidence of a contract and agreement here (RSM)	
B: I saw a counsellor a while ago, I'm doing a major change in my life at the moment, and I've gone through so much of it, and that has been working really well, but there are still things I feel anxious about	The client is showing behaviours and using words that indicate she is in her adapted child ego-state	
J: Who was it that you saw before?	The helper is changing the subject. She is not attending or hearing key emotional prompts from the client. The question is also unethical, particularly in terms of confidentiality (BACP 2013)	
B: Why do you need to know her name? I only know her by her first name		
J: Well maybe not, I was just interested . . .	The question was not for the client, it was about the helper's curiosity	
B: I only knew her by her first name		
J: I just thought it might be someone I knew	Again, the helper has not acknowledged and appears not to have noticed the client's embarrassment or reluctance to pursue this question. The helper is purely on her own agenda and not demonstrating any empathic understanding	
B: I don't know (nervous laughter)		

table 7.2 continued

Content	Process	Skills
J: Um, um, I was just trying to work out if I said to my secretary about timing wise, but we are all right, carry on, sorry, sorry I've lost you there	There is no attempt by the helper to build rapport with the client. There are instant barriers to active listening and inattention. The non-verbal communication of the helper and looking at her watch compounds this. The helper is using body language consistent with her being in her controlling parent ego-state	
B: Yes, I'm making a major change in a couple of months so there are still a few things that I'm still anxious about		
J: Yeah, OK, major change, do you know we are both in the middle of a major change, aren't we?	A 'me too' moment that deflects back to the helper. She is not listening or attending to her client's body language. Although 'major change' is reflected back, there is complete lack of empathy from the helper and the self-disclosure is inappropriate	
B: Yeah		
J: Cos we both know each other and we both know that we are going though that situation, that is really funny, really funny, because I feel, I feel about that change and I'm finding that really difficult, because I know, I just know what you are going through. I really do, so yeah, say a bit more about it, what's going on?	The dual relationship is now impacting detrimentally on the relationship. The helper is absorbed in self-interest and there is no collaborative working. The helper has shifted to her adapted child ego-state	
B: Well, I think it coincides with other changes in my life at the moment, because I've got two children – they're not children now, they are young adults and one is planning on moving out and the other one is going through change from school to college, so it seems like everything is changing at once . . .		

table 7.2 continued

Content	Process	Skills
J: What subjects are they going to be doing?	Total change of subject. Again, it is the helper's curiosity, and not of benefit to the client. There is no attempt at problem identification from the perspective of the client. Adult ego-stage	
B: What subjects?		
J: Yes	The helper has not picked up on the client's expression from this change of subject	
B: Oh gosh, I don't know, my son, er, they take so many subjects at GCSE these days and I think he is hopeful to take his A levels		
J: He is such a nice lad, you must be so proud of him	The helper again brings in their dual relationship to put words in the client's mouth. Nurturing parent ego-state	
B: I am, thank you		
J: Yeah. That's fantastic, yeah, and the kids leaving, that's a good thing	Second-guessing what the client is thinking. There are ethical considerations around autonomy	
B: Yeah		
J: You'll have a bit more time		
B: Yeah, it's a good thing, really positive, it's time, the right age and everything, but you can't help feeling kind of a bit strange that everything is changing all at the same time. I feel . . .		
J: But change is good, change is good, Becky, that's what it is all about really. And you and I are both being therapists and we work with change with other people so it's positive, and you know at the end of this it's going to be absolutely fine. You know it's going to be fine, going to be good	The helper is filtering what the client is saying and attempting to impose her own value judgement on to the client (non-autonomy). The helper is attempting to move into advice giving and having the 'right' answers for the client. Negative nurturing parent ego-state (overbearing)	

table 7.2 continued

Content	Process	Skills
B: You know, I think that's half the problem, I think that's it, I don't know it's going to be fine. I don't feel that. My head tells me everything is going to be fine, but actually I don't feel that everything is going to be fine. I haven't got that confidence. I wish I did. I think that's the major issue as I don't have that confidence that everything is going to be fine cos I've never not been employed so it feels really weird	The client is still in adapted child	
J: My old mum always says that it will be all right in the end. That phrase she always used to say, 'It'll be all right, it will all come out in the wash' she always used to say. And it's great to think about that, to thinking about the future being a positive thing. You know, we have to go forward, you know, and do it together and that. I think positive attitudes are really, really helpful. Don't you?	The helper appears oblivious to the client's non-verbal communication. She is not so much advice giving, but pressurising the client. Ethical consideration of non-maleficence (BACP 2013). The helper has shifted to mimicking her own parental influences from her nurturing parent ego-state	
B: Um, *(nervous giggle)* um, I like to think I do, yeah. . . . J: Yeah		
B: I'm quite a positive person, but at the moment I feel anxious, you know, I don't feel positive. There are days when I can't wait and it's all new and I really embrace that, but there are days when I wake up feeling quite anxious actually. My world is changing to such an extent	Remains in adapted child	
J: I don't know why you feel like that, I really don't, because you have got so much going for you, you know. Remember that conference we were in the other day, do you remember that together?	The helper pulls back to the dual relationship and changes the subject, and there is no collaborative working or understanding. Language coming from controlling parent ego-state	
B: Hmm		
J: And that you were so positive and so great about that, you know. If you could pick up some of that, that would be fantastic, that would be really good	In her attempt to encourage the client, the helper appears oblivious to her distress, and there is no attempt at problem identification from the client's perspective	

table 7.2 continued

Content	Process	Skills
B: Yeah, I do think that sometimes, I think I've got all these years' experience		
J: Yeah		
B: And I've got everything to work towards . . . and I still feel anxious, you know, I don't think that goes away		
J: (*talking over client*) You've got so much more experience than I have, you've got so much more going for you than I have. And I worry about that cos I just feel, oh, I don't know about you and I working together, I would just drag you back really. I mean I don't really feel like, I'm not sure how that is . . . you just don't know what you have going for you, you really don't, honestly	The helper has now missed many prompts that the client is giving her. The client has now used the word 'anxious' a number of times. Notice the power differential where the client is trying to remain polite to the overbearing helper while still attempting to repeat her concerns. The helper is working only with her own agenda of solutions and not exploring different possibilities or perspectives. The helper talks of her own anxieties and has moved to adapted child	
B: Hmm, yeah, I suppose, hmm yeah, I do try to stay positive, a lot of the time I am, but then there are times when I just feel anxious about it all and I don't really know how to overcome that		
J: No, well, I guess, I think you do know in yourself, you do know how to be confident with those things, you are very good at helping other people with it. It's just about taking that out and using those things yourself, that would be really good, really good, that would be fantastic	Again, the client has stated that she is 'anxious', and again the helper has remained oblivious to the client's needs. She has changed the subject, advised the client from her own opinions and had the right answers for the client	
J: And I'm really sorry, but that is all we have time for, so we need to move on. So we can perhaps make another time to talk about this because it's been fantastic meeting up with you and talking about that again, it's really great, thanks	How 'fantastic' was this session for the client! The client's facial expressions and body language reflect this	
B: OK, thanks		

Now re-watch the video while paying attention to the following analysis of the session by the helper.

Analysis of session

While the client brought real material to this session, we hope you have now realised that the helper was role-playing this session! These parodies on counselling sessions are useful to critique and to consider how we might have done things differently and what skills we might have appropriately used to provide a more empathic and skilful session. If we look closely at this session, it can be seen that there were, in fact, some counselling skills included, but the issues arise with the application of these skills – for example, there was some warmth expressed by the helper, as well as challenges and lots of self-disclosure, but, as an attempt to 'develop the relationship', these were inappropriate, unhelpful and appeared to pressurise the client rather than mutually exploring the issue.

The helper begins the session with her body language *closed* and un-empathic. Her arms are crossed; she frowns quite a lot in the beginning of the session and is also speaking quite quickly (see Chapter 2).

The helper could have done more skilful and empathic work had she responded to the strong verbal and non-verbal prompts that the client was giving. The client repeated some strong *feeling* words that would have been helpful to reflect back to her. Let us examine the use of these emotive words:

'Anxious' is used six times within this session

The helper never uses this word herself, and when the client is expressing this anxiety through both her choice of words and her non-verbal communication the helper ignores it and tries to problem-solve and change the subject. If you watch the client's hesitation and facial expressions, it is not difficult to see her discomfort. But it is interesting to note that she does not challenge the helper on this, and we might consider how this relates to the expert role and power differential between helper and client.

'Change' or 'changing' is used by the client seven times

The helper does pick up on this and reflect it back, but she uses the reflection to impose her own value judgements on the client, as well as using the word to explore her own issues about change and hijacking her client's session – for example, 'change is good', 'I'm finding it difficult' and 'I just *know* what you are going through'.

There is no attempt at problem identification; in fact, the helper seems too keen to instantly solve the problem! The core conditions are not present and there is an absence of empathy and respect. The questions that the helper asks appear to be for her own interest and take the client away from the subject that she wishes to discuss. When this happens, you may notice that the client hesitates and laughs nervously – for example, when the helper asks about the client's previous counsellor.

The helper has not established a contract or prepared for the session when she stops the client at the beginning of the session to think about whether she has checked timing with her secretary. If more preparation time had been taken 'setting up the relationship', then this interruption would not have been necessary. The client is nodding nervously when she talks about her own changes; there is no evidence of the helper getting to know the client or listening. She does ask the client to 'tell her a bit more about it', but it is evident that the helper is not listening when she then goes on to change the subject on to the client's children's choice of school subjects. The helper is continually talking over and interrupting the client.

When the helper is trying to placate the client to tell her that 'everything is going to be fine', you may notice a fleeting expression of annoyance on the client's face – this continues as the helper talks about her mother's 'sayings'. The closed question 'Don't you think?' gives the client little room to disagree. On the surface, the helper might appear friendly and encouraging, but there is no evidence of collaborative problem identification. Even though the client is agreeing that it would be helpful to have confidence in the future, she continues to tell the helper that she 'still feels anxious'. In response, the helper again interrupts and brings the subject back to herself, listening selectively to what the client is saying. The self-disclosure around the helper's own lack of experience and worries was inappropriate and disrespectful. Although the helper holds silence at this point, she appears totally unaware of the client's struggle and distress, and continues to try to impose goals with no deeper empathy or intuition. By the end of this short session, the client has practically stopped responding altogether and with her quietly spoken 'OK', she appears to sit lower in her chair with her shoulders dropped.

REFLECT, PRACTISE AND EVALUATE

How did the helper's analysis compare with your own?

Reflect on your learning from these exercises.

Discuss and compare this experience with your learning partner.

With your learning partner, take it in turns to have a session where you are distracted and/or unresponsive to your client. Do not make this too obvious or fake, but think about something else while your client is talking. Stop the session when you feel the relationship has broken down. Notice how quickly this happens.

Critically evaluate what you did and how it felt.

Video your skills session

MODEL BOX

In this chapter, we have referred to:

- The ego-state model (Berne, cited in Stewart and Joines 1987)
- Robinson's competency cycle (Howell 1982)

SUMMARY

- The use of counselling skills can have a powerful impact on the depth of the helper/client interaction.
- Helpers need to learn to evaluate their own levels of competency and assess how this relates to their client work. This includes considering dual roles.
- Helpers need to develop an awareness and broaden their knowledge of difference and diversity to work in a culturally appropriate manner.
- An awareness of TA ego-states can facilitate interactions and improve communication.
- Reflexive practice is an integral part of the helping relationship and part of the ongoing learning process.

Chapter 8
Becoming a reflexive practitioner

You will have now been using your personal journal to regularly reflect on your learning throughout this book. You will have begun to recognise any changes in yourself and have hopefully been monitoring your achievements and learning edges. You may have challenged yourself through examining your beliefs, values and assumptions. This is mainly carried out at a 'conscious' level where you are considering these insights to better reflect on their implications.

You are now at a stage of competency where you can begin to integrate all these aspects into your work. This form of self awareness is often referred to as using your 'internal supervisor', and you may already be familiar with this internal voice telling you which of your helping sessions have gone well and where you may not have felt so effective. As your counselling skills are more firmly embedded, you can begin to 'multitask' by incorporating reflective practice into your work and by listening to your internal supervisor in more depth.

This chapter of the book will examine:

- How do we learn?
- What do we mean by reflective/reflexivity?
- How can we understand ourselves better?
- The levels of reflection
- Applying a model of reflection to our case work

TEACHING

HOW DO WE LEARN?

The educational philosopher John Dewey introduced us to the concept of 'reflective thought' in 1910. Since that time, numerous philosophers and writers have developed his ideas, in particular with the introduction of the book *The Reflective Practitioner* by Donald Schön in 1983. Later, in 1984, we became aware of the term 'experiential learning' through Kolb's *Cycle of Experiential Learning*. Experiential learning has its origins in the work of Dewey, Lewin and Piaget, and Kolb drew together the characteristics of these models to define the nature of experiential learning into his own model.

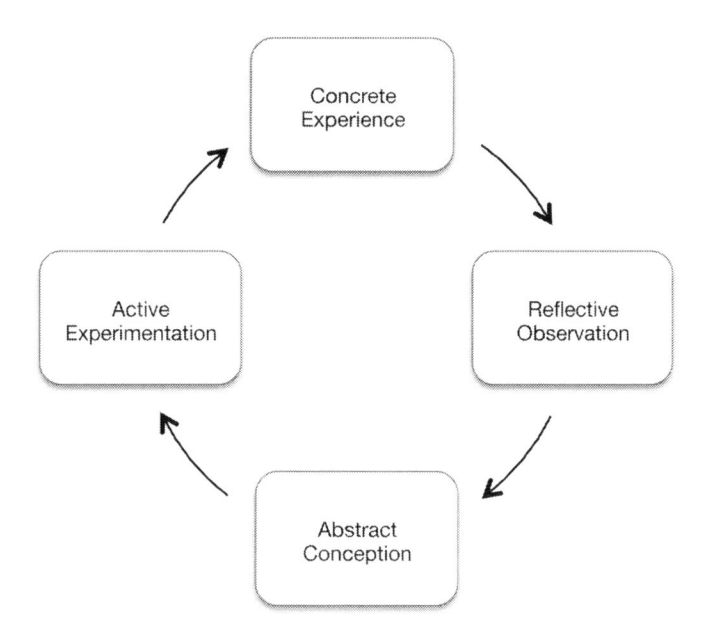

FIGURE 8.1 Kolb model of experiential learning
Source: Adapted from Kolb (1984)

Kolb suggested that if learners are to be effective, they must be able to:

> involve themselves fully, openly, and without bias to new experiences (CE). They must be able to reflect on and observe their experiences from many perspectives (RO). They must be able to create concepts that integrate their observations into logical sound theories (AC), and they must be able to use these theories to make decisions and solve problems (AE).
>
> (Kolb 1984: 30)

Honey and Mumford (2006) expanded upon Kolb's model, observing that different personality types prefer a particular learning style that fits with the four stages of the cycle of experiential learning. They created a questionnaire for people to find out what their personality type is and relate it to their learning style. For instance, someone who has been categorised as an *activist* would prefer the concrete experience stage of the cycle as he or she enjoys doing and experiencing; a *reflector* would prefer the reflective observation stage where he or she can reflect and ponder on the experience; the *theorist* wants to stay at the abstract conceptualisation stage to understand the underlying patterns, theories and relationships within the experience; and the *pragmatist* likes the active experimentation stage where he or she can test out whether the process works. While we do not wholeheartedly buy into this kind of grouping or stereotyping, it can be useful to identify your own learning preference as often we get trapped in learning via one stage of the cycle, and it is important that we privilege all aspects of the cycle. To discover your learning style, you can complete

```
      Stage 1
      Activist

Stage 4              Stage 2
Pragmatist           Reflector

      Stage 3
      Theorist
```

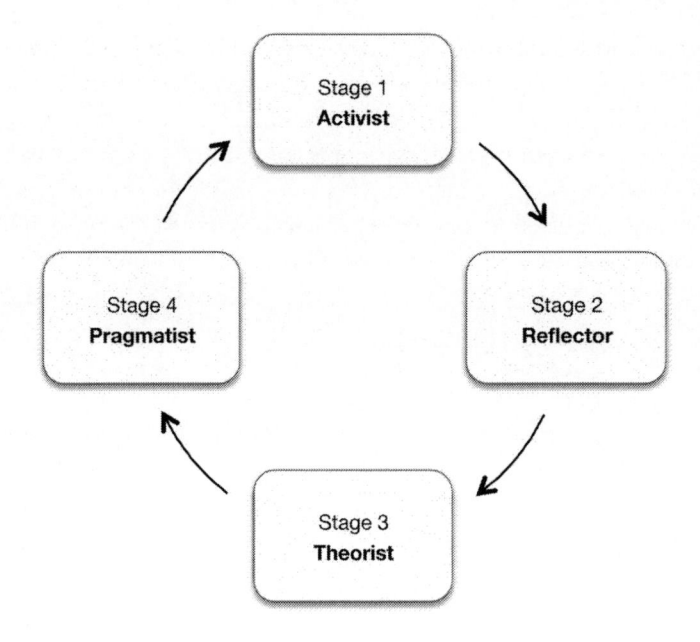

FIGURE 8.2 Learning styles

Source: Adapted from Honey and Mumford (2006)

the Honey and Mumford questionnaires, which are accessible in print (Honey and Mumford 2006) and online.

The way we learn is a very individual process, and we all do it differently. We do not enter a new experience as a blank page; we bring with us all our previous experiences of learning. We may have learned things in the past through traditional educational methods where you are taught a way of doing something, which, if followed without deviation, always leads to the same outcome. The focus of this type of 'destinational learning' is on the outcome and reaching the end of the process, without critically assimilating the process, but following the directions of an 'expert' or authoritative figure.

With experiential learning, the emphasis is on the process of learning:

> ideas are not fixed and immutable elements of thought but are formed and re-formed through experience.
>
> (Kolb 1984: 26)

We refer to this type of learning as 'transformative learning'. Mezirow (1997: 5) refers to transformative learning as:

> The process of effecting change in a frame of reference. Adults have acquired a coherent body of experience – associations, concepts, values, feelings, conditioned responses – frames of reference that define their life world. Frames of reference are the structures of assumptions through which we understand our experiences.

Transformative learning is learning that transforms our thinking, beliefs, views, attitudes, values, interests and practices about the world, others and ourselves. The nature of this kind of learning can be rewarding, evocative, academically challenging and sometimes painful. Transformative learning takes what we already know from our past experience, and allows us to reflect upon it, conceptualise it and apply it in a way that makes sense of the new experience. We question our old assumptions, allow ourselves to think differently about the values and beliefs that we may have held strongly in the past, and we create new meaning and knowledge that we apply to enhance and change our existing knowledge and skills. Transformative learning enables us to become autonomous learners and to think about learning through our own frames of reference.

> [O]ne's job as an educator is not only to implant new ideas but also to dispose of or modify old ones. In many cases, resistance to new ideas stems from their conflict with old beliefs that are inconsistent with them. If the education process begins by bringing out the learner's beliefs and theories, examining and testing them, and then integrating the new, more refined ideas into the person's belief systems, the learning process will be facilitated.
>
> (Kolb 1984: 29)

WHAT DO WE MEAN BY REFLECTIVE/REFLEXIVE?

It is important that we develop our ability to reflect in order to inform and develop our helping role. Understanding how this process works and how we learn can help us appreciate how important the use of reflection is to our learning.

At the beginning of this book, when you started your learning journal, you began the practice of *reflection and reflective learning*. This is a conscious process carried out at a cognitive level, which can be both a private internal process, or a more external shared process. You may have reflected through poetry, art, imaging and journaling, and you can decide whether you share this, explore it with others in more detail or keep it to yourself for personal reflection. While reflection is a conscious process, it also opens us up to connecting with our unconscious processing.

As a helper, we use the skill of *reflecting* back to our clients and we know that this can enable them to see parts of themselves or their responses and patterns that may have been out of their immediate awareness. They can come to understand some of their biases and prejudices and, when we draw their attention to it, they may gain insights through, for example, an awareness of the discrepancies between their body language and the emotional experience they are describing.

When we use *reflective practice* for ourselves, we may also challenge ourselves on previously held assumptions and, like our clients, we may be able to make new links between our inner feelings and outside experiences and relationships. We can also become more conscious of when we hold different world views from others and where we may want to open up our thinking to other possibilities and alternative concepts. These are not just personal views; they could also be political and cultural.

Reflection on action (Schön 1983) is when we turn experience into knowledge through retrospective thinking, self-examination and critique in order to improve our work and discover ways we might do things differently.

We might refer to this process as developing our 'know-how' and Polyani (1962) (cited in Rolfe 1997) called this 'tacit knowledge'. Tacit knowing is something that is either hard to put into words or something that we are not consciously aware of – a sort of subconscious expertise or intuitive grasp. It does not magically pop up out of nowhere, but is a result of the experience we gain from a mind-formed experience. Experiences are added on to, or selected from, other experiences in order to help us to gain a subconscious awareness of the 'right' thing to do. So an expert would be a reflective practitioner who has drawn from his or her experience in order to inform and develop his or her intuitive grasp for his or her work.

Reflection in action (Schön 1983) is thinking on your feet. This may involve more creative problem-solving drawn from an accumulation of experiences in order to form into and develop different actions. It is practice-generating theory and theory-modifying practice. This can also be referred to as *reflexivity*.

Being *reflexive* is when we apply our reflective thinking to our actions, communications and understandings. We bring it into the 'now' by simultaneous awareness, action or response. If we can appreciate this process, we can now work effectively using our *internal supervisor*. As we are talking and responding to our client, we will be noticing our reflective inner dialogue and we will be learning to apply it to our skills and relationships. We will be working both with the uniqueness of our client's situation and also with previous similar experiences of helping or client issues we may have encountered. *Reflexivity* is an action; we become aware of our inner responses and have choices about how we might use them. We can make informed choices about where to respond, how to respond or where we might not respond based on a developed awareness of relevant experiences. Reflexivity is built from past reflections on action. Reflexivity requires a lot of concentration, focus and use of our tacit knowing, or internal supervisor, to focus on the present situation and individuality of each of our clients.

An example of this may be the client that comes to us, as a manager, to discuss his or her recent redundancy notice. We may have experience of this form of helping, in which case we have an understanding that this can be a devastating experience for some people. Through reflection on action, we have honed our skills and learned how we can offer our clients as much empathy as possible. We may be consciously aware of our tendency to frown when we concentrate and we will be aware to relax our face and body language. We may also have discovered that our own experience of redundancy in the past makes it hard for us to stay impartial, and because of this we know we can feel angry for others in this situation, so we make an effort not to let this intrude into the helping relationship.

The client surprises us by strolling into the room with a big smile on his face, shakes our hand heartily and reassures us he is fine and his redundancy is not bothering him at all. Our internal supervisor's voice may now be wondering whether this is in fact the case, or whether our client is putting up a protective front. We might be aware of situations where bereaved clients have had a similar reaction, or we might have read about denial in cases of loss. At the same time, we might also be considering whether our client is genuinely not fazed by the experience. This is the point when we might notice our gut reactions. The situation might not feel right, his or her reaction might feel unrealistic, or alternatively we might consider that it could be the case that he or she hated their job and are very relieved to leave. We wait and notice our reactions; we may decide to bide our time and see where the situation goes, or we may instinctually decide to comment on his or her cheeriness in the face of job loss. Our decisions may be subtle and subconscious, but they will be based on our reflection on action and 'felt' experience or tacit knowing. We draw together the threads of knowledge and experience and use them to make considered decisions. All of these thoughts and considerations may happen very quickly, almost at the back of our awareness, but they will impact the choice of skills we use next, and we begin to use both knowledge and reflexive practice to plan the most appropriate helping response in future scenarios.

Boniface (2002) undertook a collaborative research inquiry with three different groups of occupational therapists, with the aim to determine what occupational therapists understood by 'reflection', and what encourages and what hinders that reflection.

> Reflection can be viewed in a number of ways: as a way of thinking (Dewey 1933); as natural evolution of humans (Habermas 1971); as a structure for action (Mezirow 1981; Fish and Twinn 1997); and as an evaluation tool. However, when used for evaluating the therapist's work, reflection can tend to stop at a somewhat superficial level. Such superficial reflection leads to an evaluation of a therapist's practice and work, without leading the therapist to evaluate him or herself as a therapist.
>
> (Boniface 2002: 294)

Two of the key findings of the study were that 'reflection can be taught, but there needs to be a spark of ability present' and 'reflection should lead to challenge or confirmation of belief systems'. So it is useful here to think about your own 'spark of ability' and to look at the different structures that will enable you to learn how to become a more reflective practitioner at a less superficial and more challenging level.

HOW CAN WE UNDERSTAND OURSELVES BETTER?

> O wad some Power the giftie gie us, to see oursels as ithers see us!
>
> (Burns 1786)

Developing our self-awareness is important in the helping relationship as it enables us to differentiate between the thoughts and feelings that belong to us (our material) and the material that belongs to the person we are helping. This helps us to maintain the working alliance and hold the professional boundaries. Self-awareness enables us to become aware of our own values, assumptions and prejudices, and to make choices about what we do with them. When we develop greater clarity around our thoughts and feelings, we are able to communicate clearly with the other person, rather than having to think about what needs to be filtered or shared.

As we use our reflective practice to develop our self-awareness, we can look at different ways of seeing ourselves, and understanding what is known to us and what remains subconscious or hidden to others, and sometimes ourselves. A useful tool for this is Johari's window (Luft and Ingham 1955), which is a way of exploring the four basic areas of ourselves. It was initially introduced in a presentation on group dynamics and interpersonal relationships given by two American psychologists, Joe Luft and Harry Ingham, hence the name derived from their first names Joe and Harry (Jo-hari). Using this as a model for personal development through reflective practice, we can begin a journey of self-exploration. We discover aspects of ourselves that are in and out of our awareness and see how others currently and potentially see us:

- the public or open area;
- the private or hidden area;
- the blind area; and
- the unknown or undiscovered area.

The *public area* is what everyone, including yourself, sees in you. You are usually happy to discuss this, and most of the time you share others' views about this aspect of yourself. If you are a member of a social networking site, these are the aspects you might include in your profile.

The *private or hidden area* are the parts of yourself that you are aware of but would rather keep hidden from others as you do not want this information to be freely known. These might be parts of yourself that you consider to be a weakness or that may make you look vulnerable. They may also be assets that you have but hide through modesty.

The *blind area* are the parts that you are not aware of, similar to the blind spots of your clients; they are known to others but not to yourself. These may be good qualities that others see in us or less favourable aspects of our personality. For example, we may think we are not so clever but others may recognise our intelligence. Others may see that we can be a bit stingy where we consider ourselves economical!

The *unknown or undiscovered area* are the parts of yourself that are out of your own awareness and are also unknown to others. There may have been times in your life when you have discovered something about yourself that you had no idea about. You may have now discovered that you have real 'green fingers' as a gardener when you live in a house with a garden, when previously you would not have considered it to be something you could do. It was out of your conscious awareness. When you discover this, this aspect of yourself moves from the hidden area of self to either the private or public area of self.

Knowing that there are these various parts of ourselves, some discoverable and some less so, will hopefully leave us open to a sense of curiosity about ourselves. Through these higher levels of reflection, we have the potential to develop further and gain insights into aspects of ourselves that were previously part of our blind area. Through this reflective practice, we discover more about ourselves. Some of these revelations may be welcome – others less so. But we see this as a welcome process of our evolution rather than an exercise in self-criticism. If we are open to these revelations, our Johari's window changes, becoming an exciting and ongoing journey of our personal and professional development.

	Known to self	Not known to self
Known to others	Open/free area	Blind area
Not known to others	Hidden area	Unknown area

FIGURE 8.3 Johari's window

REFLECTIVE LEARNING JOURNAL EXERCISE

In the introduction, we asked you to complete the following exercise:

Using photography, painting, poems or stories or any other metaphor to represent a portrait of you at the beginning of your journey, begin your reflective learning journal by asking yourself the following questions:

- Who am I?
- Where am I at this moment in time?
- Where have I come from?

We invite you to look back in your journal and recall what you put. What are your thoughts and feelings now about where you were in your journey then? How has this changed? Complete the exercise again today as you come to the end of this book. What were your blind areas? Do you now understand any parts of you that were unknown to you at the time of completing the exercise? We hope you discover something new and different about yourself, as we have in sharing this journey with you.

THE LEVELS OF REFLECTION

There are several 'layers' to reflective practice. Boniface (2002) drew together various models (Mezirow 1981; Schön 1983; Fish and Twinn 1997) to differentiate between the different levels of reflection.

TABLE 8.1 Levels of reflection (Boniface)

1 Setting the scene	Lowest level of reflection
2 Telling the story of the event to be reflected upon	Lowest level of reflection
3 Identifying critical occurrences	Lowest level of reflection
4 Linking the story and critical occurrences to previous events or knowledge	Middle level of reflection
5 Identifying feelings associated with the story or critical occurrences	Middle level of reflection
6 Identifying and challenging blind spots associated with those feelings such as prejudices	Middle level of reflection
7 Identifying what has been learned from the reflection	Middle level of reflection
8 Deciding whether a change is now necessary as a result of reflection	Middle level of reflection
9 Identifying and critiquing the belief system upon which our actions are based	High level of reflection (reflecting on reflection)

Most of the time, we are involved in the 'doing' of our work and we have little time to think about being reflective. Many of our jobs do not include reflective time within their daily timescales. Often, we reflect at the lowest levels of reflection, to enable us to quickly move forward to our next action:

- What has just happened?
- What do I need to think about?
- Are there any issues I need to think about?

As we allow ourselves more time to focus and reflect on our experience, we are able to reflect at a higher level:

- How does that experience relate to other experiences I have had?
- How do I feel about the new experience and how does it relate to past experiences?
- What have I learned from exploring the experience in more depth?
- Are there any changes I now need to make to put any new learning and understanding into future practice?

On occasions, an experience or action makes us stop in our tracks and we have the urge to stop and reflect at the highest level – often referred to in counselling as the 'light bulb' moment. We take time to think about the gaps in our knowledge – the blind spots where we notice that the experience or new learning does not seem to fit with our sense of knowing, either intellectually or in a more tacit way. Our reflection becomes more purposeful and we spend time questioning our values and belief systems and ponder on how the experience has impacted on these. It is usually after such reflection that we really feel that we understand the experience and we can therefore act upon our new learning with a sense of confidence and achievement.

the simple perception of experience is not sufficient for learning; something must be done with it. Similarly, transformation alone cannot represent learning, for the must be something to be transformed, some state or experience that is being acted upon.

(Kolb 1984: 42)

There are various frameworks or models that you can use to help you be more reflective/reflexive in your role as a helper. It may well be that we only reach the level of reflection that enables us to make choices about changes that we need to make to help us to work better.

How we reflect is a unique experience, but the frameworks provided by theorists may guide you to understand the reflective process better. Models or frameworks for reflection must be used flexibly to fit your own learning style.

EXAMPLE

Here is an example of our experience of writing this book, using the levels of reflection model (Boniface 2002) as a tool for our reflection.

1 Setting the scene

Janie and Becky are writing a book together. Both are new to writing manuscripts that will be published, but they are familiar with both academic writing and reflective journaling.

2 Telling the story of the event to be reflected upon

We initially had a contract in April 2012 from a publisher to write the book by January 2014. It was a joint authorship and our aim was to write a book to capture the experience of teaching counselling skills, through the use of video clips and teaching materials.

3 Identifying critical occurrences

One of the major occurrences was the change of publisher midway through the writing process. Another was negotiating the timing of writing around the submission of student dissertations, a critical point in the academic year. The main tension throughout the process was our differing work styles and the way that we approached our writing.

4 Linking the story and critical occurrences to previous events or knowledge

It seemed important to us both that we did not lose all our experience of teaching together over the last 10 years, and we wanted to record in some way the things that we had learned and ensure that our knowledge and experience was passed on. Writing the book was a way of ensuring this happened, and it was therefore more than an 'academic' piece of writing. We were also aware that this was a critical time in the academic calendar, where all students would be submitting their dissertations and this would be a great pull on our time and resources. One important aspect that we needed to negotiate throughout was the different ways that we approached the writing process and the impact this had on our joint authorship and business relationship.

5 Identifying feelings associated with the story or critical occurrences

We knew that by the end of the writing process, we would have left the university where we were both working. The book became about offering a legacy of our time and experiences spent teaching. It therefore felt exposing – that we were sharing ourselves with the reader and therefore open to appraisal and criticism. The times when the book chapters went to the reviewers were tense and our confidence and self-esteem dipped. However, receiving the constructive feedback that the reviewers returned was affirming and we were open to reviewing our chapters based on the feedback, which felt collaborative and liberating.

There were also practical events that caused us high levels of anxiety and stress. While most of our writing was done outside of our academic time, trying to continue to write in the evenings while being at the busiest time of the academic year was impossible, and we both realised that we needed to concentrate on getting the students through the academic process and leave the writing until after all students had submitted.

As we finished at the university, we both felt that we had fulfilled our duties to the students and now was the time to concentrate fully on the writing of the book. Instead of it feeling like a drag and a chore, we once again became excited about the process, with time to dedicate to the task without feeling pulled in different directions.

The change in publisher became a smooth transition that, despite our initial concerns, caused little anxiety and led to feelings of delight at the reputable final choice.

Negotiating our different ways of writing was much trickier. One of us is an 'activist' who prefers doing and experiencing, and the other a 'reflector' whose preference was to observe and reflect (Honey and Mumford 2006: 19). It was difficult to privilege both ways of working, and this caused some frustration and irritation for both of us.

6 Identifying what has been learned from the reflection

The main thing that we learned was the necessity to prioritise and acknowledge what needs to be done and when. That it is impossible to do everything at the same time. Also to recognise that achieving emotional stability is really important when there is so much change and transition happening at once. To notice there are times when it is appropriate to pause and to regain equilibrium before pressing on. To recognise each other's differences. To look out for signs of stress in the other and to negotiate a way of working through the process that fits both learning styles.

7 Deciding whether a change is now necessary as a result of reflection

Once we had an understanding of where the friction lay in our collaborative writing experience, we needed to implement a plan that enabled us both to feel secure in reaching deadlines but that allowed space to work in a way that felt comfortable to both. Part of this required us to discover and discuss where we were individually within the process and share honest and congruent feedback.

8 Identifying and challenging blind spots associated with those feelings or prejudices

This needed to be reflected upon together. We felt it was important that we both supported each other in looking for and being able to identify our blind spots. Individually, we went for coaching support to help us do this and then we went for coaching support together. The knowledge we gained from those experiences had a profound effect on our relationship. We were able to identify that, under stress, we went to opposite ends of the spectrum – one of us being motivated through altruistic and nurturing thinking and the other through assertive and directive thinking. This knowledge gave us an empathic understanding of the other's position and allowed us to accept and embrace these differences.

9 Identifying and critiquing the belief system upon which our actions are based

It takes time to identify a belief system upon which our actions are based. These are often at a very unconscious level. It was enlightening for both of us to realise the value base of our approach to becoming business partners. The *activist* discovered that she needed to be less independent, to slow down and reflect more on the process and place trust in her business partner's way of working. The *reflector* became insightful to the fact that, when under pressure, she had a tendency to give over her 'power' to others and 'go with the flow'. Through this, she realised that she had an overdeveloped sense of responsibility based on an inherited value base of putting others before herself. She began to think about strategies that she could use to privilege her own desires and needs, and be collaborative and aware of the needs of others.

APPLYING A MODEL OF REFLECTION TO OUR CASE WORK

In Chapter 7, we reflected on a 'session to critique' (p. 181), examining this from the perspective of skills application and stages of relationship. In order to demonstrate the use of reflective practice, we will look again at this session, applying Gibbs' model of reflection (Gibbs 1998) to examine what feelings the helper (Janie) was experiencing, what she thought was happening in the sessions and what her learning was from this session for future reference and/or application. Gibbs very helpfully breaks down the stages of reflection into questions we can ask ourselves and explore. In the example that follows, the helper (Janie) has answered the questions (in italics) in relation to this helping session.

A brief summary of Gibbs' model

Stage 1: We set the scene in detail, rather like a play with a plot and players. This starts the reflective process and guides the associated imagery.

Stage 2: We start to develop our awareness of the situation by exploring our thoughts and feelings more deeply.

Stage 3: We move into evaluating or critiquing our session. It is important to find a balance between areas for development and acknowledging our strengths.

Stage 4: Through further analysis we break down the session by examining our feelings and insights in even more detail. We may go back between stages 3 and 4 in order to do this thoroughly and effectively.

Stage 5: Having explored all the previous stages, we are now able to evaluate whether we might have done things differently. This stage needs honesty and self-awareness.

Stage 6: Action plan. We now project about future similar occurrences or situations. We could be happy with our session and feel it was effective and a good template for future work, or we might conclude that we would work differently in future. This we bring forward into our learning, and the process can be gone through again with future work to further hone our expertise.

EXAMPLE

Here is an example of Gibbs' model applied to the 'session to critique' from Chapter 7.

Stage 1: description of the event

Describe in detail the event you are reflecting on.

Include, for example, where were you; who else was there; why were you there; what were you doing; what were other people doing; what was the context of the event; what happened; what was your part in this; what parts did the other people play; what was the result.

In an attempt to replicate the teaching models that we have used within numerous skills training courses, we included a session to critique in this handbook. Becky brought *real* material and I (Janie) was not aware beforehand what the issue might be. We were being filmed in a studio setting and the only person in the room with us was the cameraman. After the camera was turned off, Becky joked with me that I was 'far too convincing', and this felt quite a relief to be back into our usual relationship.

Stage 2: feelings and thoughts (self-awareness)

At this stage, try to recall and explore those things that were going on inside your head. Include:

How you were feeling when the event started?
The thoughts that were going through my head were to tell myself not to be phased by the situation, but there was also an anxiety about how many 'takes' we might need to do and that this might have an impact on Becky. I was very consciously aware that this was not 'pretend' for her, and was a real issue she was bringing. I began to notice a real feeling of inner conflict and discomfort when turning off my usual empathic responses.

However, I am used to working with Becky and demonstrating skills in front of classes of students, as well as sessions for them to critique, so I felt reasonably comfortable with the setting.

What you were thinking about at the time?
Of course this was in front of a camera and I was conscious of the less usual scenario of a cameraman in the room with us and the microphones and lights. This felt a bit strange but, as I do in the classroom with the students, I attempted to fade him out of my awareness and concentrate on my client. I think I am quite good at concentrating on my clients and tuning out outside distractions and noise as I have good focus. It occurs to me writing this that playing the piano and meditation helps with that concentration and focused attention. I am not sure if I had really made that connection so clearly before now.

What I had in mind was doing the opposite of what I would normally do, but not to make it too obvious by being cold and detached, but attempting a sort of unskilled empathy by not using the skills that I would normally use.

I consciously closed my body language by folding my arms and waving my hands around a lot. I was also frowning and interrupting.

How did it make you feel?
I found it surprisingly hard emotionally, particularly as I was aware of how important this issue is to Becky. I didn't really like myself in this role. I was trying to frown and look distracted, and I felt, at that point, not genuine. Initially, I think Becky was quite taken aback by my responses and I thought she might laugh but as we went on it felt like she was quite annoyed with me.

How did other people make you feel?
Watching Becky's facial expressions when I interrupted her or changed the subject was really horrible. I felt really uncomfortable in my stomach and quite cruel. I realise that I respond strongly to facial expressions on my client and I am aware that I can recognise quite subtle aspects of this. So 'turning this off' and doing the opposite took effort.

How did you feel about the outcome of the event?
By the end of the session, I was beginning to feel like a real bully. Becky was being really polite but at that exact moment I felt like she didn't really like me at all! I felt the incongruity of her politeness and facial expressions, and she looked to me as though she felt frustrated, unappreciated and neglected. I was aware that Becky was being open and congruent in her

responses to me and there was a part of me that wanted to do the session properly when the cameras stopped rolling!

What do you think about it now?
I think as a session to critique, it works quite well. But it has been interesting having had a conversation with people about it. Others have commented that it 'must have been quite fun to do', but it didn't feel like that at all. However, it has given me cause to reflect again more deeply on my role as a helper.

Stage 3: evaluation

Try to evaluate or make a judgement about what has happened. Consider what was good about the experience and what was bad about the experience, or what did or did not go so well.

As an exercise, this felt 'fit for purpose', but as an emotional experience it has given me quite a lot of food for thought. Occasionally, I think I slipped into giving more empathic responses than I had planned but I felt that I then slipped back 'into role' when I became more opinionated and imposed my views on the session. After years of being tentative in self-disclosure, this session felt incongruent. I was trying to be 'inappropriate' with our dual roles and make it all about me instead of Becky. In that way, the session went well as a teaching aid, but for my own feelings it was difficult and challenging to play this role.

Stage 4: analysis

Break the event down into its component parts so they can be explored separately. You may need to ask more detailed questions about the answers to the last stage. Include:

What went well?
I think mostly this session went to plan. When halfway through the session I told Becky 'It will be fine', I could see a real flash of irritation on her face. This showed clearly that she was not feeling listened to but she was still too polite to challenge me. I think this demonstrated the power differential very well.

What did you do well?
I think I maintained a surface friendliness alongside a lack of skills and bad non-verbal communication quite effectively!

What did others do well?
My client (Becky) tried very hard to respond to me and not get angry with me.

What went wrong or did not turn out how it should have done? In what way did you or others contribute to this?
The effect of my ploughing on and my attempt to impose my 'positive' world view seemed to bully Becky into agreeing with me and losing any voice or opinion of her own. It felt like I was beating her down into agreeing with me. I wanted to appear unskilful rather than cruel. When you are working with people's real feelings, I am not sure how you could avoid this result.

Stage 5: conclusion (synthesis)

This differs from the evaluation stage in that now you have explored the issue from different angles and have a lot of information to base your judgement. It is here that you are likely to develop insight into your own and other people's behaviour in terms of how they contributed to the outcome of the event. Remember the purpose of reflection is to learn from an experience. Without detailed analysis and honest exploration that occurs during all the previous stages, it is unlikely that all aspects of the event will be taken into account and therefore valuable opportunities for learning can be missed. During this stage, you should ask yourself what you could have done differently.

I am not sure at this stage what I could have done differently when providing a session to critique, so this stage is hard to evaluate. However, it has been an interesting exercise to reflect on this session because it has brought some things back into my awareness that I don't often consider these days.

Stage 6: action plan

During this stage, you should think yourself forward into encountering the event again and plan what you would do – would you act differently or would you be likely to do the same?

Here, the cycle is tentatively completed and suggests that should the event occur again, it will be the focus of another reflective cycle.

When I reflect on exercises like this, I have two internal supervisors, one is concerned with my role as a helper or counsellor and the other is as a trainer of counselling skills. I have asked myself how best to demonstrate this session without becoming too much of a parody of a helper because when we practice bad skills or lack of them, it is not because we want to be cruel and uncaring. What I have realised is as a helper today, it feels really uncomfortable and contradictory when I ignore the verbal and non-verbal responses from my client. I have also learned to appreciate the transferable skills between concentration as a helper and developing concentration in other areas in my life, which I do through music and mindfulness, and I have an awareness of how important that concentration is. Gibbs' model incorporates all the core skills of reflection. Arguably, it is focused on reflection on action, but with practice it could be used to focus on reflection *in* and *before* action.

REFLECT, PRACTISE AND EVALUATE

We would like you to try applying a framework to your own reflective practice, choosing either the Boniface model (Appendix 8) or the Gibbs model (Appendix 9). Both templates are included within the appendices for you to complete. Think of a helping session you have had with a client, or with your learning partner. Work through one of the templates, as we have in our examples, to think reflectively about that piece of work.

Once you have completed the template, share it with your learning partner. Discuss:

- How easy was it to do?
- What are the barriers to you undertaking reflective practice?
- What have you learned about yourself and how you undertake reflective practice?
- What are the implications for future reflective practice?

MODEL BOX

> In this chapter, we have referred to:
>
> - Cycle of experiential learning (Kolb 1984)
> - Learning styles (Honey and Mumford 1992)
> - Transformative learning (Mezirow 1997)
> - Levels of experiential learning (Boniface 2002)
> - Johari's window (Luft and Ingram 1955)
> - Model of reflection (Gibbs 1998)

SUMMARY

- Recognising and understanding our own learning styles is an integral aspect of the helping relationship.
- It is important that we develop our ability to reflect in order to inform and develop our helping role.
- Taking time to explore the known and unknown aspects of ourselves provides us with insights into aspects of ourselves that were previously part of our blind area.
- Recognising and enhancing our innate 'spark of ability' to be reflective enables us to learn how to become a more reflective practitioner at a less superficial and more challenging level.
- Models or frameworks for reflection must be used flexibly to fit your own learning style.

Conclusion

> Experience teaches only the teachable.
>
> (Aldous Huxley 1931)

> Communication is central to successful caring relationships and team working. Listening is as important as what nurses say and do and critical to decisions about a patient.
>
> (NHS Careers 2014)

In this chapter, the authors reflect on their own learning journey and the development of the Relational Skills Model, and consider its impact and application for future training. This chapter includes:

- Future learning
- Further reading
- Appendices

FUTURE LEARNING

The conception and writing of this book over the last two years has been a reflexive practice for us both. We can remember a time when counselling skills training was predominantly a precursor to, or module in, a professional training in counselling or psychotherapy. Some professional training did, of course, include a counselling or communication skills module, or students individually opted for this kind of training as part of their CPD, but equally we have spoken to professionals who never had these opportunities during training. As we began to have conversations about our book with a variety of other professionals, we were encouraged by their interest and enthusiasm. Many times, the response has been, 'We could use a training like that for our work!' This response has often come from unexpected sources — teachers, alternative therapists and nutritionists — as well as other medical and welfare professionals. In response to this, our list of proposed readership has grown. It seems to us that the counselling profession needs to be more generous in sharing its knowledge of communication and listening skills. We believe that learning to take an active and skilled helping role is an essential aspect of any helping profession, and we hope that now you have worked through this textbook and developed and practised your own skills that you may want to pass your knowledge and skills on to others.

The Relational Skills Model was also a result of this reflexive practice and of our combined teaching experiences. Our model arose from a growing process of observing the videos of helpers and clients working through 10-minute sessions as would be usual in many health-care settings. We began by trying to fit these examples of using skills with existing skills models and were constantly challenged. These were not 'perfect' sessions, just because they were real. It was good that the helpers made some 'mistakes' or that there were 'areas for development' because we intended these sessions to be critiqued. We started to examine the videos more carefully. What was good about that intervention? What made that paraphrase work? Why did the helper challenge at this point? Why did they not challenge here? We almost got to the point of giving up the project altogether because the videos were not fitting with the counselling skills models that underpinned current training. But then we both had a light bulb moment. It was not about applying the skills to a model; it was about applying the skills to the relationship! How could we not have seen that? The interventions had to be applicable to the phases of the relationship otherwise they would not be effective. We realised that this mirrored the challenges experienced by students on our counselling skills courses. It was all about timing and awareness. In order to challenge, there needed to be an appropriate relationship between helper and client. Skills needed to be appropriately applied within phases of the relationship. And so the new model was conceived.

We do not want our Relational Skills Model to be prescriptive; as practiced professionals, we all know that this is not an exact science. But the reality of today's time constraints for busy professionals means that professional helpers need to have a framework to start from. Students that we have taught to use the Relational Skills Model have welcomed a framework that fits neatly on to a piece of A4 paper. It is a useful prompt when practising skills, and the feedback we have had is that it is a confidence boost in the learning process when they have felt confused about which skills they might be using. Understanding that a relationship can be formed in quite a short time, but equally that it also has phases that they need to be aware of, has helped the students to be more fluent in their skills practice through using this as an aide memoire.

We think this model provides a good framework to develop awareness of helping strategies, and importantly to learn about good 'timing'. With today's culture of limited time for client contact and the likelihood of only having 10 or 15 minutes for a consultation or appointment, we needed to demonstrate the important understanding that even these small sound bites constitute a 'relationship'.

The skills we teach in this book are not rocket science, but they are impacting. It might be the first time a client has been asked, 'And how do you feel about that?' or, 'And why is that important to you?' and those questions can lead to a depth of exploration of meaning for the client. We strongly believe that anyone who works professionally with the welfare of others should be fully trained in embedding counselling and communication skills – not as an add-on or CPD training, but a mandatory unit in a core training programme with appropriate and recognisable learning outcomes. Our aim would be to see a mandatory counselling and communication skills unit in every professional training programme that incorporates a need for a person-centred approach.

In order to implement the person-centred approach, professionals must be proficient in using verbal and non-verbal communication skills, enabling them to recognise and respond to a client's needs and to have empathic and congruent counselling skills that demonstrate to the client that he or she has been heard and understood. We have a hope and a desire that training in our Relational Skills Model will go some way to assisting helping professionals to keep the client at the heart of the intervention and to embrace this person-centred model of care.

Most people who have been involved in or who have been following the development of the NHS over the last few years would acknowledge that the reforms have been many and they have been implemented with dizzyingly fast speed.

Changes in health-care education, practitioner training programmes, skills for health career frameworks and the introduction of the new BSc in Healthcare have resulted in the development of a more generic training entry and degree level that, it is hoped, will provide an opportunity to address one of the visions for the 2010 Government White Paper *Equity and Excellence: Liberating the NHS*, which sets out the long-term vision for the NHS, putting the patient at the heart of the NHS with the evocative statement: 'no decision about me without me'.

We would hope that this would encourage a universal approach for mandatory integration of counselling and communication skills into all basic training. We feel that practitioners who work with the welfare of others are disadvantaged without this training. When a health professional can practise basic counselling skills with a degree of self-awareness, the consequence for the patient is that he or she may feel in a better position to be involved in the decision-making process of his or her treatment plan, and he or she can gain a sense of empowerment in a potentially anxiety-provoking experience. If we have been in the patient's position, we may have had personal experience of helping professionals who have empathically listened and discussed our issues and anxieties and know the reassurance this can give of being in a 'safe pair of hands'. For the professional, he or she can feel confident that he or she is using the skills to his or her best advantage and that embedding this knowledge into his or her role will enhance his or her everyday working practice.

Reflexive practice continues to be an integral part of our learning and professional development. We would hope to always remain teachable and, as such, adaptable in the way we work and learn. The research we have undertaken for the development of this book has led us to a greater awareness of the wider relevance of these skills and their need to be embedded within the toolbox of a multitude of helping professionals, and we have a curiosity and excitement on where this will go forward.

FURTHER READING

Bond, T. (2000). *Standards and Ethics for Counselling in Action* (2nd edn), London: Sage.

Boyd, D. and Bee, H. (2012). *Lifespan Development* (6th edn), London: Prentice Hall.

Davies, D. and Neal, C. (eds) (1996). *Pink Therapy: A Guide for Counsellors and Therapists Working with Lesbian, Gay and Bisexual Clients*, Maidenhead: Open University Press.

Etherington, K. (2004). *Becoming a Reflexive Researcher*, London: Jessica Kingsley.

Feltham, C. (ed.) (1999). *The Counselling Relationship*, London: Sage.

Goodman, J., Schlossberg, N. K. and Anderson, M. (2006). *Counselling Adults in Transition: Linking Practice with Theory* (3rd edn), New York: Springer.

Greenberg, L. S., Rice, L. N. and Elliott, R. (1993). *Facilitating Emotional Change: The Moment-by-Moment Process*, New York: Guilford Press.

Lago, C. (ed.) (2011). *The Handbook of Transcultural Counselling and Psychotherapy*, Maidenhead: Open University Press.

Lendrum, S. and Syme, G. (1992). *Gift of Tears: A Practical Approach to Loss and Bereavement Counselling*, London: Routledge.

Nelson-Jones, R. (2012). *Introduction to Counselling Skills* (4th edn), London: Sage.

Reeves, A. (2013). *An Introduction to Counselling and Psychotherapy: From Theory to Practice*, London: Sage.

Saunders, P. (2009). *First Steps in Counselling: A Students' Companion for Basic Introductory Courses*, Ross-on-Wye: PCCS.

Stewart, I. (1996). *Developing Transactional Analysis Counselling*, London: Sage.

Appendix 1
The Relational Skills Model

The Relational Skills Model

Phases of relationship development	Process	Skills
Setting up the relationship	Contacting/meeting the client Getting to know the client Communicating with and contracting with the client	**Initial core skills:** Attending skills Active listening skills and contracting skills
Developing the relationship	Developing the relationship Problem identification and assessment	**Additional core skills:** Presence and communication of the core conditions Paraphrasing Summarising Identifying and reflecting feelings, content and meaning Asking questions
Working with the relationship	Challenging and creating new meaning, different possibilities and perspectives	**Enhanced skills:** Challenging Confronting Use of self-disclosure, immediacy and silence Clarifying Reassessing Probing Giving feedback and sharing information
The established relationship	Clarifying and focusing on likely changes Working collaboratively to make plans, set goals, and consider and evaluate possible strategies and directions	**Intuitive and learned skills:** Deeper empathy Focusing Use of metaphor and hunches Drawing together themes Clarifying and developing goals Action planning
Maintaining and ending the relationship	Implementing and maintaining change Supporting self-management strategies	**Embedded skills:** Encouragement, support and affirmations Review, monitor, evaluate and facilitate ending Signposting/referring on

© Copyright 2012 Midwinter and Dickson. All Rights Reserved.

Appendix 2
The qualities of a helper

Think of someone who has helped you in the past.

What qualities do you think he or she had that enabled him or her to be of help?

1 _____

2 _____

3 _____

4 _____

5 _____

6 _____

7 _____

8 _____

9 _____

10 _____

Appendix 3
Skills sheet

Skill used	Examples
Identifying and reflecting content	
Identifying and reflecting feelings	
Identifying and reflecting meaning	
Phrases that helped communication	
Phrases that hindered communication	
Paraphrasing	
Summarising	
Open questions	
Closed questions	
Challenging questions	
Probing questions	

Appendix 4a
Working with the relationship (Video Clip 4d) (blank transcript)

Content	Process	Skills
G: Rob, just so I'm sure I understand everything that's going on here. Your mum and brother have just recently moved. You've got some very mixed feelings about that we've talked about. Just wondered where you are with it all. Where does it feel it is for you now?		
R: Yeah, I feel more isolated now and, um, as I said, I moved to Reading, which isn't too far away, and it was nice being close to them. Not too close, they can't turn up for a cup of tea every five minutes but it was nice being close to them, you know. Cos I've been away for a long time so I guess I'm kind of used to that, um, and it was nice to get some of it back because when I moved away I also felt like I sort of lost something with my mum and the rest of my family, you know		
G: What do you feel you lost?		
R: Just growing up with them, spending time in the same rooms, just doing everyday stuff. I don't know what that is, in a way I do know what that is with my brother but I don't know what it is with all of us. And I will never know because it's gone. Um. And it didn't happen. We saw each other but it's not the same as coming home from school and stuff. So it was nice being back near and even though I'm used to being away from my mum and my brother and my family it was just nice to have it. So now it's a bit, yeah, I know this feeling		
G: Yeah		
R: So I can cope with it. Doesn't mean I like it		
G: OK, can you tell me about what the feeling does to you?		
R: What it does?		
G: What does it present to you?		
R: Um		
G: Cos you said you felt isolated		

continued

Content	Process	Skills
R: Yeah, um, it makes things a bit hard to do, it's difficult to explain but it's like a . . . I just want to go 'umph'		
G: OK		
R: You know, and . . . yeah, I feel heavier and I feel a bit sort of more tired. It's not quite hopeless, it's not that bad, but it's just like . . . you know, I miss them		
G: You miss them		
R: Miss them, yeah. I felt like I had . . . as much as we argue all the bloody time, it's like I had a bit of support, you know it's like you know, it's that thing about family are a pain but at the same time you love them. And I er, I didn't know until I just said it but I guess I feel like that		
G: So you feel that you miss them and that makes you feel heavy		
R: Yeah bit of a struggle		
G: So what do you want to do about that?		
R: (*deep breath*) Phew. That's a big question. Um		
G: What do you think will reduce some of that for you?		
R: Um, I was going to say to see them and in a way that would, but it's more that I want to be happier without that, if you see what I mean. Where I kind of, where I don't rely on them. Although I can kind of feel myself getting tied up in knots here because it's not that I don't want to be with them and it's not that I want to dismiss how I am feeling, but I want to be OK. I mean, I am OK but I want to be just anyway		
G: So it sounds like you need some autonomy but you still want to be close to your family		

continued

Content	Process	Skills

R: Well that's the thing. I have loads of autonomy I have loads of it, you know it's . . . I'm very used to being on my own and doing things on my own and, you know, if something needs doing I'll do it. And it's nice to be close to them but I . . . what I want is the autonomy plus . . . plus the closeness just for the sake of us being who we are. My family being who we are, you know. I guess, and this is when I start tearing up and feeling sad again, it's like, when I talk about, when I talk about them now . . . and it's getting really difficult to say, um. It's almost nostalgic whereas when we are living day to day I can kind of see why I don't, um. Why I don't see them all the time. You know, there's a kind of a . . . not that we argue with each other but . . .

R: . . . the way that we talk is pretty straightforward really. My mum can be quite, um. I kind of see it as quite critical. She tells me I'm being too sensitive and it's just like kind of – OK! *(laughs)* But that's kind of the way we get on, um. Sorry, I don't know whether I'm getting a bit lost but I've kind of forgotten

G: So what do you want here? What is it you want? So you say you've got your autonomy but you say you want your autonomy and closeness, so what is it you want?

R: I want to feel happy in myself so that I can go and do what I want to do without the feeling that I'm missing out on something, the feeling that I owe somebody something, that I owe my family something while I'm at it. Part of the thing about moving away is . . . is I always kind of had a sense in some way of what I'd lost. It's like every time I do something it's a choice, you know, and there's only so much time. There's only so much life that I have and that sounds quite . . . like it might be a bit much but it's not. Literally, there's only so long that we live and I really feel it when I choose to spend my time with my family or alone. I really wonder what else could be you know. When they move away and I have that kind of emptiness, that hole, it really hurts

G: So how can we simplify that? How can we put that into something that you want that's going to make things better for you?

continued

Content	Process	Skills

R: I think for me what would really work is, you know, like I've just said about life being short, to kind of break that down a bit instead of having some kind of abstract idea that kind of life is short, it's actually about day to day stuff and about actually just accepting that bit and rather than just dwelling on the fact that actually time is just slipping away. It's a case of actually time is slipping away, time is slipping away for everybody, you know, we are all here but I can use it to do what I want, that's it, I can use it to do what I want and that's the bit about not owing other people something

G: OK

R: Does that make sense?

G: Yeah. Can I? Just to make sure I understand what you were looking for. You have this loss here that it feels like you're working with and you want to be able to have your autonomy that you've got but also still have the ability to sort of move on in your life by some sort of acceptance of that

R: It's that acceptance that really hits me when you were telling me that

G: OK

R: You know cos the autonomy and the things I can do for myself since I've grown up. I can do all of that and I know I have done for ages but it's the, it's the acceptance and the being comfortable in myself that actually this is my time and I can spend it how I want and that might mean an afternoon in front of the telly, that might mean that I can choose what I do and that's OK and it doesn't have to be anything huge but it's OK to want something just because I want it

G: OK

R: You know?

G: Yeah

Appendix 4b
Working with the relationship (Video Clip 4d) (completed transcript)

Content	Process	Skills
G: Rob, just so I'm sure I understand everything that's going on here. Your mum and brother have just recently moved. You've got some very mixed feelings about that we've talked about. Just wondered where you are with it all. Where does it feel it is for you now?	Creating new meaning	Probing Open questions
R: Yeah, I feel more isolated now and, um, as I said, I moved to Reading, which isn't too far away, and it was nice being close to them. Not too close, they can't turn up for a cup of tea every five minutes but it was nice being close to them, you know. Cos I've been away for a long time so I guess I'm kind of used to that, um, and it was nice to get some of it back because when I moved away I also felt like I sort of lost something with my mum and the rest of my family, you know		
G: What do you feel you lost?		Open question
R: Just growing up with them, spending time in the same rooms, just doing everyday stuff. I don't know what that is, in a way I do know what that is with my brother but I don't know what it is with all of us. And I will never know because it's gone. Um. And it didn't happen. We saw each other but it's not the same as coming home from school and stuff. So it was nice being back near and even though I'm used to being away from my mum and my brother and my family it was just nice to have it. So now it's a bit, yeah, I know this feeling		
G: Yeah		
R: So I can cope with it. Doesn't mean I like it		
G: OK, can you tell me about what the feeling does to you?		Open question
R: What it does?		
G: What does it present to you?		Open question
R: Um		
G: Cos you said you felt isolated		Challenging

continued

Content	Process	Skills
R: Yeah, um, it makes things a bit hard to do, it's difficult to explain but it's like a . . . I just want to go 'umph'		
G: OK		
R: You know, and . . . yeah, I feel heavier and I feel a bit sort of more tired. It's not quite hopeless, it's not that bad, but it's just like . . . you know, I miss them		
G: You miss them		Empathic reflection
R: Miss them, yeah. I felt like I had . . . as much as we argue all the bloody time, it's like I had a bit of support, you know it's like you know, it's that thing about family are a pain but at the same time you love them. And I er, I didn't know until I just said it but I guess I feel like that		
G: So you feel that you miss them and that makes you feel heavy		Paraphrase
R: Yeah bit of a struggle		
G: So what do you want to do about that?	Challenging and creating new meaning, different possibilities and perspectives	Challenge
R: (*deep breath*) Phew. That's a big question. Um		
G: What do you think will reduce some of that for you?		Probing
R: Um, I was going to say to see them and in a way that would, but it's more that I want to be happier without that, if you see what I mean. Where I kind of, where I don't rely on them. Although I can kind of feel myself getting tied up in knots here because it's not that I don't want to be with them and it's not that I want to dismiss how I am feeling, but I want to be OK. I mean, I am OK but I want to be just anyway		
G: So It sounds like you need some autonomy but you still want to be close to your family		Paraphrase

continued

Content	Process	Skills
R: Well that's the thing. I have loads of autonomy I have loads of it, you know it's . . . I'm very used to being on my own and doing things on my own and, you know, if something needs doing I'll do it. And it's nice to be close to them but I . . . what I want is the autonomy plus . . . plus the closeness just for the sake of us being who we are. My family being who we are, you know. I guess, and this is when I start tearing up and feeling sad again, it's like, when I talk about, when I talk about them now . . . and it's getting really difficult to say, um. It's almost nostalgic whereas when we are living day to day I can kind of see why I don't, um. Why I don't see them all the time. You know, there's a kind of a . . . not that we argue with each other but . . .	The client is exploring different perspectives now	
R: . . . the way that we talk is pretty straightforward really. My mum can be quite, um. I kind of see it as quite critical. She tells me I'm being too sensitive and it's just like kind of – OK! *(laughs)* But that's kind of the way we get on, um. Sorry, I don't know whether I'm getting a bit lost but I've kind of forgotten		
G: So what do you want here? What is it you want? So you say you've got your autonomy but you say you want your autonomy and closeness, so what is it you want?		Challenging through confronting the client by questioning what he wants
R: I want to feel happy in myself so that I can go and do what I want to do without the feeling that I'm missing out on something, the feeling that I owe somebody something, that I owe my family something while I'm at it. Part of the thing about moving away is . . . is I always kind of had a sense in some way of what I'd lost. It's like every time I do something it's a choice, you know, and there's only so much life that I have and that sounds quite . . . like it might be a bit much but it's not. Literally, there's only so long that we live and I really feel it when I choose to spend my time with my family or alone. I really wonder what else could be you know. When they move away and I have that kind of emptiness, that hole, it really hurts	The client picks up the challenge and begins to question what it is he does want	

continued

Content	Process	Skills
G: So how can we simplify that? How can we put that into something that you want that's going to make things better for you?	Problem identification	Clarifying
R: I think for me what would really work is, you know, like I've just said about life being short, to kind of break that down a bit instead of having some kind of abstract idea that kind of life is short, it's actually about day to day stuff and about actually just accepting that bit and rather than just dwelling on the fact that actually time is just slipping away. It's a case of actually time is slipping away, time is slipping away for everybody, you know, we are all here but I can use it to do what I want, that's it, I can use it to do what I want and that's the bit about not owing other people something	The client is creating new meaning	
G: OK		
R: Does that make sense?		
G: Yeah. Can I? Just to make sure I understand what you were looking for. You have this loss here that it feels like you're working with and you want to be able to have your autonomy that you've got but also still have the ability to sort of move on in your life by some sort of acceptance of that	Working with the relationship	Summary to create new meaning
R: It's that acceptance that really hits me when you were telling me that	The client is responding to the helper's recognition of the concept of 'acceptance' and recognising its importance	Reassessing
G: OK		
R: You know cos the autonomy and the things I can do for myself since I've grown up. I can do all of that and I know I have done for ages but it's the, it's the acceptance and the being comfortable in myself that actually this is my time and I can spend it how I want and that might mean an afternoon in front of the telly, that might mean that I can choose what I do and that's OK and it doesn't have to be anything huge but it's OK to want something just because I want it	The client continues to explore the meaning of 'acceptance'	
G: OK		
R: You know?		
G: Yeah		

Appendix 5
Blank milestone table

Main goal	Milestones	Action by	Completion date	Comments

Appendix 6
Prejudices and judgements

(a) Think of three things, off the top of your head, that might bias you *towards* someone:

(i) _____

(ii) _____

(iii) _____

(b) Think of three things, off the top of your head, that might bias you *against* someone:

(i) _____

(ii) _____

(iii) _____

(c) Do any of these fall into categories that you have listed above?

Appendix 7
Session to critique – Janie and Becky (Video Clip 7a)

Content	Process	Skills
J: So, Becky, hi		
B: Hi		
J: So you were going to be talking about something you talked about before in counselling?	There is no evidence of a contract and agreement here (RSM)	
B: I saw a counsellor a while ago, I'm doing a major change in my life at the moment, and I've gone through so much of it, and that has been working really well, but there are still things I feel anxious about	The client is showing behaviours and using words that indicate she is in her adapted child ego-state	
J: Who was it that you saw before?	The helper is changing the subject. She is not attending or hearing key emotional prompts from the client. The question is also unethical, particularly in terms of confidentiality (BACP 2013)	
B: Why do you need to know her name? I only know her by her first name.		
J: Well maybe not, I was just interested . . .	The question was not for the client, it was about the helper's curiosity	
B: I only knew her by her first name		
J: I just thought it might be someone I knew	Again, the helper has not acknowledged and appears not to have noticed the client's embarrassment or reluctance to pursue this question. The helper is purely on her own agenda and not demonstrating demonstrating any empathic understanding	
B: I don't know (nervous laughter)		
J: Um, um, I was just trying to work out if I said to my secretary about timing wise, but we are all right, carry on, sorry, sorry I've lost you there	There is no attempt by the helper to build rapport with the client. There are instant barriers to active listening and inattention. The non-verbal communication of the helper and looking at her watch	

continued

Content	Process	Skills
	compounds this. The helper is using body language consistent with her being in her controlling parent ego-state	
B: Yes, I'm making a major change in a couple of months so there are still a few things that I'm still anxious about		
J: Yeah, OK, major change, do you know we are both in the middle of a major change, aren't we?	A 'me too' moment that deflects back to the helper. She is not listening or attending to her client's body language. Although 'major change' is reflected back, there is complete lack of empathy from the helper and the self-disclosure is inappropriate	
B: Yeah		
J: Cos we both know each other and we both know that we are going though that situation, that is really funny, really funny, because I feel, I feel about that change and I'm finding that really difficult, because I know, I just know what you are going through. I really do, so yeah, say a bit more about it, what's going on?	The dual relationship is now impacting detrimentally on the relationship. The helper is absorbed in self-interest and there is no collaborative working. The helper has shifted to her adapted child ego-state	
B: Well, I think it coincides with other changes in my life at the moment, because I've got two children – they're not children now, they are young adults and one is planning on moving out and the other one is going through change from school to college, so it seems like everything is changing at once . . .		
J: What subjects are they going to be doing?	Total change of subject. Again, it is the helper's curiosity, and not of benefit to the client. There is no attempt at problem identification from the perspective of the client. Adult ego-stage	
B: What subjects?		
J: Yes	The helper has not picked up on the client's expression from this change of subject	

continued

Content	Process	Skills
B: Oh gosh, I don't know, my son, er, they take so many subjects at GCSE these days and I think he is hopeful to take his A levels		
J: He is such a nice lad, you must be so proud of him	The helper again brings in their dual relationship to put words in the client's mouth. Nurturing parent ego-state	
B: I am, thank you		
J: Yeah. That's fantastic, yeah, and the kids leaving, that's a good thing	Second-guessing what the client is thinking. There are ethical considerations around autonomy	
B: Yeah		
J: You'll have a bit more time		
B: Yeah, it's a good thing, really positive, it's time, the right age and everything, but you can't help feeling kind of a bit strange that everything is changing all at the same time. I feel . . .		
J: But change is good, change is good, Becky, that's what it is all about really. And you and I are both being therapists and we work with change with other people so it's positive, and you know at the end of this it's going to be absolutely fine. You know it's going to be fine, going to be good	The helper is filtering what the client is saying and attempting to impose her own value judgement on to the client (non-autonomy). The helper is attempting to move into advice giving and having the 'right' answers for the client. Negative nurturing parent ego-state (overbearing).	
B: You know, I think that's half the problem, I think that's it, I don't know it's going to be fine. I don't feel that. My head tells me everything is going to be fine, but actually I don't feel that everything is going to be fine. I haven't got that confidence. I wish I did. I think that's the major issue as I don't have that confidence that everything is going to be fine cos I've never not been employed so it feels really weird	The client is still in adapted child	

continued

Content	Process	Skills
J: My old mum always says that it will be all right in the end. That phrase she always used to say, 'It'll be all right, it will all come out in the wash' she always used to say. And it's great to think about that, to thinking about the future being a positive thing. You know, we have to go forward, you know, and do it together and that. I think positive attitudes are really, really helpful. Don't you?	The helper appears oblivious to the client's non-verbal communication. She is not so much advice giving, but pressurising the client. Ethical consideration of non-maleficence (BACP 2013). The helper has shifted to mimicking her own parental influences from her nurturing parent ego-state	
B: Um, *(nervous giggle)* um, I like to think I do, yeah . . .		
J: Yeah		
B: I'm quite a positive person, but at the moment I feel anxious, you know, I don't feel positive. There are days when I can't wait and it's all new and I really embrace that, but there are days when I wake up feeling quite anxious actually. My world is changing to such an extent	Remains in adapted child	
J: I don't know why you feel like that, I really don't, because you have got so much going for you, you know. Remember that conference we were in the other day, do you remember that together?	The helper pulls back to the dual relationship and changes the subject, and there is no collaborative working or understanding. Language coming from controlling parent ego-state	
B: Hmm		
J: And that you were so positive and so great about that, you know. If you could pick up some of that, that would be fantastic, that would be really good	In her attempt to encourage the client, the helper appears oblivious to her distress, and there is no attempt at problem identification from the client's perspective	
B: Yeah, I do think that sometimes, I think I've got all these years' experience		
J: Yeah		
B: And I've got everything to work towards . . . and I still feel anxious, you know, I don't think that goes away		

continued

Content	Process	Skills
J: (*talking over client*) You've got so much more experience than I have, you've got so much more going for you than I have. And I worry about that cos I just feel, oh, I don't know about you and I working together, I would just drag you back really. I mean I don't really feel like, I'm not sure how that is . . . you just don't know what you have going for you, you really don't, honestly	The helper has now missed many prompts that the client is giving her. The client has now used the word 'anxious' a number of times. Notice the power differential where the client is trying to remain polite to the overbearing helper while still attempting to repeat her concerns. The helper is working only with her own agenda of solutions and not exploring different possibilities or perspectives. The helper talks of her own anxieties and has moved to adapted child	
B: Hmm, yeah, I suppose, hmm yeah, I do try to stay positive, a lot of the time I am, but then there are times when I just feel anxious about it all and I don't really know how to overcome that		
J: No, well, I guess, I think you do know in yourself, you do know how to be confident with those things, you are very good at helping other people with it. It's just about taking that out and using those things yourself, that would be really good, really good, that would be fantastic	Again, the client has stated that she is 'anxious', and again the helper has remained oblivious to the client's needs. She has changed the subject, advised the client from her own opinions and had the right answers for the client	
J: And I'm really sorry, but that is all we have time for, so we need to move on. So we can perhaps make another time to talk about this because it's been fantastic meeting up with you and talking about that again, it's really great, thanks B: OK, thanks	How 'fantastic' was this session for the client! The client's facial expressions and body language reflect this	

Appendix 8
Boniface levels of reflection

1	Setting the scene	Lowest level of reflection
2	Telling the story of the event to be reflected upon	Lowest level of reflection
3	Identifying critical occurrences	Lowest level of reflection
4	Linking the story and critical occurrences to previous events or knowledge	Middle level of reflection
5	Identifying feelings associated with the story of critical occurrences	Middle level of reflection
6	Identifying and challenging blind spots associated with those feelings such as prejudices	Middle level of reflection
7	Identifying what has been learned from the reflection	Middle level of reflection
8	Deciding whether a change is now necessary as a result of reflection	Middle level of reflection
9	Identifying and critiquing the belief system upon which our actions are based	High level of reflection (reflecting on reflection)

Source: Taken from Mezirow (1981), Schön (1983) and Fish and Twinn (1997)

Appendix 9
Gibbs' framework for reflection

Stage 1: Description of the event

Describe in detail the event you are reflecting on.
Include, for example, where were you; who else was there; why were you there; what were you doing; what were other people doing; what was the context of the event; what happened; what was your part in this; what parts did the other people play; what was the result.

Stage 2: Feelings and thoughts (self-awareness)

At this stage, try to recall and explore those things that were going on inside your head. Include:

- How were you feeling when the event started?
- What were you thinking about at the time?
- How did it make you feel?
- How did other people make you feel?
- How did you feel about the outcome of the event?
- What do you think about it now?

Stage 3: Evaluation

Try to evaluate or make a judgement about what has happened. Consider what was good about the experience and what was bad about the experience or what did or did not go so well.

Stage 4: Analysis

Break the event down into its component parts so they can be explored separately. You may need to ask more detailed questions about the answers to the last stage. Include:

- What went well?
- What did you do well?
- What did others do well?

- What went wrong or did not turn out how it should have done?
- In what way did you or others contribute to this?

Stage 5: Conclusion (synthesis)

This differs from the evaluation stage in that now you have explored the issue from different angles and have a lot of information to base your judgement. It is here that you are likely to develop insight into your own and other people's behaviour in terms of how they contributed to the outcome of the event. Remember the purpose of reflection is to learn from an experience. Without detailed analysis and honest exploration that occurs during all the previous stages, it is unlikely that all aspects of the event will be taken into account and therefore valuable opportunities for learning can be missed. During this stage, you should ask yourself what you could have done differently.

Stage 6: Action plan

During this stage, you should think yourself forward into encountering the event again and to plan what you would do – would you act differently or would you be likely to do the same?

Here, the cycle is tentatively completed and suggests that should the event occur again, it will be the focus of another reflective cycle

Gibbs' model incorporates all the core skills of reflection. Arguably, it is focused on reflection on action, but with practice it could be used to focus on reflection in and *before* action.

Core reading

BACP (British Association for Counselling and Psychotherapy) (2013). *Ethical Framework for Good Practice in Counselling and Psychotherapy*, Lutterworth: British Association for Counselling and Psychotherapy.

Boniface, G. (2002). Understanding reflective practice in occupational therapy, *British Journal of Therapy and Rehabilitation* 9 (8): 294–8.

Culley, S. and Bond, T. (2004). *Integrative Counselling Skills in Action* (2nd edn), London: Sage.

Egan, G. (2002). *The Skilled Helper: A Problem-Management and Opportunity-Development Approach to Helping* (7th edn), Pacific Grove, CA: Brooks/Cole.

Egan, G. (2010). *The Skilled Helper: A Problem-Management and Opportunity-Development Approach to Helping* (10th edn), Belmont, CA: Brooks/Cole, Cengage Learning.

Honey, P. and Mumford, A. (2006). *The Learning Styles Questionnaire*, London: Pearson.

McLeod, J. and McLeod, J. (2011). *Counselling Skills: A Practical Guide for Counsellors and Helping Professionals* (2nd edn), Maidenhead: Open University Press.

Rogers, C. R. (1957). The necessary and sufficient conditions of therapeutic personality change, *Journal of Consulting Psychology* 21 (2): 95–203.

Rogers, C. R. (1961). *On Becoming a Person*, London: Constable.

Rogers, C. R. (1964). Toward a modern approach to values: the valuing process in the mature person, *The Journal of Abnormal and Social Psychology* 68 (2): 160–7.

Rogers, C. R. (1980). *A Way of Being*, New York: Mariner Books.

Schön, D. (1995). *The Reflective Practitioner: How Professionals Think in Action*, Aldershot: Arena.

References

Aldridge, S. and Rigby, S. (eds) (2001). *Counselling Skills in Context*, London: Hodder & Stoughton.
BACP (British Association for Counselling and Psychotherapy) (2012). *Accreditation of Training Courses Including the Core Curriculum*, Lutterworth: British Association for Counselling and Psychotherapy.
BACP (2013). *Ethical Framework for Good Practice in Counselling and Psychotherapy*, Lutterworth: British Association for Counselling and Psychotherapy.
Barr, F. M. N. (2000). Introduction to Counselling Skills Course University of Bristol, unpublished essay.
Beck, A. T., Rush, J., Shaw, B. F. and Emery, G. (1979). *Cognitive Therapy of Depression*, New York: Guildford Press.
Berne, E. (2010). *Games People Play: The Psychology of Human Relationships*, London: Penguin.
Board, R. (1998). *Counselling for Toads*, London: Routledge.
Boniface, G. (2002). Understanding reflective practice in occupational therapy, *British Journal of Therapy and Rehabilitation* 9 (8): 294–8.
Burns, R. (1786). To a Louse. On Seeing One on a Lady's Bonnet at Church, available at: www.gutenberg.org/files/18500 (accessed 2 January 2015).
Carkhuff, R. (1969). *Helping & Human Relations Vol. 1*, New York: Holt, Rinehart & Winston.
Carkhuff, R. (1979). *The Skills of Helping: An Introduction to Counseling Skills*, Amherst, MA: Human Resource Development Press.
Carter, E. and McGoldrick, M. (1989). *The Changing Family Life Cycle*, Boston, MA: Allyn Bacon.
Carver, C. S. and Baird, E. (1998). The American dream revisited: is it what you want or why you want it that matters? *Psychological Science* 9 (4): 289–92.
Centre for Coaching (2011). *Coaching Development Programme*, course held by Centre for Coaching, London, 31 October–4 November.
Charles, C., Gafni, A. and Whelan, C. (1999). Decision-making in the physician-patient encounter: revisiting the shared treatment decision-making model, *Social Science & Medicine* 49 (5): 651–61.
Clarkson, P. (2003). *The Therapeutic Relationship* (2nd edn), London: Whurr.
Culley, S. and Bond, T. (2004). *Integrative Counselling Skills in Action* (2nd edn), London: Sage.
D'Ardenne, P. and Mahtani, A. (1999). *Transcultural Counselling in Action* (2nd edn), London: Sage.
De Shazer, S. (1988). *Clues: Investigating Solutions in Brief Therapy*, London: W. W. Norton & Co.
Dewey, J. (1910). *How We Think. A Restatement of the Relation of Reflective Thinking to the Educative Process*, Boston, MA: DC Health.
Doran, G. T. (1981). There's a S.M.A.R.T. way to write management's goals and objectives, *Management Review* 70 (11): 35–6.
Edgerton, N. and Palmer, S. (2005). SPACE: A psychological model for use within cognitive behavioural coaching, therapy and stress management, *The Coaching Psychologist* 2 (2): 25–31.

REFERENCES

Egan, G. (2002). *The skilled helper: a problem-management and opportunity-development approach to helping* (7th edn), Pacific Grove, CA: Brooks/Cole.

Egan, G. (2010). *The Skilled Helper: A Problem-Management and Opportunity-Development Approach to Helping* (10th edn), Belmont, CA: Brooks/Cole, Cengage Learning.

Ekman, P. (2008). *Emotional Awareness: A Conversation Between the Dalai Lama and Paul Ekman*, New York: Holt Paperback.

Ellis, A. (1962). *Reason and Emotion in Psychotherapy*, New York: Lyle Stuart.

Feirn, R. (2013). Breaking news and communicating with families, PowerPoint presentation, BSc in Audiology, University of Bristol.

Feltham, C. and Horton, I. (eds) (2000). *Handbook of Counselling & Psychotherapy*, London: Sage.

Fink, S. L., Beak, J. and Taddeo, K. (1971). Organizational crisis and change, *Journal of Applied Behavioral Science* 7 (1): 15–37.

Fish, D. and Twinn, S. (1997). *Quality Supervision in the Health Care Professions: Principled Approaches to Practice*, Oxford: Butterworth-Heinemann.

Fisher, T. D., Davis, C. M., Yarber, W. L. and Davis, S. L. (2010). *Handbook of Sexuality-Related Measures*, New York: Routledge.

Gabriel, L. and Casemore, R. (2009). *Relational Ethics in Practice: Narratives from Counselling and Psychotherapy*, Hove: Routledge.

Gibbs, G. (1998). *Learning by Doing: A Guide to Teaching and Learning*, London: Further Education Unit.

Great Britain Department of Health (2010). *Liberating the NHS: Legislative Framework and Next Steps*, London: The Stationary Office (CM7993).

Greenson, R. R. (1965). *The Technique and Practice of Psychoanalysis Vol. 1*, New York: International Universities Press.

Guttman, H. A. (1991). Systems theory, cybernetics and epistemology, in A. S. Gurman and D. P. Kniskern (eds), *Handbook of Family Therapy Vol. 11*, New York: Routledge, pp. 41–64.

Hawkins, P. and Shohet, R. (2012). *Supervision in the Helping Professions* (4th edn), Maidenhead: Open University Press.

Holly, M. L. (1988). Reflective writing and the spirit of inquiry, *Cambridge Journal of Education*, 19 (1): 71–80.

Holman, P., Devane, T. and Cady, S. (eds) (2008). *The Change Handbook: The Definitive Resource on Today's Best Methods for Engaging Whole Systems*, San Francisco, CA: Barrett-Koehler.

Honey, P. and Mumford, A. (2006). *The Learning Styles Questionnaire*, London: Pearson.

Hopson, B. and Adams, J. (1976). Towards an understanding of transition: defining some boundaries of transition dynamics, in J. Adams, H. Hayes and B. Hopson (eds), *Transition: Understanding and Managing Personal Change*, London: Martin Robertson. pp. 3–25.

Howell, W. S. (1982). *The Empathic Communicator*, Minnesota, MN: Wadsworth.

Jahoda, M. (1979). Impact of unemployment in the 1930s and the 1970s, *Bulletin of the British Psychological Society* 32 (August): 309–14.

Johns, H. (1996). *Personal Development in Counsellor Training*, London: Continuum.

Kelly, B. (2003). *Worth Repeating: More Than 5,000 Classic and Contemporary Quotes*, Grand Rapids, MI: Kregel.

Knaus, W. J. (1973). Overcoming procrastination, *Rational Living* 8 (2): 2–7.

Kolb, D. (1984). *Experiential Learning*, Upper Saddle River, NJ: Prentice Hall.

Lapworth, P. and Sills, C. (2011). *An Introduction to Transactional Analysis*, London: Sage.

Lazarus, A. (1976). *Multimodal Behavior Therapy*, Oxford: Springer.

Lewin, K. (1951). *Force Field Analysis*, New York: Harper & Row.

REFERENCES

Luft, J. and Ingham, H. (1955). The Johari window, a graphic model of interpersonal awareness, proceedings of the Western Training Laboratory in Group Development, Los Angeles, UCLA.

McDermott, I. and Jago, W. (2005). *The Coaching Bible*, London: Piatkus.

McKay, M., Davis, M. and Fanning, P. (1995). *Messages: The Communication Skills Book* (2nd edn), Oakland, CA: New Harbinger.

McLeod, J. (1998). *An Introduction to Counselling* (2nd edn), Buckingham: Open University Press.

McLeod, J. (2007). *Counselling Skill*, Maidenhead: Open University Press/McGraw-Hill Education.

McLeod, J. and McLeod, J. (2011). *Counselling Skills: A Practical Guide for Counsellors and Helping Professionals* (2nd edn), Maidenhead: Open University Press/McGraw-Hill Education.

Mearns, D. and Cooper, M. (2005). *Working at Relational Depth in Counselling and Psychotherapy*, London: Sage.

Meyer, P. J. (2003). *Attitude is Everything: If You Want to Succeed Above and Beyond*, Waco, TX: The Meyer Resource Group.

Mezirow, J. (1981). A critical theory of adult learning and education, *Adult Education* 31 (1): 3–24.

Mezirow, J. (1997). Transformative learning: theory to practice, *New Directions for Adult & Continuing Education* 74 (Summer): 5–12.

Neenan, M. and Dryden, W. (2002). *Life Coaching: A Cognitive Behavioural Approach*, London: Brunner-Routledge.

NHS Careers (2014). Skills required, available at: www.nhscareers.nhs.uk/explore-by-career/nursing/skills-required (accessed 1 October 2014).

Parkes, C. M. (1972). *Bereavement Studies of Grief in Adult Life*, London: Tavistock.

Philpott, J. (2012). Counting the cost of the jobs recession, *Work Audit Issue 42*, available at: www.cipd.co.uk/binaries/5795workauditWEB.pdf (accessed 26 May 2014).

Prochaska, J. O. and DiClemente, C. C. (1983). Stages and processes of self-change of smoking: toward an integrative model of change. *Journal Consulting & Clinical Psychology* 51 (3): 390–5.

Prochaska, J. O. and DiClemente, C. C. (1986). Towards a comprehensive model of change, in W. R. Miller and N. Heather (eds), *Treating Addictive Behaviors*, New York: Plenum Press, pp. 3–27.

Robinson, W. L. (1974). Interview, *Personnel Journal* 53 (7) (July): 538–9.

Rogers, C. R. (1957). The necessary and sufficient conditions of therapeutic personality change, *Journal of Consulting Psychology* 21 (2): 95–203.

Rogers, C. R. (1961). *On Becoming a Person*, London: Constable.

Rogers, C. R. (1964). Toward a modern approach to values: the valuing process in the mature person, *The Journal of Abnormal and Social Psychology* 68 (2): 160–7.

Rogers, C. R. (1980). *A Way of Being*, New York: Mariner Books.

Rolfe, G. (1997). Beyond expertise: theory, practice and the reflexive practitioner, *Journal of Clinical Nursing* 6 (2): 93–7.

Sanders, D. and Wills, F. (2005). *Cognitive Therapy: An Introduction* (2nd edn), London: Sage.

Schlossberg, N. K., Waters, E. B. and Goodman, J. (1995). *Counseling Adults in Transition: Linking Practice With Theory* (2nd edn), New York: Springer.

Schmid, P. F. (2002). Knowledge or acknowledgment? Psychotherapy as 'the art of not knowing' prospects on further development of a radical paradigm, *Person Centred and Experiential Psychotherapies* 1: 56–70.

Schön, D. (1983). *The Reflective Practitioner*, New York: Basic Books.

Schön, D. (1995). *The Reflective Practitioner: How Professionals Think in Action*, Aldershot: Arena.

Stewart, I. (2000). *Transactional Analysis Counselling in Action*, London: Sage.

Stewart, I. and Joines, V. (1987). *TA Today: A New Introduction to Transactional Analysis*, Nottingham: Russell Press.

Stroebe, M. and Schut, H. (1995). The dual process model of coping with loss, paper presented at the International Workshop on Death, Dying and Bereavement, Oxford.

Sue, D. W. and Sue, D. (1977). Barriers to effective cross-cultural counselling, *Journal of Counseling Psychology* 24 (5): 420–9.

Tonkin, L. (1996). Growing around grief: another way of looking at grief and recovery, *Bereavement Care Journal* 15(1): 10.

West, D. (2012). *Signs of Hope: Deafhearing Family Life*, Newcastle-upon-Tyne: Cambridge Scholars.

Williams, H., Palmer, S. and Edgerton, N. (2008). May the force be within you: harnessing the power of the mind to combat stress by using the cognitive behavioural SPACE model of coaching, counselling and training, *Stress News* 20(3): 29–31.

Wilson, C. and McMahon, G. (2006). What's the difference? TJ September: 54–7.

Worden, J. W. (2009). *Grief Counseling and Grief Therapy: A Handbook for the Mental Health* (4th edn), New York: Springer.

Index

Page numbers in *italics* denotes a figure/table

acceptance 13
action plan/planning 123–6; and reflection 199; writing an 126
active listening 25; barriers to 28–30
Adams, J. 132–5
adapted child 165, 166, 171, 172
addiction 136
adult ego-state 164, 165, 166, 167
affirmations: and empathy 98
alcohol: clients under the influence of 172
Aldridge, S. 78
analysis 198
Angelou, Maya 88
angry clients 172
attending skills 25–30; being attentive 27; being fully engaged 26; being responsive 27; body posture 27–8; eye contact 27–8; facial expression 27–8; and SOLER 25
attentive, being 27
audiologists 12
autonomy 36, 157

BACP (British Association for Counselling and Psychotherapy) 10; Ethical Framework for Counselling and Psychotherapy 36, 157
Baird, E. 113
Barr, F. M. N. 156
Beck, A. T. 65
beneficence 36, 157
bereavement 144–6
Berne, Eric 164
black-and-white thinking 109
blind area 190
blind spots 65, 66, 85
blue sky thinking 108–9
Board, R. 166

body language/communication 27–8, 30, 181; expressing empathy through 99–100; and use of silence 78
body listening 30
body posture 25, 27–8
Bond, T. 17–18, 71, 73, 160–1
Boniface, G. 189, 191, 192, 227
brainstorming 108–9
British Association for Counselling & Psychotherapy *see* BACP
Burns, R. 189

Carkhuff, R. 68
Carver, C. S. 113
catastrophising 109
challenging 20, 64–96; and blind spots 65, 66, 85; clarifying 84–5, 86; and confrontation 66–8; examples 74–7, 79, 80–3, 90, 91–4; giving feedback and sharing information 88–90; probing 87–8; and reassessing 87; skill of 64–5; use of immediacy 68–71, 74–7; use of self-disclosure 71–3, 74–7; use of silence 78–9, 80–3
change/change models 123, 129–55; ABCDE model 146; and choice in transition 130; and cultural influence 149; cycle of change model 136–7, 138–43; example 138–43; final stages of transition 151–4; four quadrants of 131; grief and loss models 144–5; maintaining positive 149–50; nature of 129–30; rate and extent of 129; and redundancy 133–5; resistance to 123, 131, 137, 147–9; seven-stage model of transition 132–5; SPACE model 146–7; theory of 131–47
changing the subject 30

Charles, C. 89
child: adapted 165, 166, 171, 172; natural 165, 166, 171
child ego-state 164, 165, 167, 169
CIPD: World Audit (2013) 134
clarifying 84–5, 86
Clarkson, P. 31
climate setting 24–5
closed mind 123–4
closed questions 56–7
cognitive behavioural therapy (CBT) 65, 146
comfort zones 124
communication: body *see* body language/communication; phases that help/hinder 47–8
communication skills 9–22
competence cycle 111
competence model 158
competencies: working within your 158–61
concentration, losing 29
confidentiality 31, 33–4, 72
confrontation 66–8
congruence (genuineness) 13, 65, 70, 97
consciously competent 111, 158
consciously incompetent 111, 170
content: identifying 51
contracting 31–6; confidentiality 31, 33–4; cultural expectations and diversity 35; ethical issues and guidelines 35–6; realistic expectations and dual relationships 34–5; self-disclosure 32; space 32; time boundaries 32; touch/touching 33
controlling parent 165–6, 171, 172
Cooper, M. 97
CORBS feedback 43–4
core conditions 13–14, 97
counselling: differences between counselling skills and 10–11, 13, 161; training in 10
counselling menu 18–19
counselling skills 107; differences between counselling and 10–11, 13, 161; embedding 11–12; powerful tool of 156–7
counselling tasks 19
critical (controlling) parent 165–6, 171, 172
crying 78
Culley, S. 17–18, 71, 73, 160–1
cultural differences 25, 35; and use of silence 78–9
cultural influence: and change 149
cycle of change model 136–7, 138–43

denial stage 132, 135
depression 132–3
description of the event 196
destinational learning 186
Dewey, John 184
DiClemente, C. C. 132, 136–7
difference 97; working across 161–3
difficult clients 170, 172–4; angry clients 172; 'passive' or 'sent' clients 173; under the influence of alcohol or drugs 172
distractions 26, 29
diversity 35; working across 161–3
Doran, G. T. 112
dreaming 29
drugs: clients under the influence of 172
Dryden, W. 125
dual relationships 31–2, 34–5, 160–1
dual roles 158–9, 160

Egan, Gerard 14–16, 65, 68, 100, 108
ego-states 163–70; adult 164, 165, 166, 167; child 164, 165, 167, 169; clues to identifying 171; parent 164, 165, 167, 169
Ellis, A. 146
embedded counselling 12
emotions: dealing with our own strong 173–4
empathy 14, 65, 97–100, 173; demonstrated through immediacy and self-disclosure 98; expressing through body language 99–100
emphatic opportunities 12
engaged: being fully 26
equality 161
Equity and Excellence: Liberating the NHS (White Paper) (2010) 203
established relationship 20, 97–128; action planning 123–6; clarifying and developing goals 111–13; drawing together themes 108–9, 110; examples 104–7, 110, 114–17, 119–22; and focusing 100–1; force field analysis 118, 119–22; use of metaphor and hunches 101–3, 104–7; working emphatically 97–100
ethical issues 32, 35–6, 157
evaluation 198
expectations: cultural 35; realistic 31
experiential learning 184–5, 186
'expert hat', wearing our 159–60
eye contact 25, 27–8

facial expression 27–8
failure: embracing both success and 125; fear of 125
family system 148
fear 124–5
feedback 43–4, 88–90; CORBS 43–4

INDEX

feelings: identifying 51–2; sharing 71
Feirn, R. 90
'felt sense' 99
filtering 29
Fink, S. L. 135
focusing 100–1
force field analysis 118, *119–22*
free child (natural child) 165, 166, 171
future learning 201–3

genuineness 13, 65, 70, 97
Gibbs, G. 195–6, 228
goals: clarifying and developing 19, 111–13; and milestones 126, *127*; SMART 16, 111–13
going along with everything 30
grief models 144–5
guidelines 35–6
Guttman, H. A. 148

Holly, M. L. 7
homeostasis 148
Honey, P. 185
hope 108
Hopson, B. 132–5
hunches 101–3, 108

immediacy 89; and empathy 98; use of 68–71, 74–7
impatience 124
information, sharing 89–90
Ingham, Harry 190
integrative skills model 17–18
internal supervisor 7, 158, 174, 184, 188
internalisation 133

Jago, W. 124
Jahoda, M. 135
Johari's window 190, *191*
Johns, H. 7
Joines, V. 164
justice 36, 157

Kanter, Moss 123
'know-how' 188
Kolb, D. 184–5, 186, 187, 193

learning 184–7; common blocks to 123–5; destinational 186; experiential 184, 185, 186; future 201–3; transformative 186–7
learning journal 7

learning partner relationship: setting up the 43–5, 89
learning styles 185–6
letting go 133
leverage 100
Lewin, Kurt 118
'light bulb' moment 87, 192
listening 25, 28, 48; active 25; barriers to active 28–30
loss models 144–5
Luft, Joe 190

McDermott, I. 124
McLeod, J. 18–19; *Counselling Skills* 12
'me too' responses 28, 97
meaning, identifying 52
Mearns, D. 97
metaphors 101–2, 104–7
micro-counselling 18
milestones 126, *127*
miracle imagery questions 109
mirroring 30–1
mistakes, making 174
Mumford, A. 185

natural child 165, 166, 171
Neenan, M. 125
non-events 130
non-maleficence 36, 157
non-verbal communication 30–1; and empathy 99
nurturing parent 165, 171, 172

open questions 56–7, 87–8

paraphrasing 48–9, 101
parent: controlling 165–6, 171, 172; nurturing 165, 171, 172
parent ego-state 164, 165, 167, 169
Parkes, Murray 144, 145
'passive' clients 173
person-centred approach 13–14, 203
personality types: and learning styles 185
Philpott, J. 134
planning what we are going to say next 29
Polyani 188
'possible selves' 108
posture *see* body posture
private/hidden area 190
probing 87–8
Prochaska, J. O. 132, 136–7
psychological contact 13, 170, 172

psychosynthesis theory 131
public area 190

questions 56; closed 56–7; miracle imagery 109; open 56–7, 87–8; Socratic 57, 87–8, 101; unhelpful 58

rapport building 23–4
realistic expectations 31, 34–5
reality, accepting 133
reassessing 87
redundancy 133–5
reflection/reflective practice 6–8, 69, 184–200; action plan 199; analysis stage 198; applying model of to case work 195–9; Boniface model 191–5; conclusion stage 199; description of the event 196; evaluation stage 198; Gibbs' model 195–9; and Johari's window 190, 191; levels of 191–5; meaning 187–9; and self-awareness 189–90, 197–8; understanding ourselves better 189–91
reflective journal 7
relational depth 97
Relational Skills Model (RSM) 2–4, 3, 12–13, 202; phases 20–1, 205
relationship(s): established 20, 97–128; maintaining and ending 20–1, 129–55; working with the *see* challenging
relationship, developing the 20, 47–63; asking questions 53, 56–8; examples 53, 54–5, 58–9, 60–2; identifying and reflecting feelings, content and meaning 50–2, 54–5; paraphrasing 48–9; phases helping/hindering communication 47–8; summarising 49–50
relationship, setting up the 20, 23–46; attending and listening skills 25–30; barriers to active listening 28–30; climate setting 24–5; contracting 31–6; example 36–7, 38–42; non-verbal communication 30–1; rapport building 23–4; setting up the learning partner relationship 43–5
resonance 173–4
respect 85
responsive, being 27
Rigby, S. 78
risk: taking a 125
Robinson, W. L. 111
Rogers, Carl 13–14, 113
role-play 45
room setting 26, 32

Sanders, D. 57
Schlossberg, N. K. 130
Schön, Donald 6, 184
Schut, H. 145
scripts 113
seating 26
second-guessing 29
self-awareness 24, 68, 89, 189, 197–8
self-disclosure 32, 71–3, 74–7, 98
self-esteem: and seven-stage model of transition 132–5
self-reflexive 35, 161
self-respect 36, 157
self-sharing 71
shared treatment decision-making model 89
sharing feelings 71
sharing information 89–90
silence(s) 56; cultural variations 78–9; use of 78
skilled helper model 14–16
SMART goals 16, 111–13
Socratic questions 57, 87–8, 101
SOLER acronym 25
space, contracting 32
SPACE model 146–7
stereotyping 35, 161
Stewart, I. 164
Stroebe, M. 145
Sue, D. 78
summarising 49–50, 84, 87
systems awareness 147–9
systems theory 148

tacit knowledge 188, 189
TERMS acronym 1, 4–6
theoretical underpinnings 12–19
three-stage skills model 14–16
time boundaries, contracting 32
timing, monitoring 26
Tonkin, L. 145
touch/touching 33, 159
training 10
transactional analysis (TA) 163–70
transformative learning 186–7
transition/transition models 131–9; final stages of 151–4; and redundancy 133–5; seven-stage model of 132–5
trustworthy 36, 157

unconditional positive regard 13, 97
unconsciously competent 111, 158

unconsciously incompetent 111, 158
unknown/undiscovered area 190

value judgements 29, 85
verbal language 30
visual mental imagery 102

'what if' scenario 161
Wills, F. 57
Worden, J. W. 145
wrong, getting it 174–82

'yes, but' reply 123

eBooks
from Taylor & Francis

Helping you to choose the right eBooks for your Library

Add to your library's digital collection today with Taylor & Francis eBooks. We have over 50,000 eBooks in the Humanities, Social Sciences, Behavioural Sciences, Built Environment and Law, from leading imprints, including Routledge, Focal Press and Psychology Press.

Free Trials Available

ORDER YOUR FREE INSTITUTIONAL TRIAL TODAY

We offer free trials to qualifying academic, corporate and government customers.

Choose from a range of subject packages or create your own!

Benefits for you
- Free MARC records
- COUNTER-compliant usage statistics
- Flexible purchase and pricing options
- 70% approx of our eBooks are now DRM-free.

Benefits for your user
- Off-site, anytime access via Athens or referring URL
- Print or copy pages or chapters
- Full content search
- Bookmark, highlight and annotate text
- Access to thousands of pages of quality research at the click of a button.

eCollections
Choose from 20 different subject eCollections, including:
- Asian Studies
- Economics
- Health Studies
- Law
- Middle East Studies

eFocus
We have 16 cutting-edge interdisciplinary collections, including:
- Development Studies
- The Environment
- Islam
- Korea
- Urban Studies

For more information, pricing enquiries or to order a free trial, please contact your local sales team:

UK/Rest of World: online.sales@tandf.co.uk
USA/Canada/Latin America: e-reference@taylorandfrancis.com
East/Southeast Asia: martin.jack@tandf.com.sg
India: journalsales@tandfindia.com

www.tandfebooks.com

Printed in Great Britain
by Amazon